HOLY SPIRIT
PNEUMA HAGION

A STUDY OF

THE MANIFESTATIONS AND
THE HOLY SPIRIT FIELD
FROM CORINTHIANS AND ACTS

VICTOR PAUL WIERWILLE

Originally taught live—March 1967

© 2017 Eternally Blessed

All rights reserved. No new contribution to this publication may be reproduced, stored in a retrieval system, or transmitted, in any form or by any means, electronic, mechanical, photocopying, recording, or otherwise, without the prior permission of the publisher except in the case of brief quotations embodied in articles or reviews.

TABLE OF CONTENTS

FOREWORD	v
EDITOR'S PREFACE	ix
Session One: THE DAY OF PENTECOST—WHAT, WHERE, WHO	11
Session Two: FILLED WITH *PNEUMA HAGION*	47
Session Three: YE SHALL RECEIVE	99
Session Four: FREED FROM THE LAW	151
Session Five: SPIRITUAL MATTERS	207
Session Six: WHAT'S THE PROFIT	255
Session Seven: BENEFITS OF SPEAKING IN TONGUES	315
TONGUES, INTERPRETATION AND PROPHECY	341
SCRIPTURE INDEX	357

Foreword

One of the most misunderstood subjects in the Bible is the holy spirit and the operation of the nine manifestations. Yet the Christian's knowledge and application of the holy spirit dictates whether this endless power from on high lies dormant or is utilized. Jesus Christ stated, the works that I do shall you do also, and greater works than these because I go unto the Father. Therefore, it must be and is available to do the works that Jesus Christ did. The lessons in this book give the background to the power base and training that Christians need on how to manifest power from on high.

In March of 1967, Dr. Victor Paul Wierwille taught a class entitled "Special Study on PNEUMA HAGION (Holy Spirit)" at the Biblical Research Center to a live audience for seven evenings, with two sessions each night. Dr. Wierwille utilized his book on *Receiving the Holy Spirit Today* as the framework for this class. In addition to referencing his book, he expounded in great detail many truths regarding the holy spirit field during the class. This class was recorded live over approximately 14 hours of teaching during these two weeks. This manuscript was meticulously taken from these recordings. Every effort to preserve the words and intent that Dr. Wierwille spoke was taken into consideration.

Dr. Victor Paul Wierwille's life was dedicated to helping people attain a greater understanding of the Word of God. He would often say, "the Word of God is the will of God."

As a young minister fresh out of seminary, Reverend Wierwille found himself ill-equipped to really take care of his people. That led to a fervent quest to intimately know God through His Word and to manifest His power in his life and ministry; and then in turn, to teach others also. For over forty years, Wierwille enlightened people all over the world through classes, books, live teachings, radio and television broadcasts. He imparted to his students and listeners a deep understanding of the Word of God. But he accomplished even more than that as he opened up the Scriptures. He made it live!

Dr. Wierwille was a master teacher in every regard. He electrified audiences of over 30,000 people with his dynamic presentation of the Word, while at the same time elucidating substantial doctrinal matters. He stood alone in the field of Biblical research for his unmatched ability to put the whole Word of God together so that it cohesively fit without any contradiction from Genesis to Revelation. Moreover, as a teacher, he excelled at making even the most difficult verses easily understood. With an extra-ordinary ability to communicate simply, Victor Paul Wierwille made tenets of doctrine that theologians have strenuously wrestled with throughout the course of Christianity easily accessible to even the youngest neophyte.

He connected with the common man so readily because he spoke on their level. With honesty and frankness, Victor Paul Wierwille never watered down the Word, nor shied away from controversial subjects or truths some might have found difficult to swallow. Rather, his disarmingly warm, paternal manner made even strong reproof and correction somehow palatable to the honest hearers.

To some extent, Wierwille's ability to communicate in simple terms may have obscured both his intellect and education to some people. Dr. Wierwille received his Bachelor of Arts and Bachelor of Theology degrees from present day Lakeland College, and conducted graduate studies at the University of Chicago and Princeton Theological Seminary. It was at Princeton that Wierwille earned the Master of Theology degree in Practical Theology. He later completed his Doctor of Theology degree at Pike's Peak Bible Seminary and Burton College in Manitou Springs, Colorado.

His greatest learning, however, did not come from his formal education but instead his personal quest for truth. A voracious reader, Victor Paul Wierwille consumed two or three theological works a week, week after week for years, until he finally came to the place where he realized that the Bible must be the only rule for faith and practice. For nearly twelve years of his life, he then worked the Word, studying from fourteen to eighteen hours a day in his search for answers. Throughout his life, Dr. Wierwille extensively studied the primary Biblical languages of Hebrew, Greek, and Aramaic; figures of speech used in the Bible; Eastern manners and customs; and many other resources and disciplines relevant to Biblical research. As he searched for enlightenment, he consulted and worked with some of the most outstanding individuals in Biblical studies and Christianity of his day; including Karl Barth, Joseph Bauer, Glenn Clark, Karl J. Ernst, Joseph Friedli, Louis C. Hessert, Elmer G. Homrig-hausen, E. Stanley Jones, George M. Lamsa, Richard and Reinhold Niebuhr, K. C. Pillai, Paul Tillich, Ernst Traeger, and many others.

The scope of his major works irrefutably stand as proof of Dr. Wierwille's achievements in the field of Biblical research. Rather than drown in the stagnant pools of tradition, he chose to honestly allow the Word of God to speak for itself, and that unbiased approach enabled him to uncover truths that had been hidden for centuries. Dr. Wierwille was the author of numerous books, including *Are the Dead Alive Now?; Receiving the Holy Spirit To-*

day; Jesus Christ is Not God; Jesus Christ Our Passover; and *Jesus Christ Our Promised Seed.* Additionally, he developed and taught several comprehensive classes directed toward helping people to understand the Bible and to increase the power of God in their lives, such as the Power for Abundant Living series, Living Victoriously, and the University of Life courses.

Editor's Preface

In March of 1967, Dr. Victor Paul Wierwille taught a series of teachings. His live presentation was recorded at the time, and subsequently a verbatim transcript was made directly from those recordings. That exact transcript has been preserved in an unedited form for posterity. This book is now an edited version of those teachings. In order to make the teachings more accessible for a wider audience, the work has been edited simply for the sake of grammar and readability, as is typical when converting spoken words to a written form.

Great care has been taken to preserve Dr. Wierwille's actual words and teaching style along with the logical content as much as possible during the editing process.

Like most speakers, the way that Dr. Wierwille spoke often differed from the way that he wrote. In general, his books especially were more formal than the usual style of his live presentations. Having been delivered in a class setting, these particular teachings on the holy spirit were even more casual at times. A fundamental decision was made to retain the informal tone of the audio teachings in the approach to editing the transcript, rather than "polish" the words a bit more to better match the style found in his other books. In doing so, the relaxed atmosphere of the class setting has been allowed to reverberate through the teacher's words onto the pages of the book, and the reader enjoys a sense of intimacy and familiarity with him that would otherwise be missing. Beyond that, the subject matter of the holy spirit is most effectively communicated through the narrative setting of the Special Study on PNEUMA HAGION (Holy Spirit) Class.

In keeping with that approach, certain remarks that were directly relevant to the immediate audience at the class have been retained in the book. Although not commonly found in the pages of a book, the opening and closing prayers in their entirety are included for the same reason. However, some comments and references are no longer pertinent to the present time, and they have been changed or eliminated. Additionally, the audience interaction with the teacher has been removed from the manuscript simply to improve the flow of thought.

A few other notes of explanation:

Dr. Wierwille did not originally entitle the individual teachings at the Special Study on PNEUMA HAGION (Holy Spirit) Class. Also the chapter titles that appear in the book have been added for reference sake.

Dr. Wierwille often made reference to the fifth edition during his teaching. Footnotes in this book reflect the seventh edition.

Unless otherwise noted, all Scriptures quoted in the transcript are taken from the King James Version (KJV) of the Bible, also known as the Authorized Version (AV).

Italic type is used in the KJV Bible to indicate words that have been added by the translators to the Scriptural text, for which there are no words found in the original language.

Italic type is additionally used for Greek, Hebrew or Aramaic words, as well as the names of figures of speech.

( ) Parentheses are used in the KJV Bible to indicate explanatory statements within the actual Scriptural text.

[ ] Brackets are used within quoted scriptures to indicate the teacher's explanatory comments.

THE DAY OF PENTECOST— WHAT, WHERE, WHO

We're beginning the field of the holy spirit which will be covered in every segment. This field of the holy spirit is the field of the church. The church came into being on the Day of Pentecost. This was the day on which the greatness of God's power came to live, to be born in men and women. Ever since the Day of Pentecost this has been the age of the holy spirit. These things should be known by the Church, because this is where the Church's power is. There is no question in the holy spirit field, to which God has not given to me the answer from the Word of God that I can read to a man, line by line and word by word. It was in this field, I believe that God raised me up to teach again to God's hungry people the inerrant accuracy, the greatness of His wonderful power, glory and majesty in this day, time and hour in which we live and have been called to.

This field of the holy spirit [1] is about as misunderstood and as wrongly divided as anything can be. And yet, somehow or other once the principles are understood, and you read these principles from the Word of God, the field becomes real simple and real easy. It is error which is complicated; truth is always simple. The more we get to the truth of God's Word, the more questions we have

---

1. In other writings "the Holy Spirit field" is capitalized. Since this field is the whole package of the 25 different usages of *pneuma* in the Greek New Testament, the operation of the manifestations, the Giver and the gift, walking by the spirit, fruit of the spirit, the rights and abilities inherent in the new nature, this phrase will be referenced as "the holy spirit field" (lower case) throughout this book.

12 HOLY SPIRIT—*PNEUMA HAGION*

answered, the greater the power of God is able to live within us and we are able to make it manifest.

For those of you who have registered or are still registering tonight for this week, (I'm speaking now to the grads only, who have taken the foundational classes on Power for Abundant Living.) there is an assignment that has to be kept by tomorrow night, so you might as well go to work on it. Pages 219 to 227 in the new book (fifth edition) on receiving the holy spirit[2] deals with the word "receive"—the Greek word *lambanō* and the Greek word *dechomai*. Take every place in the New Testament where the word "receive" is used, and it's either *lambanō* or *dechomai*, either one of those two Greek words. Go through your Bible and if it's the word *lambanō*, put an "L" on top of it, so you'll be able to recognize it. If it's the word *dechomai*, put a "D" on top of it. The reason you'll be able to do this is because I have given all of them to you in the appendix, starting with page 219. They're all in here: Matthew 10:14, Matthew 10:40, and so on. So you just take this book[3] and your Bible and you can go right through from Matthew to Revelation and you can mark them. This is an absolute requirement by tomorrow night.

The second requirement—which perhaps you will not be able to finish by tomorrow night, all of you, some of you may if you get up an hour earlier tomorrow morning which will not hurt you—is that you will take the references from page 240 on. Every place in the Bible in the New Testament where the word *pneuma* or the word *hagion* are used, you mark them. *Pneuma* is the word "spirit"; *hagion* is the word "holy." Every place where the word "holy" or the word "spirit" is translated in the New Testament, you go to your pages in the appendix

---

2. See also *Receiving the Holy Spirit Today*, seventh edition, p. 225-231.
3. See also *Receiving the Holy Spirit Today*, seventh edition, p. 225.

THE DAY OF PENTECOST—WHAT, WHERE, WHO   13

of the holy spirit book,[4] and take your Bible next to you and you mark in the following.

First of all, if there is no article "the" preceding it, that you will know because I have given it to you in the appendix. If the article "the" precedes the words "holy" and "spirit" it's in here, in the book. The first one for instance is Matthew 1:18. And there you will see Matthew 1:18, then just the words *pneuma hagion*, no article. That will immediately tell you that in every critical Greek text, as well as in the Aramaic texts, there is no article "the" in any of the texts.

Take a look at Matthew 1 while you keep your finger in Acts. Since I'm teaching you how to do it, I want you to do it accurately and write it in your Bible. Because once you do this, you'll have it as long as you have that particular Bible and use it. In Matthew 1:18 it says:

> **Matthew 1:18c**
> …before they came together, she was found with child of [what's the next word?] the Holy Ghost.

The Holy Spirit is the text, but "ghost" is the Greek word *pneuma*, translated "ghost." There is no article "the"—once again, there is no article "the" so I want you to take that article "the" in verse 18 and scratch it out. And above the words "Holy Ghost" I simply want you to put for the word "holy" a small "h" and for the word "ghost" a small "p." *Pneuma*. So the "h" stands for "holy" or *hagion*; the "p" stands for *pneuma*. Then every time you read in your Bible, you'll know whether there's an article supposed to be there or whether it isn't. Understand? That is the assignment that has to be done this week. One of them by tomorrow night and as much of this second assignment from page 240 on as you can take care of. Then

---

4. See also *Receiving the Holy Spirit Today*, seventh edition, p. 233.

the balance we'll take care of in a day or so, so that you'll all have them.

Now tonight, in Acts 1, the best way for me to teach you this field is just to begin with the first verse of Acts chapter 1. I'm interested specifically tonight to set before our people the greatest understanding once again, so that no matter how many times you may have learned it that you may learn it once more and never to forget it: what it was that came on the Day of Pentecost. This is the first thing you have to decide if you're really going to tap resources in the holy spirit field. Exactly what was it that came on the Day of Pentecost? It cannot have been the "Holy Spirit" with a capital H and a capital S, because the "Holy Spirit" is God. God did not specifically come on the Day of Pentecost; God is from the beginning. Genesis 1:1 says "In the beginning…" was who?—God. "In the beginning God…" so therefore we will have to find out from the Word of God WHAT came on the Day of Pentecost.

Secondly, we will have to find out WHERE it occurred. Where did this experience of the Day of Pentecost occur? And the third thing you will have to really know is WHO were present on the day when the holy spirit was given?

Acts 1:1
The former treatise…

The word "treatise" is the word *logos*, the former word, the former treatise. The former treatise is the Gospel of Luke. The Gospel of Luke was written by the same writer who wrote the Book of Acts. It was originally given in a scroll form, not in a book form like you and I have it. A scroll is rolled up. The former treatise, the former word (I'm real interested that you know that the word "treatise" is the Greek word *logos*); the Gospel of Luke. You see the Gospel of Luke is the Word of God. So is

THE DAY OF PENTECOST—WHAT, WHERE, WHO   15

the Book of Acts, the "Word of God" because the Bible is "The Word of God." Understand?

Acts 1:1a
The former treatise [the Book of Luke] have I made, O Theophilus,...

The word "Theophilus" means beloved of God. The Book of Acts is not addressed to an individual, like the Word of God in Luke is not addressed to an individual. It's addressed to the "beloved of God": *"The former word, have I made O beloved of God, of all that Jesus began both to do and to teach."* [5]

The word "all" is not all without exception, but all without distinction. He gave all in the Gospel of Luke, that God by revelation gave to him and told him to write.

Acts 1:1b, 2
...all that Jesus began both to do and to teach,
Until the day in which he was taken up,...

The day in which he was taken up was the Ascension. The Ascension is forty days after the Resurrection.

So the Gospel of Luke, as does all the gospels, terminates with the Ascension. The gospels do not go beyond the Ascension. But very specifically here dealing with the Gospel of Luke, he tells us that he goes as far as unto the day in which he was taken up.

Acts 1:2b
...after that he through the Holy Ghost...

Now here you have the first one. If you had it marked

---

5. A literal translation according to usage of Acts 1:1.
A literal translation according to usage is that which reproduces the thoughts and meanings of the original, based on the words in the original in relation to the verse, the context, the remote context and to whom it's written. (The editors have chosen to identify them by quotation marks and italics. This is not KJV text.)

in your Bible, you would have the word "the" scratched out because the word "the" does not appear in any of the critical Greek texts or any of the Aramaic texts. The word "holy" is the Greek word *hagion* and the word "ghost" is the Greek word *pneuma*. By the way, they are always in the Greek written *pneuma hagion* (spirit holy). In English you translate it so it would read "holy spirit" changing the order of the words for the English language.

Now, there is a word here that I would like to share with you in Acts 1:2.

> **Acts 1:2a**
> Until the day in which he was taken up, after that he through…[Holy Spirit]…

The Greek word for "through" is the word *dia* meaning "by" or "proceeding from"; by or proceeding from *pneuma hagion*—Holy Spirit, which in this instance has to be the Giver, and if we were to bring it over into English you would have to capitalize "Holy" and "Spirit" because in English they are proper nouns.

> **Acts 1:2b**
> …that he through…[Holy Spirit] had given commandments…

Or as you could translate it very beautifully: "…*after that he through, or by way of the Holy Spirit had commanded the apostles whom he had chosen.*"[6] You see, it is God by revelation that gave commandments to the apostles whom he had chosen.

There is a record in Luke 6 which you ought to check and mark in your Bible after Acts 1:2. In Luke 6:13, this is talking now about the ministry of Jesus.

---

6. A literal translation according to usage of Acts 1:2b.

The Day of Pentecost—What, Where, Who   17

Luke 6:13
And when it was day, he called *unto him* his disciples: and of them he chose [Jesus Christ chose how many?] twelve, whom also he named apostles;

A disciple is a follower; an apostle is a follower "plus." An apostle is one who is called of God, who has a ministry to God's people bringing new light; it may be old light, but it is new to the generation to whom he speaks. Verse 13—he chose out from among the disciples, the followers, these twelve and he called them apostles. And he named them in verses 14, 15 and in 16, especially notice. And one of those twelve was Judas Iscariot, which also was the traitor.[7]

In Acts 1:2 this becomes remarkably unique when it said:

Acts 1:2c
...he...had given commandments unto the apostles whom he had chosen:

How many apostles did he choose? Twelve. How many were present then here? Twelve. If the apostles whom he chose were still present then Judas Iscariot could not have been dead at the time of the Ascension. For in verse 3 you read, "To whom also..." To whom? to whom the apostles, whom he had chosen.

Acts 1:3, 4
To whom also he shewed himself alive after his passion [his death] by many infallible proofs, being seen of them forty days, and speaking of the things pertaining to the kingdom of God:
And being assembled together with *them* [the apostles whom he had chosen], [he] commanded them...

---

7. Luke 6:16—And Judas *the brother* of James, and Judas Iscariot, which also was the traitor.

This is why we read in verse 2—until the day in which he was taken up, after that he through Holy Ghost had given COMMANDMENTS unto the apostles whom he had chosen. Now verse 4.

Acts 1:4
And being assembled together with *them* [on the day of the Ascension, forty days after the Resurrection], commanded them that they should not depart from Jerusalem, but wait for the promise of the Father, which, *saith he*, ye have heard of me.

Now there is the first great truth regarding the holy spirit field. These apostles were instructed to return to Jerusalem after the Ascension and there they were to wait. They were to wait. And what were they to wait for? It says they were to wait for "THE promise of THE Father." That's what they were to wait for. The promise of the Father, which God had given before to the Lord Jesus Christ and had communicated to them. We'll cover some of these things from the Gospel of John tomorrow night perhaps, in John 14, 15 and 16, so that we get it all lined up.

Tonight I'm after three great truths, namely: What was it that came on the Day of Pentecost? Where did it occur? And who were present to receive?

He told them to go back to Jerusalem and wait for THE promise of THE Father. They were to wait. You and I looking back, we know how long they waited. But put yourself in the shoes of those men on the day in which the commandment of the Lord was given to them. Just think that way for a moment. If the Lord said to you today, "Go to Jerusalem and wait for the promise of the Father." You would not know when it was going to occur. You might wait a day, you might wait two days, you might wait three days, you might wait three years. You

THE DAY OF PENTECOST—WHAT, WHERE, WHO 19

don't know. Once again, you and I looking back, we know how long they waited. But did they know that day how long they would have to wait? No. He simply told them to go back to Jerusalem and "wait for the promise of the Father, which, *saith he*, ye have heard of me."

Then comes verse 5.

Acts 1:5a
For John [talking about John the Baptist] truly baptized with water; but ye [the apostles] shall be baptized with the Holy Ghost...

Now here is the second usage, we have no definite article "the" so we scratch it out. Holy Ghost again is *pneuma hagion*.

Acts 1:5b
...[holy spirit] not many days hence.

The word "with" in this particular verse is the Greek word *en* meaning "in." Ye shall be baptized "with." And really, if you're literally going to translate it, it's beautiful: "ye shall be baptized within!" Not on the outside. Got it? "...*baptized within, or in pneuma hagion* (*holy spirit*), *not many days hence.*" [8]

Now this is a remarkable truth and that's the second truth you will have to put down in your mind. That THE promise of THE Father equals whatever it is to be baptized with or in *pneuma hagion* or holy spirit. That's the second truth given in that fifth verse. This tells us that "the promise" of the Father is the same as "baptized with holy spirit." It's the same. Those two verses (4 and 5) give you that. He told them also in this verse that they would be baptized with this holy spirit not many days hence. Not too far in the distant future.

---

8. A literal translation according to usage of Acts 1:5b.

Now keeping your finger in the Book of Acts, we go to that Word of God which is "the former treatise," to the Gospel of Luke. Remember, he is saying this to his apostles before he has ascended. You understand? The Ascension Day is here but Christ has not yet ascended. He is giving his last minute instructions to the apostles who are gathered with him. It's like a coach getting his team around him, and just before they win the ball game, they have a time out. Eight seconds before the game ends, he gives them the final word on how he wants the ball to be brought in and who is going to shoot it. That's exactly like Jesus is operating here. He is ready to ascend. They will never see him again, until his return. But there is something coming to replace the personal presence of Christ and preparing them for this. He gives them these last minute instructions in the 24th chapter of the Gospel of Luke, in verse 49:

> **Luke 24:49a**
> And, behold, I send the promise of my Father upon you:…

Here he is talking to the apostles, the same as he is in Acts 1. It's the day of the Ascension and he uses the same words just before he ascends: "I send the promise of my Father upon you."—He is talking about the promise of the Father which is to be sent upon them not many days hence.[9] And here it says,

> **Luke 24:49b**
> …but tarry ye in the city of Jerusalem, until ye be endued with power from on high.

In the Book of Acts it said they were to wait for the promise in verse 4, remember? Here in Luke it uses the word "tarry." Same word. The reason they had to wait

---

9. Acts 1:5.

and had to tarry was because it had not yet been given. It had not yet come. If I said to you, next Tuesday morning at nine o'clock I will give you something, then you would have to wait from now till next Tuesday nine o'clock. You would have to wait for, wait until, you would have to tarry for one reason only—because I haven't got it yet to give. So it was with this holy spirit field. And all of this teaching that you have to wait and tarry for the holy spirit today is an absolute contradiction of God's Word! You don't have to wait and tarry because God gave it 1900 years ago on the Day of Pentecost!

This is addressed to the apostles before the Day of Pentecost. Just at the time of the ascension of our Lord and Savior Jesus Christ, when he told them to wait, to tarry. The reason they had to tarry is because it had not yet come, and he did not want them running all over the country. He wanted them back there where he was in Jerusalem. So he said, you go on back there and you wait; you tarry in Jerusalem for the promise of the Father. Then he says in Luke, tarry until ye be endued with power from on high. That's tremendous. Did their tarrying bring the power? No. When God's fullness of time came, he sent forth the gift on the Day of Pentecost.

It was not their tarrying in prayer; it was not their agonizing for the holy spirit that made the holy spirit come. It was not their waiting for it that brought it. It was simply that the time had not yet come. That's all! So he said, "tarry ye…until ye be endued with power from on high." And that's the third explanation of what it was that would come on the Day of Pentecost. The promise of the Father equals to be baptized with the holy spirit (*pneuma hagion*) which equals to be endued with power from on high. And that is the total explanation that is given in the Book of Acts chapter 1, verses 4 and 5 when he talks about "THE Promise of THE Father" which is to "be baptized with *pneuma hagion*." This one phrase explains that completely. Before I break down the greatness of this phrase for you, grammatically, logically, semantically and every other way that I know, let me remind you of a mathematical axiom: "Things equal to the same things are equal to each other." Therefore, the promise of the Father equals to be baptized with *pneuma hagion* equals endued with power from on high. Therefore, things equal to the same things are equal to each other.

Therefore, that which came on the Day of Pentecost must always be and always is and always will continue to be, until Christ comes back again to be endued with power from on high.

Now I'm going to handle this last phrase for you "…endued with power from on high." The first word is the word "endue." This word means "clothed with"; "to be clothed with." Before the Day of Pentecost, were they born again? They had no "Christ in them." They were dead in trespasses and sins,[10] without God and without hope.[11] On the Day of Pentecost Christ came in, they were born again of God's spirit—that anointing, that "Christ in you, the hope of glory,"[12] the epistles said. That is the enduement, that is the clothing with; that's what the enduement is, the "enclothing with." You are no longer spiritually naked. You are no longer spiritually dead. For now you are endued with, clothed with.

Now that clothing is not something on the outside, because the clothing on the outside until this time has been manifested in the senses realm by a baptism of John which was by water. But now something better came than water and that something better was not an external

---

10. Ephesians 2:1.
11. Ephesians 2:12.
12. Colossians 1:27.

THE DAY OF PENTECOST—WHAT, WHERE, WHO   23

clothing. It was an internal reality! To be endued with, clothed on the inside with power—power. Endued or clothed with power! The word "power" is the word *dunamis* in the Greek which is almost translated literally into the English language in our word "dynamite." Endued with power (*dunamis*).

Now this word "power" is uniquely and marvelously accurate. There are other words for power in the Bible. Like the one Greek word is the word *exousia*. Another Greek word for power is the word *energēmata*. If either one of those words were used here, nobody could put the Word of God together! They could only guess; they couldn't put it together. As a matter of fact it would fall to pieces. This one word is the only word that could possibly fit! Why? Because *dunamis* always means "inherent power." If the entire basement of this teaching center was filled with dynamite, would it hurt us? Not as long as someone didn't ignite it. It would have a lot of potential, a lot of power. But it couldn't hurt anybody and it couldn't do anybody any good either until somebody would do something to it. Look, that is one of the greatest keys in the holy spirit field you will ever know! And this will explain a thousand things (that's a figure of speech) if you sit down and think it through, because it is to be "clothed with" *dunamis* power, inherent power! It's only potential. And unless you know what to do with it, it never becomes kinetic. It will just be in you as long as you live physically, and it will never do one lousy thing for you if you aren't using it! It is *dunamis* power, it's "inherent" power, it's "potential" power. It becomes "kinetic" when you and I do something about it!

The inherent, potential power has to be this because God is spirit, and God doesn't take a man by the nap of the neck and shove him down a hole or shove him someplace else. If He did, that kind of power would have to be what kind of power? Kinetic, not potential; it couldn't be *dunamis* at all. But on the Day of Pentecost when the new birth came and we were endued with, clothed with, we were clothed spiritually with power, *dunamis* power! Wow, you're loaded with *dunamis* power! Everything that God is in Christ is in the believer! But it's spirit. You can't feel spirit, you can't smell it, you can't taste it, you can't touch it because God is spirit and God gives that *dunamis*, that power which is spirit power, the new birth! It's all wrapped up, endued with power, *dunamis*! "Power from on high." Jesus had said in the Gospel of John that he was going up, and when he would go up the Father would send a "comforter," a *paraklētos*, one who would be alongside and was in you. This is what the Father God would do! So the phrase "from on high" tells us where it came from. It didn't come from the corner drug store and it didn't come from the Jewish synagogue, or the Temple. It didn't come from the believing of the people, but this which came on the Day of Pentecost was to be "clothed with" spiritual power, *dunamis* power from on high, from God.

That's why it says:

> **Acts 1:4c, 5a**
> …wait for the promise of the Father, which, *saith he*, ye have heard of me.
> For John…baptized with water; but [you are going to be] baptized [in or] with…

…you're going to be baptized with "water and…"— no, sorry, it doesn't say "water and…."! Anybody that puts water into the Word of God in that place is all wet! And they have sure been that way, but that's their privilege. I'm not interested in what people put in or take out. I'm interested in the integrity and accuracy of God's Word! For if it's God's Word then it will have to fit like a hand in a glove all the way through. And it will have worked with a mathematical exactness and with a scientific precision else it cannot be God's Word.

So, that which is to be "baptized with *pneuma hagion*" is to be endued, clothed with. That's what the word "baptized with" means, to be "clothed with"! And ladies and gentlemen it is a lot better to be clothed with the Lord Jesus Christ than all the water in the Atlantic and Pacific Oceans. It is a lot better to have Christ in you, than just to have enough water around the place to wash the outside. This "endued with" is his power, which is Christ in you the hope of glory! This is what came on the Day of Pentecost.

Three verses of scripture take all the guess work out, all the private interpretation, and this is all that you can know from God's Word regarding what came on the Day of Pentecost. All the other stuff is just talk—hot air. Anything a man could say about it would just be what he would say. Once again, this is all there is in the Word of God that can be known as to what it was that came on the Day of Pentecost. And those three verses take all the guess work out, all the private interpretation. For "the promise of the Father" equals whatever it is to be baptized with or in *pneuma hagion* (holy spirit) which is equal to that which is endued with, clothed with, power (*dunamis*) from on high!

Now, keep your finger in Luke and go back to Acts, verse 6.

Acts 1:6
When they therefore were come together [this is at the day of the Ascension], they [the apostles] asked of him, saying, Lord, wilt thou at this time restore again the kingdom to Israel?

Jesus Christ was talking to them about the greatest thing coming in the whole world, and you know what they were concerned about? They didn't understand him at all. It went over their heads. It's really shocking when you think it through. Here is Jesus' last minute on earth with them and he is so concerned about giving them this last minute information and instruction, really getting them all lined up on it, and you know what they're concerned about? Who's going to be the new treasurer, and who will be secretary of state. That's right. For they asked of him, "Wilt thou at this time restore...the kingdom to Israel?" For had the kingdom of Israel been restored, the apostles would have been in seats of rulership and authority.

I've always marveled at the answer Jesus gave them. Had it been anybody else but the Lord Jesus Christ he'd have balled them out. He would have said "Why aren't you listening to me? I'm not talking about that stuff. I'm talking about something a lot bigger!" But they asked him a very unimportant question at that moment and he gives them a very wonderful answer, lovingly.

Acts 1:7
And he said unto them, It is not for you [the apostles] to know the times or the seasons, which the Father [God] hath put in his own power [authority].

The word power is not *dunamis* at all—the word "power" is authority. He put it in His own authority. I love that answer because all through the years people come up to me from all over, and they're always talking about knowing the time when the Lord is coming back. Some told me he came back in 1918. Somebody else said that he's coming back in 1966. Somebody wrote me less than a month ago that he's coming back in 1967. Every time I get these letters and hear from people like that, I wish we had a betting organization. There is one sure thing that I could bet; he's not coming when they say he's coming! Why? The Word of God says so! So any time a man comes along and he says Jesus Christ is coming next Tuesday morning at 8:17 and a half, he's not coming! The reason he isn't coming is because the Word of God says that *nobody*, but God himself, the Father, knows the time or the seasons which the Father has put in his own power.

Acts 1:8
But ye shall receive power, after that the Holy Ghost is come upon you: and ye shall be witnesses unto me both in Jerusalem, and in all Judea, and in Samaria, and unto the uttermost part of the earth.

"But ye shall"—talking to the apostles, "ye shall receive power." Now, let's settle this word "shall." It becomes very important that you understand the word "shall." If the Word says "ye will" receive power, it would mean "perhaps." But when it says "ye shall" it puts it into the absolute. I'd like for you to mark this in your Bible or in your notes, something I have written in the back of my Bible. In the singular and plural, first and second person: "I will" means absolute; "I shall" means simple future. Now we are in the singular. "You" or "they will" denotes simple future. When you say "you will" or "they will" it denotes simple future time. "You" or "they shall" denotes absolute. You have it? Those are the things you must remember grammatically. "You" or "they will" denotes simple future. "You" or "they shall" denotes absolute. You see, in the singular it's one thing, in the plural the order is just reversed. So if you can remember the singular, then you can just reverse the plural. "I will" means absolute in the singular. "I shall" means simple future.

Now "you" or "they" means simple future. "You" or "they shall" denotes absolute. In Acts chapter 1, verse 8 it says: "But ye shall"—"ye shall" is plural putting it into the absolute. Do you see it? "But ye shall [absolute] receive" and there comes that word that I asked you to mark, because the word "receive" is the word meaning "to manifest."

There are two Greek words translated "receive" that affect us in the work of the holy spirit field. The one is the word *dechomai* which means I as a believer subjectively receive. The subject receives what God makes available. This then would be for me to be endued with power from on high. Right? That's right. Now the other word translated "receive" is the word *lambanō*. The word *lambanō* means to manifest out here in the senses realm. You know you can receive something spiritually without ever receiving it into evidence or into manifestation, without it ever being seen in the senses realm. Because that which you receive spiritually is spirit, and you can't see spirit, you can't smell it, you can't taste it, you can't touch it. Therefore, when you *lambanō* it, you manifest it. To *lambanō* is for the subject to make it manifest in the senses realm, which is to receive it into the world, into evidence so that others can see it. And the word "receive" in verse 8 is the word *lambanō*.

"But ye shall *lambanō*"—do you know why it has to be this? Because he has already told them that they would be baptized in *pneuma hagion*, endued with power from on high. So the moment they got endued with power from on high, had they received spiritually? Yes! They would have received spiritually, but had they received into the senses realm? So he puts the whole thing together here in Acts. He says, not only will you receive it spiritually, be baptized in *pneuma hagion* (holy spirit) but, ye shall —absolutely—receive it into manifestation into the senses realm! Ye shall absolutely receive, then the next word "power" is the Greek word *dunamis*. You shall receive this inherent power in manifestation. You've got it in here, now you bring it out here, you *lambanō* it!

Acts 1:8a
...ye shall receive [*lambanō*] power, after...

The word "after" is the word "when"; it's the same word. Now, ye shall receive power after (or when that) the *pneuma hagion*. Now the article "the" remains in here.

Acts 1:8b
...the Holy Ghost [holy spirit] is come upon you:...

Why does the article "the" remain in here grammatically? It is a very wonderful usage of the article "the." Not to make it "The Holy Spirit," who is God. It's not God he is talking about. Then why the article? Because he's already given us this *pneuma hagion* (holy spirit). Ye shall be baptized (in verse 5) with *pneuma hagion* (holy spirit). Now the emphasis is in verse 8. To emphasize that it will be the same which they have received into manifestation, now he puts the article "the" in front of it. This is to identify it as the same thing that they have received spiritually. It's like saying, you have received holy spirit, now make THE holy spirit, manifested. He just put an article to it to emphasis it. This is a grammatical usage permissible in language, and this is exactly why it is done that way in this particular verse: "*Ye shall receive power, when that the pneuma hagion is come upon you:...*"[13] You see, you shall receive it into manifestation is what this verse is talking about. For you have already received it spiritually when it comes to pass (what will occur in verse 5). Do you understand?

Now then, "as ye shall"—ye shall again is absolute. Not simple future, it's absolute.

Acts 1:8c
...ye shall be [what?] witnesses...

It does not say "defense attorneys"; it does not say that

---

13. A literal translation according to usage of Acts 1:8.

you become an apologist (to apologize for what you have received). It says you don't even have to argue about it, you just witness—witness! Witness is one who bears testimony, that's all. But this witness here is entirely different than what I was taught. It's entirely different than any commentary I've ever read, because of the context in which we are dealing. It is to witness! It is to bring into manifestation what you have spiritually. In Acts 2, when we get to it, I'll show you again and again that the witness was they spoke in tongues.

This is what he is talking about in this verse when he says you shall *lambanō* the power, manifest the power when this is come upon you. You shall absolutely thereby as you manifest be a what? Witness—a witness, a witness! The witness in the senses world that the apostles were born again on the Day of Pentecost and had received the power of the holy spirit in Acts 2:4 says "for they spake with tongues"! That's the witness. My talking about the Bible, my talking about the new birth is not the witness. The witness in the senses world that you've got the "real McCoy" on the inside, the witness, is the speaking in tongues. "Ye shall" absolutely, no ifs, ands or buts about it.

> **Acts 1:8c**
> …you shall [absolutely] be witnesses unto me both in Jerusalem,…in all Judaea,…in Samaria, and unto the uttermost part of [what?] the earth.

And if you enlarge this a little bit the "uttermost part of the earth" might include where you and I live.

Verse 9.

> **Acts 1:9, 10**
> And when he had spoken these things, while they [the twelve apostles] beheld, he [Jesus Christ] was taken up; and a cloud received him out of their sight.

THE DAY OF PENTECOST—WHAT, WHERE, WHO 31

And while they [the twelve apostles] looked steadfastly toward heaven [looked up] as he went up, behold, two men [angels] stood by them [the twelve apostles] in white apparel;

This is the Ascension, this is the description thereof. In the Gospel of Luke, chapter 24, it says in verse 50: "And he led them out as far as to [where?] Bethany." Bethany is on the east side of the Mount of Olives. Bethany was the city which was the home of Mary and Martha and Lazarus.

Luke 24:50
And he led them out as far as to Bethany,...

And people this becomes important, like the whole Word of God is important, because if you went to the holy land today on a trip they will always show you where Jesus ascended from and it's absolutely contrary to the Word of God! The Word of God tells you where he ascended from, so why argue. But see they never read the Word of God. They just go looking for footprints and sand or something. That's right. Over in Jerusalem they you take right up there and show his footprint in the stone. And they say that's where he ascended from. And you pay them a buck and a half an hour to tell you those errors, or two bucks. Then they hold out their hands for extra gifts. Good deal—unbelievable!

This is what the Word says, verse 50.

Luke 24:50b, 51
...and he lifted up his hands, and blessed them.
And it came to pass, while he blessed them, he was parted from them, and carried up into [what?] heaven.

Which means he went up. Where is heaven? Any place above earth, it's up! That's what the Word means, that's what is says.

Now back to Acts.

Acts 1:10
…stood by them in white apparel;

And here we come into a mighty change between verse 10 and 11 because when Jesus ascended Judas Iscariot was still there. As we have followed very carefully on the pronouns, I've hit them every time they've come up. But now in verse 11, after Jesus' Ascension these angels spoke to the men who were remaining. Judas must have left because in verse 11 the angels addressed them saying:

Acts 1:11a
…Ye men of Galilee,…

There's the switch, a change of nouns. Because the first noun that we approached was "the apostles whom he had given" way back in verse 2.[14] And from then on it was simply a pronoun describing the apostles whom he had chosen. The pronoun is always controlled by closest associated noun, grammatically.

Now these men (angels) could no longer say "you apostles" as they had said before whom he had chosen, because they were not all present, one had gone away. That one that had gone away was Judas. The other eleven men that were remaining were all Galileans! Judas was the only one of the twelve who was not a Galilean. He was a Judean. He came from the city of Iskar in southern Judea and this is why he was called Judas Iscariot. He came from the city of Iskar or as it is many times called Kerioth[15] in southern Judea. So in verse 11 we're rid of Judas.

---

14. Acts 1:2—Until the day in which he was taken up, after that he through the Holy Ghost had given commandments unto the apostles whom he had chosen:
15. Joshua 15:25.

The Day of Pentecost—What, Where, Who 33

And now in verse 11 we have the record of what these angels said to the men of Galilee, the eleven apostles now remaining:

Acts 1:11b
...why stand ye gazing into heaven? this same Jesus, which is taken up from you into heaven, shall [absolutely] so come in like manner [in the same way] as ye have seen him go [up] into heaven.

Is he coming back? If he went up, he is coming back! So when the critics say "he is not coming," when they say "that the Passover was only a prop," when they say "there is nothing to the resurrection of the Lord Jesus Christ," or to the "new birth," or "to speaking in tongues," somebody is a liar! Somebody has got to be wrong! Either the men who say that or the Word of God. I know you must feel like I do, like the prophet of old who said that he would stand on the Word of God with his house if nobody else believed. Remember when Joshua said that as for me and my house, we shall serve the Lord.[16] As for me and my house we shall believe God's Word! We believe that God's Word is God's will; it means what is says.

If the whole world says Jesus Christ is not coming back, I believe he is—in the same manner in which the eleven apostles saw him go up. Verse 12 says, "Then returned they unto..." New York? No. Had they been modern theologians they most likely would have. Why did they go back to Jerusalem? Because Jesus Christ had said go back to Jerusalem and wait. The Word of God meant what it said, and said what it meant! When he said go back to Jerusalem, what did he mean? Go back to Jerusalem, and to these men they believed that the Word of God was the will of God. When he said Jerusalem, they said that's what he meant.

---
16. Joshua 24:15.

Today, when people read the Word of God they say "Oh that may be in the Bible but that doesn't mean what it says!" Is that right? No. If it were, you might as well write yourself another book called "The Key to Scripture." It either means what it says and says what it means or we have no meaning to learn anything!

It's remarkable that all through the Bible the men of God who received anything from God literally believed when God said something! God told Noah once we're going to have a little shower. He told him to go build himself a little boat. Everybody laughed at him but Noah believed the Word of God was the will of God, and he built that ark. Only Noah, his wife, and their three sons and their three wives made it through the little shower, remember? Follow it through the Bible; they are all like that. Here you have another one. Jesus said to go back to Jerusalem and wait. So when it's all over with, they go back to Jerusalem. Remarkable!

> **Acts 1:12, 13a**
> Then returned they unto Jerusalem from the mount called Olivet, which is from Jerusalem a Sabbath day's journey.
> And when they [they who? the men of Galilee]...

Now watch your pronouns. We're now talking about Galileans, the eleven, were come into Jerusalem, they, the men of Galilee, "went up into an upper room." Is it the Day of Pentecost? No! I was taught that the holy spirit was poured out to a hundred and twenty, on the Day of Pentecost, in the upper room. Those teachings are wrong on every count! It isn't the Day of Pentecost at all!

> **Acts 1:13a**
> ...when they...[came] in, they went into an upper room, where abode...

THE DAY OF PENTECOST—WHAT, WHERE, WHO   35

It's the day of the Ascension when they went up into the upper room. And the upper room is the place where the apostles abode. The word "abode" means where they slept. That's where they put on their pajamas and brushed their teeth. The upper room was the place where they abode.

The eleven apostles' names are given in verse 13. The only one that's missing out of that list is who? Judas Iscariot. The other eleven are all Galileans and now their names are given. The upper room was a place where they abode. That's what the Word says. That's where they slept! No women would be allowed in the quarters of this upper room. Not even a woman servant would clean the place. Wherever there were groups of men gathered together, they had to have a male servant. This is an Eastern custom. And therefore, this upper room as it says in the Word of God was just a place where the apostles abode. Please remember this! You say "What difference does it make where it occurred?" It makes all difference in the world! If I say it occurred in the upper room, when the Bible says something else, then somebody is wrong—either V.P. Wierwille or the Word of God! And down through the centuries they've always said "The Word of God is wrong!" I say people have been wrong and the Word of God is right!

Keep your finger here and go to Acts, chapter 2. Verse 41. On the Day of Pentecost after Peter gets through preaching that sermon, it says in the last part of verse 41:

Acts 2:41b
...and the same day there were added *unto them* about three thousand souls.

About 3,000 people got converted. That would take a pretty big upper room just to handle the 3,000 converted ones, right? Take it a step further, if the proportion of salvation was as bad then as it is today, how many must they have had in the upper room listening to Peter preach, that by the time Peter got finished 3,000 were converted? Would you like to guess? 30,000? That would take a pretty good size upper room, wouldn't it? You multi-millionaires here with me tonight, have you got an upper room that will take care of 30,000 people? Why don't you just let the Bible say what it means and means what it says! The upper room was a place where they abode! Eleven men could stay in a room, 40 x 30, or 10 x 10.

Now back in Acts 1, verse 14.

> **Acts 1:14**
> These all [the eleven apostles] continued with one accord [one accord means "unity of purpose."] in prayer and supplication, with the women, and Mary the mother of Jesus, and with [Jesus' brethren] his brethren.

In the upper room? No! It could not be the upper room because the verse just ahead of it said the upper room was where men abode only! It had to be a place where women could meet with men, where they were allowed to come. There is only one place mentioned in the Bible where women could come to pray with men in a public place. And that was the Temple and its environment, the area of the Temple which had a women's court in it and so forth.

Verse 15, "And in those days"—what days? It's the days between the Ascension and the day that they were tarrying for, which we know as the Day of Pentecost.

> **Acts 1:15**
> And in those days Peter stood up in the midst of the disciples, and said, (the number of names together were about an hundred and twenty,)

Is it the Day of Pentecost? No! It's in the days between the Ascension and the Day of Pentecost. It is not yet the

The Day of Pentecost—What, Where, Who   37

Day of Pentecost! Were they in the upper room? No. Wherever they were they had to be at a place where women could be present also. That could only have been in the Temple area when they prayed. And in verse 15, they had to be present at a place where the names together were about a hundred and twenty.

Is it the Day of Pentecost? Nope! It isn't the Day of Pentecost. Were there 120 present? No! It says "about" a hundred and twenty. Those who teach that there were 120 on the Day of Pentecost use verse 15. They use this verse to teach that on the Day of Pentecost there were 120 present in the upper room. It doesn't say that in the Bible at all! It says the upper room was a place where the apostles abode and sometime between the day of the Ascension and the Day of Pentecost, they were gathered together at some place *about* a hundred and twenty. If it's about a hundred and twenty, is it a hundred and twenty? Nope! It could have been a hundred and nineteen. It could not have been a hundred and twenty. It could have been a hundred and seventeen but not a hundred and twenty. And it still is not the Day of Pentecost. And you know what they do with this "about" a hundred and twenty? They select someone to take Judas Iscariot's place. Why would they want to elect someone to take Judas Iscariot's place if Judas Iscariot hanged himself immediately after he betrayed the Lord Jesus Christ and threw the 30 pieces of silver back into the Temple?

It seems to me, if Judas had done that—as all the commentaries teach and everybody else teaches, except the accuracy of the Word. Had Judas done that, then Jesus, during those 40 days while he ministered among the apostles, would have chosen someone to take Judas's place because he chose the twelve to begin with. But Judas had just gone out and killed himself after the Ascension. Jesus was no longer here! Peter and James and John and the other apostles, eleven in all, were in Jerusalem in the upper room waiting for the promise of the Father and they remembered a little scripture. And the scripture that they remembered is verse 16.

> **Acts 1:16-20**
> Men *and* brethren, this scripture must needs have been fulfilled, which the Holy Ghost [*pneuma hagion* (the article "the" meaning God, the Giver) spoke] by the mouth of David spake before concerning Judas, which was guide to them that took Jesus.
> For he was numbered with us, and had obtained part of this ministry.
> Now this man [Judas] purchased a field with the reward of iniquity; and falling headlong, he burst asunder in the midst, and all his bowels gushed out.
> And it was known unto all the dwellers at Jerusalem; insomuch as that field is called in their proper tongue, Aceldama, that is to say, The field of blood.
> For it is written in the book of Psalms, Let his habitation be desolate, and let no man dwell therein; and his bishoprick [his rulership, his ministry] let another take [*lambanō*].

The word "take" is the word *lambanō*. You'll see that tomorrow when you take your notes.

> **Acts 1:21, 22**
> Wherefore of these men that have companied with us all the time that the Lord Jesus went in and out among us,
> Beginning from the baptism of John [when John baptized Jesus], [until] unto that same day that he was taken up from us [the Ascension], must one be ordained to be a witness with us of his [what?] resurrection.

Hallelujah! Every time I speak in tongues, I am a witness of his resurrection! That's it! You have no proof

Jesus Christ arose. You've never seen the Lord Jesus Christ. You have no proof in the senses world at all, except the witness! The witness is the men or women who speak in tongues; that man or that woman has the witness. He is a witness of the resurrected Christ.

I told you in my Foundational Class,[17] I've got more proof of the resurrection of the Lord Jesus Christ than any man or woman I've ever met has proof that George Washington was the president of the United States. I have no proof, whatsoever, that George was the president or that he chopped down a cherry tree. I have no proof, except what a man has written in a book. What he wrote in a book, he could have lied about. Then if all the books lied about it, then I believed a lie. I have no proof. I have built my believing that he was president upon what I've read in books. That's all.

I do not have to build my believing of the Lord Jesus Christ on what I've read in books. (I have to read "The Book" to find out how to operate it!) But, I have a witness. I have a proof! I have a guarantee, a certainty and an assurance which cannot be contradicted or counterfeited of the eternal reality of the Lord Jesus Christ, because he arose again from the dead! And of all the great religious leaders of the world, Buddha and all the rest, there has only ever been one whom God raised from the dead and that's the Lord Jesus Christ! And the proof that God raised him from the dead, he is alive today, he ascended into heaven and coming back is because we have the God given privilege of speaking in a tongue! Bless your heart, I didn't write the Book. Verse 23.

Acts 1:23, 24
And they appointed [the word "appointed" means

---

17. Dr. Wierwille is referring to the *Foundational Class on Power for Abundant Living.*

made to stand] two, Joseph call Barsabas, who was surnamed Justus, and Matthias.
And they prayed, and said, Thou, Lord, which knowest the hearts of all *men*, shew whether [whether is "if either"] of these two thou hast [what?] chosen,

An apostle is one who must be chosen of God. I cannot make an apostle by sending him to my classes. Nor, can any man be made an apostle by going to a college or seminary. These apostles must be called and chosen of God.

Acts 1:25
That he may take part [the word "take part" again is *lambanō*—that he may manifest] of this ministry and apostleship, from which Judas by transgression fell, that he might go to his own place.

Judas committed suicide. Verse 26.

Acts 1:26a
And they gave forth their lots [another text reads their ballots]; and the lot fell upon Matthias;…

In another text it reads: "They gave forth their ballots and the ballot was for Matthias"; and I don't believe that "ballot" is where you get a slip of paper and you write whether you want Barsabas or Matthias. I think it was done entirely by revelation, but that's neither here nor there in the holy spirit field right now.

Acts 1:26b
…and he was numbered with the eleven apostles.

If he was numbered with the eleven then now we have again how many? Twelve—twelve apostles. Is it the Day of Pentecost? No. It's in the days between the Ascension and the Day of Pentecost when this was done. Now they've gotten twelve back, one to replace Judas. Now the next verse we get to the Day of Pentecost.

THE DAY OF PENTECOST—WHAT, WHERE, WHO   41

Acts 2:1a
And when the day of Pentecost was fully come, they...

They who? The pronoun is controlled by its closest associated noun. And the closest associated noun is the eleven apostles to which Matthias was added therefore the noun is apostles making twelve.

Acts 2:1b-4
...they [the twelve apostles] were all with one accord in one place.
And suddenly there came a sound from heaven as of a rushing mighty wind, and it filled all the house where they [They who? the twelve apostles] were sitting.
And there appeared unto them [Them who?—the twelve apostles] cloven tongues like as of fire, and it sat upon each of them [Them who?—the twelve apostles].
And they [the twelve apostles] were all filled with the Holy Ghost [*pneuma hagion*—holy spirit], and began to speak with other tongues, as the Spirit gave them [Them who? the twelve apostles] utterance.

And that's the end of Pentecost! Four verses. In Acts 2, how many were present on the original outpouring? Twelve! And these twelve were all apostles. That's what the Word says, that's what it means. All you have to be able to do is read! And anybody with an ounce of brains can see it. But you've got to read the Word, not your theology.

Before the Day of Pentecost, there were about 120 present when they selected somebody to take Judas Iscariot's place. But after they had selected that one "...he [Matthias was joined] was numbered with the eleven apostles, And when the day...they..." They—they—they (Acts 2:1)—the twelve apostles. That's how the Word fits!

Well, now we have only one question left. Where did it occur? In Acts, chapter 2, verse 2, it says:

> **Acts 2:2**
> And suddenly there came a sound from heaven as of a rushing mighty wind, and it filled all the house where they were sitting.

And from that word "house" they have read and inserted the error that it is the upper room. It doesn't say "upper room," it says "the house." Had God meant "upper room" you know what it would say? Upper room. You know how I know He had this in His vocabulary? Because He used it in Acts 1. Right? So God must have had it in His vocabulary, or the men he gave it to. And had God meant "upper room," He would have said "upper room." He didn't mean "upper room," He meant "the house." And the only thing in the Bible that's called "the house" is the Temple.

> **Luke 19:46**
> Saying unto them, It is written, My house is the house of prayer: but ye have made it a den of thieves.

Jesus Christ himself referred to the Temple as "the house of prayer." This last statement reflects the writing of the prophet Isaiah in which the Lord called His house a house of prayer. The Temple is always the house of Prayer. This is covered in the holy spirit book in more depth.[18]

I'm going to illustrate this from our teaching ministry. There are many of you in here tonight who have groups in your home during the week. Your house and my house may be "a house" or "an house." Two, three, four, five, or six people come into your house and you teach them

---

18. *Receiving the Holy Spirit Today*, seventh edition, p. 56.

The Day of Pentecost—What, Where, Who   43

the Word of God. You share with them the greatness of God's Word, right? Now that is "a" teaching center. That is a teaching place or that is a place where they are taught. But you will say, "I'm teaching you the accuracy of what the ministry represents." But for the ministry (this place in which you are gathered tonight), it is "the" teaching center. Your home would be "a" teaching center, but this place here would be "the" teaching center. So the Temple was "the house," while all the rest of the places where the synagogues were "an house" and so forth, but the Temple was "the house."

There they would have plenty of room! There they would be able for it to be "noised abroad." There it would be possible for 30,000 people to gather at the feast of Pentecost. There it would be possible for 3,000 people to get converted. And there is no question about it if you will turn to Luke 24:52 again.

> **Luke 24:52, 53**
> And they worshipped him, and returned to Jerusalem with great joy:
> And were continually [where?] in the temple, praising and blessing God....

Yet, in Acts 1, verse 13 it says: When they came back into Jerusalem, they went into an upper room. Do you have an apparent contradiction? No, it is not an apparent contradiction; it's just been a lack of understanding! It does NOT say in Luke 24, "they were *continuously* in the temple." It says they were in the Temple, when? *Continually*. The word "continuously" would mean they were there ALL the time. But they weren't there ALL the time in the Temple. It says in Luke, they were in the Temple "continually." To continually be some place is to be there when you are supposed to be there! Not all the time, but all the times you are supposed to be there.

These are hours of the day. In the Old Testament, and even to this day in 1967 among Mohammedans,[19] as well as Orthodox Jews, there are still five hours of prayer (the first hour, the third hour, the sixth hour, the ninth hour, and the twelfth hour). The first hour corresponds to our 6:00am. The second hour corresponds to our 9:00am. The third hour corresponds to our 12:00pm. The fourth hour corresponds to our 3:00pm. The fifth hour corresponds to our 6:00pm. They were continually in the Temple in the first hour, the third hour, the sixth hour, the ninth hour and the twelfth hour. The five hours of prayer —that's when they were at the Temple, praying after the Ascension until the Day of Pentecost.

Now on this Day of Pentecost, in verse 1 of Acts 2.

Acts 2:1b
...they [the twelve apostles] were all with one accord [unity of purpose] in one [what?] place.

Now that "place" was called in verse 2 "the house," right? And I said to you this was "the Temple," and they were in the Temple at the hours of prayer. The reason I know this is because when Peter gets up to preach, some short time after this experience on the Day of Pentecost, in verse 14 it says:

Acts 2:14a, 15
But Peter, standing up with the eleven [and one

---

19. This was the term used in 1967 for Muslim. "Mohammedan is a term for a follower of the Islamic prophet Muhammad. It is used as both a noun and an adjective, meaning belonging or relating to, either Muhammad or the religion, doctrines, institutions and practices that he established. The word was formerly common in usage, but the terms Muslim and Islamic are more common today. Though sometimes used stylistically by some Muslims, a vast majority consider the term a misnomer."
(https://en.wikipedia.org/wiki/Mohammedan)

makes twelve], lifted up his voice, and said unto them,...

...these are not drunken, as ye suppose, seeing it is *but* [what?] the third hour of the day.

And the third hour was an hour of what? Prayer. Where were they? They were in the Temple, the third hour of the day, an hour of prayer. They were in the Temple at the first hour and received. The receiving of the holy spirit occurred at this first hour. They were in the Temple. And this is why the women could be there. It's why it could get noised abroad. We will read all of this as we get deeper into the class: how it could be noised abroad, how all Jerusalem could come together, how there could be 3,000 converted. After they had received here it got noised abroad. And by this third hour of the day, Peter was already doing what? Preaching! Had he been in his office and outlined his sermon, read all of his commentaries, and written it out in long-hand? No! By the third hour of the day he was already preaching.

I haven't handled anything except Acts 1 and five verses from the Gospel of Luke. This is how the wonderful Word of God (without any private interpretation and with just a little bit of understanding) puts this whole thing together; to let you not only know WHAT it was that came on the Day of Pentecost, but that you know WHO were present, and that you are fully aware of WHERE it occurred.

God has never had to do anything behind closed doors. He never needs to put us up into an upper room, lock the doors and turn the lights out! If it's of God, it can stand the light. And where would have been a more wonderful place for God to pour out the greatest gift the world has ever received, than to do it publicly right out in the open where *everybody* could see it! Everybody could be a part of it. Everybody who wanted to could be blessed by it. He has *never* had to do anything in the dark. And He promised to meet His people and so forth in the Temple. By the way, class, this is the last time that God ever brought (to God's own people Israel) the light of God's Word back to the Temple. This is it. From here on out because they rejected, from here on out, He never comes back there again. Jesus Christ is coming back some day to where the Temple was built on Mount Zion, but when he comes back then he will come as King of Kings and Lord of Lords.

This is the beginning of this class, and I think you all know what a tremendous time it's going to be. Because all we are going to do is just work this Word and let this Word live abundantly. So, I thank God for the privilege of teaching, for the health and strength to do it.

[Prayer] *Father, I thank thee for thy Word and thy greatness and thy presence and power. I thank thee Father that this Word of God is a lamp unto our feet and a light to our path. I thank thee for its greatness among our people. And let this Word live abundantly in our lives. So we praise thee and thank thee for it, through Christ Jesus our living Lord. Amen.*

FILLED WITH
PNEUMA HAGION

We begin with the deeper parts of some of these great truths in the holy spirit field. In the Introduction of *Receiving the Holy Spirit Today*, there is a notation regarding the usage of the words *pneuma* and *hagion*. It says: In our Authorized King James Version, the word *pneuma* is used 385 times. It is translated with a capital "S," Spirit—133 times. (This is in your King James Version, the ones that you bring to class with you.) With a small lower case "s", spirit—153 times. (So in 133 times the King James translators said it referred to God.) This 153 times, the King James men said it did not refer to God. Same word, same word.) Once they translated it "spiritual." Twice they translate the word *pneuma* as "ghost." Once it is translated as "light." Once it is translated "wind" in the Gospel of John, and once adverbially as "spiritually." And with the word *hagion*, holy, it is rendered in your King James translation "Holy Spirit" 4 times and "Holy Ghost" 89 times.

Now this you have to put into your mind. You've got to understand these words *pneuma* and *hagion*. In the critical Greek texts, as well as in the Aramaic texts, these words *pneuma* and *hagion* are never, never capitalized! The word *pneuma* is "spirit"; the word *hagion* is the word "holy." Those two words you've got to memorize. Those you have to know. Those you have to be absolutely sure of! These two words are used, as I have just told you in that introductory paragraph—they are used so differently in the King James Version that you cannot go to the King James and understand the holy spirit field! Nor can you go to any other translation and understand it, because every other translation is as confused as the King James.[1]

So we're going to have to go much deeper, but it's real simple once we get to the principle; it is real simple so you can understand it! These two words are never capitalized in any original, critical Greek text. Therefore, all capitalization thereof, will immediately be private interpretation. The first thing we have to know regarding any scripture, the prophecy of the scripture, is that it is of no private interpretation! Now, that is true but we run into a problem in the English language, because, in the English language the requirement is that when we have a proper noun we have to capitalize it. The word "holy" and the word "spirit" are nouns. Now it's never capitalized in Greek but in English what are you going to do with it? You see if it becomes a proper noun in English, we will have to capitalize it.

Take an ordinary noun like the word "dog." To capitalize the word "Dog" wouldn't make that dog any "dogier" and wouldn't make it any more effective. Take the noun "cat." To capitalize the word "Cat" doesn't make the cat any "catier." But, when it comes to a study of the noun *pneuma hagion* and you capitalize the word "Spirit" or leave it in lower case, it makes all the difference in the world! Because if you capitalize "Holy" and "Spirit" or you write it in lower case "holy" and "spirit," there is a tremendous difference in English. If it's capitalized, it's always equal to God. Always! So whenever those words "holy" or "spirit" refer to God, we in English would always have to capitalize it.[2]

This usage of these two words for both "the Giver" and "His gift" have caused no end of confusion. This is be-

---

1. Referring to the King James Version of the Bible.
2. Holy Spirit.

cause the same words are used in the Bible for the Giver who is "The Holy Spirit," or the same words are used for His gift which is "holy spirit." This is the "Giver" and this is His "gift."

If I gave you this piece of chalk, would you get the giver or the gift? You would get the gift. Now, "The Holy Spirit" is God. He is the Giver. On the Day of Pentecost was the first time in the history of the world that He could give what "He is" in people, and that was the "new birth" and it is called His gift which is "holy" and which is "spirit." For it is God-in-Christ-in-you which is "spirit" and God is "Holy." God is "Holy" and God is "Spirit." John 6:24 says just as plain as day, God is a what? Spirit.[3]

So, these two words you must understand. Then you have to recognize the difference between the Giver and His gift. The Giver is "The Holy Spirit"; His gift is "holy spirit." This is why every time after the Day of Pentecost (or before) when it talks about that which came on the Day of Pentecost, it should always be translated with a small "h" and a small "s." It is never the Giver, it's always His gift! In one verse of scripture you have the usage of these two words uniquely set apart. In John, chapter 3, verse 6.

John 3:6
That which is born of the flesh is flesh; and that which is born of the Spirit is spirit.

The first word "Spirit" is capitalized, the second is lower case. In the original text they are both *pneuma*, both lower case. Now why did they capitalize the first "spirit"? Because they said it is who? God. And they said that the second one was "His gift." And they are right grammatically in English. There, in the first one the Spirit is the

---

3. John 4:24—God *is* a Spirit: and they that worship him must worship *him* in spirit and in truth.

Giver. The second word "spirit" is His gift. You see how that is accurate there? So you must always distinguish between the "Giver" and His "gift." Always! The same words are used, the word *pneuma* and the word *hagion*, but you will always have to find out from context whether it's talking about God or whether it's talking about what God gave. If it's talking about what God gave, it's always "holy spirit" (lower case—small "h," small "s"). If it is God, it would have to be a capital "H" or a capital "S."

Now, as I told you in that paragraph they translated it "holy spirit" 4 times, and "holy ghost" 89 times. It is this word *pneuma* (spirit) which they translated "ghost." And that is a poor translation for us today, because with the word "ghost" you think about something hanging up in the closet! But, that's what they did in the King James Version and this is what we are working so you have to understand it. It's the word *pneuma*. And as I told you in the last session, these two words *pneuma* and *hagion* when they translate it, it's just reversed. You see *pneuma hagion* is "spirit holy" but in English we don't say "spirit holy"; we say "holy spirit."

In the last session from Acts 1:4-5, and from the Gospel of Luke 24:49, we discovered out of three verses that what it was that came on the Day of Pentecost was to be endued, spiritually clothed with power (*dunamis*—inherent or potential power) from "on high" (from God). That's what it was. And that which came was to be "baptized with"—to be baptized with is a one-time deal because you are born again just once. It's an "inside job" to be baptized with or in *pneuma hagion* (holy spirit) which is His gift.

Now in Acts, chapter 1, we also learned that in those days between the days of the Ascension and the Day of Pentecost was when Peter stood up with the "about" 120 and that it was not yet the Day of Pentecost. Then in the last session I deliberately hurried over a section in the first chapter in the Book of Acts, because I did not want to touch it until the whole class was in session now. Acts chapter 1, verse 18. Talking about Judas, I would suggest you read the Study in Abundant Living[4] entitled "When Judas Hanged Himself." But for those of you who have or haven't read it, I'll give you the essence of it and the truth of it here from the text (even as it is written in that little booklet).[5]

In Acts 1:18 it's talking about Judas.

Acts 1:18
Now this man purchased...[6]

The word "purchased" here is also used in Matthew 10:9. The same Greek word there is translated "provided." And I can understand this because he purchased for himself, and when you purchase something for yourself you provide it for yourself. Judas purchased for himself "a field." The word "field" is the Greek word *chorion*. You ought to put in it in the margin or up on top of the page in your Bible. The word *chorion* means "lot," a "lot" or property. That's the meaning of the word. Now this man purchased (or he provided for himself) a property, a "lot." In the King James it says "field" but it isn't quite a field. You get the wrong impression of a "field." He bought himself a "lot" in town or something, a property. That's what he bought. And he bought this in the next phrase, it says: "...with the reward of iniquity;..."

All the commentaries say that the "reward of iniquity" was the thirty pieces of silver that he got for betraying

---

4. The Bible Tells Me So, Chapter 16, "When Judas Hanged Himself."
5. When Judas Hanged Himself. (New Knoxville, Ohio: American Christian Press. 1965, 14 pp.)
6. Acts 1:18—Now this man purchased a field with the reward of iniquity; and falling headlong, he burst asunder in the midst, and all his bowels gushed out.

the Lord Jesus Christ. This is not true. He bought this property with money he had stolen out of the purse because he was the treasurer of the apostles. He stole money from the purse of the apostles. And that money that he stole is called "the reward." The word reward is the word "wages" also. This is what he stole; it's the wages of iniquity. He stole this from the purse. The side reference is Matthew 10:9 and John 12:6, if you want them, and perhaps you ought to look it up now. Will someone please read Matthew 10:9 and someone else John 12:6.

> **Matthew 10:9**
> Provide neither gold, nor silver, nor brass in your purses,

The word "provide" is the same word for "purchase" that I told you about a little while ago. It's the same Greek word.

Now John 12:6.

> **John 12:6**
> This he said, not that he cared for the poor; but because he was a thief, and had the bag, and bare what was put therein.

See, it states Judas was a "thief." He carried the purse or "bag of money" that belonged to the apostles. This is what the verse is talking about. It is that money that he stole from the apostles' purse which is called the "reward of iniquity." So with that reward of iniquity money, he purchased (or he provided for himself) a property on which he could retire when he got old.

> **Acts 1:18b**
> …and falling headlong, he burst asunder in the midst, and all his bowels gushed out.

Falling headlong on his own property, impaling himself upon a stake (a pointed object like a sword or a piece of wood that had a real sharp point like a spear). He put that stake in the ground and then threw himself on that stake. That is how Judas "hanged" himself. To hang yourself in the Bible does not mean a rope! It means to "impale" yourself, to commit suicide by impaling yourself upon a sharp instrument. *Life* magazine, a year or so ago at the Easter season had the pictures of the impaling of the early Christians and it said underneath, "They hanged themselves," which is right. So he committed suicide on his own property, in his own back yard. When he impaled himself on that pointed object, his bowels gushed out.

> **Acts 1:19**
> And it was known unto all the dwellers at Jerusalem; insomuch as that field [property—*chorion*] is called in their proper tongue, Aceldama [Remember the name of the field—Aceldama], that is to say, The field of blood.

Was it called this when he bought his property? No, but later on after he had committed suicide there and his bowels had gushed out, when he was dead and gone, then the people walking by said, "See that Judas's place where he committed suicide, that's Aceldama. That's the field of blood because he committed suicide there."

Now, this is all that's to the story in Acts 1. But in Matthew 27 is the other record that they have confused with it which I would like to share with you and straighten out. Isn't it wonderful to be able to pattern this?

> **Matthew 27:3-5**
> Then Judas, which had betrayed him [Jesus], when he saw that he was condemned, repented himself [repented himself is "felt sorry"; he felt sorry that he got tripped up], and brought again the thirty pieces of silver to the chief priests and elders,

> Saying, I have sinned in that I have betrayed the innocent blood. And they [the chief priests and elders] said, What *is that* to us? See thou *to that*.
> And he [Judas] cast down the pieces of silver in the temple, and departed and went and hanged himself.

Does it say *where* he hanged himself? Does it say *when* he hanged himself? No. It just says "he threw the thirty pieces of silver and he departed and went and hanged himself." It does not say when. Matthew is simply giving the record of what Judas did with the 30 pieces of silver, and how afterwards he hanged himself. But you and I know from Acts, which we studied in the last session that Judas was still present on the day of the Ascension.

Now, verse 6 tells you what they did with this thirty pieces of silver.

> **Matthew 27:6a**
> And the chief priests took the silver pieces,...

The word "took" is the Greek word *lambanō*—manifested. They bought something with the money. They put it in circulation.

> **Matthew 27:6b**
> ...the silver pieces, and said, It is not lawful for to put them into the treasury, because it is the price of blood.

Why was it the price of blood? Because this is what they paid Judas for betraying the Lord Jesus, so they could crucify Jesus. This is why the 30 pieces of silver was "blood money." They had paid this for the blood, the life of Jesus Christ! That's why it is called "blood money," the price of blood.

> **Matthew 27:7**
> And they [the chief priests and elders] took counsel

[the word "took" is again the word *lambanō*], and bought [bought where? in the market place, publicly] with them [the thirty pieces of silver] the potter's field, to bury strangers in.

They deliberately took the thirty pieces of silver that Judas had thrown back into the Temple and after consultation among themselves (the chief priests and the elders), they said, "We can't put that money back into the treasury, but we have it on our hands. It's blood money, what can we do with it? Well, we will spend it on the real poor, those who haven't even got a place to be buried in. We'll buy them a place to be buried in." Real religious! It sounds just like the modern outfit! So they took the 30 pieces of silver and deliberately went to the public market place and bought the potter's field. The word "field" is the word *agros*, not property, not a little lot, but they bought a whole field! An *agros*. Remember in Latin where *agricola* is the "farmer"; the same root word comes from the Greek word *agros*—the farmer who farms the field. The word "field" in Latin is the same word *agros*, just transliterated over from the Greek.

Matthew 27:7b
...the potter's field, to bury strangers in.

Foreigners, the so called "no ones" who had a place to be buried.

Matthew 27:8
Wherefore that field [*agros* which those chief priests and elders bought with the 30 pieces of silver] was called, The field of [what?] blood, unto this day.

Now this field of blood is not the same field of blood as the one in Acts, because this one was not bought with the same money. This was the field of blood, called so later by the people, when the people found out that they (the priests and elders) had bought this *agros* with blood money, the thirty pieces of silver to bury strangers in. Therefore, that field was called by the public "the field of blood." In Acts, I told you to remember it was called "Aceldama." Here the words are *agros hacmatos. Agros* is the word "field"; *hacmatos* is "blood" and that's "field of blood," an entirely different word. Is there a contradiction between the record in Matthew and the record in Acts? No. The contradiction is in the concordances, not in the Word of God. The contradiction is in men's minds, not in God's Word. They are two entirely different things being talked about.

In Acts, the record is regarding Judas: where Judas hanged himself, who's property it was, how he got it, and that he committed suicide on his own property. While the record in Matthew is regarding what the chief priests and elders did with the 30 pieces of silver. That's all. No contradiction.

Now Acts, chapter 2. All the rest I covered with you in the last session. But now we know from the accuracy of the Word, that the outpouring of the holy spirit on the Day of Pentecost was in the Temple. We know that there were twelve apostles present who received the original outpouring. Furthermore, we know that it was God's gift *pneuma hagion*, endued with power from on high, which was given.

Now we're ready to understand the experience of Pentecost as it's given in only four verses of the Book of Acts. Chapter 2, verse 1. You know, the word "and" is a conjunction. The word "and" is the same Greek word as the word "but." I am sure that here it should be the word "but." You know why class? Because "and" is a conjunction, tying that which went before with that which follows, setting it in correspondence with. While the word "but" sets it in contrast with. And here, I believe it's set in contrast with. Verse 26, "And they gave forth their lots; and the lot fell upon Matthias; and he was numbered with the eleven apostles."⁷ Period. I believe that is the end of the experience.

Now to set it in contrast with that experience of the selection of the twelfth apostle, the first word of Chapter 2 would be the word "But," and that would set it in contrast. This is why I believe it's the word "But."

Acts 2:1a
[But] when the day of Pentecost was fully come,...

Which was 10 days after the Ascension, and 40 days after the Resurrection for a total of 50 days, that's what the word "pente" means—50.

Acts 2:1b
...they [the twelve apostles] were all with one accord in one place.

Pentecost was a Jewish (Hebrew) celebration which was observed every year.⁸ It was one of the great feasts of the Jewish year. It lasted a total of 7 days. Fifty days after the Passover they had a Pentecost feast which lasted 7 days. And it was during this feast, when they were all at Jerusalem again, when the Day of Pentecost was fully come.

As far as you and I are concerned from the accuracy of the Word, Pentecost, that which we are now going to see which occurred, was in the process of coming ever since Genesis 3 when man fell. When Adam and Eve succumbed to Satan's intrigue, from that day on God had planned and God put forward the best He could. But the best never came until this day that we are going to read about. It was in the process of coming but it never fully came. This is why in the Old Testament, at times you read about the holy spirit being "on" men, to a degree. In the

---
7. Acts 1:26.
8. Pentecost was one of the three yearly celebrations.

Old Testament at various times, men could prophesy. Men at various times could receive word of knowledge, word of wisdom, discerning of spirits, faith, miracles and healing in the Old Testament. But it never fully came. It was two different senses, class. It never fully came.

Number one: it was completely complete. Number two: it could be and would be in everybody who was a believer. There are believers in the Old Testament who never gave a word of prophecy, who never received word of knowledge, word of wisdom, discerning of spirits, etc. This, in the Old Testament, was reserved for the men of God, the prophets. But, you saw all of this in the Old Testament in part but it never fully came until this day.

The fullest that it was in the Old Testament was upon our Lord and Savior Jesus Christ. The Lord Jesus Christ had everything that was available up until that time. But, the Lord Jesus Christ could not be born again because it was not yet available. He came to make it available. But the new birth, the power of his holy spirit as an indwelling reality and anointing, never became a reality until the Day of Pentecost that we are going to read about.

Where is that scripture that it has the word "measure" —upon him by measure? You know what I'm after class? John, chapter 3.

> **John 3:34**
> For he whom God hath sent speaketh the words of God: for God giveth not the Spirit by measure *unto him*.

"God giveth not the Spirit by measure *unto him*"— "*unto him*" is in italics but it's done very well. "God giveth not the Spirit by measure" means that he had everything that was available. Up before this time, to a prophet like Isaiah, it was measured out; like Saul was numbered among the prophets, it was measured and metered out. All through the Old Testament and Gospels you will find this truth. But on the Day of Pentecost, now we're at the place for the first time in the history of the world that something is able to become fully-full.

And I believe you will remember that I've taught you in the Foundation Class, that the reason God had to wait so long is because God couldn't find a man or a woman to believe. Had someone believed, the Lord Jesus Christ would have been born nine months after Adam and Eve sinned! But they did not believe! Nobody believed until Mary came along. And it was Mary who was the first woman who absolutely ever believed God that she was able to say, "Be it unto me according to thy word."[9] This is why she brought forth the Christ.

And God knew that when Jesus Christ would be born, he would always do his Father's will, therefore he became our savior. And he made available what God then was able to give to man on this day that we are reading about!

> **Acts 2:1a**
> And when the day of Pentecost was fully come [fully come], they [the twelve apostles] were all with one accord…

"…one accord" means unity of purpose because it was an hour of prayer. So they were in the Temple.

> **Acts 2:1b**
> …in one place [the Temple].

And they were in the posture (or in the attitude) of prayer. That's what it means.

> **Acts 2:2a**
> And suddenly there came a sound from heaven as of a rushing mighty wind,…

---

9. Luke 1:38.

It was a sound from heaven as of a heavy breathing. I believe the word "came" could be translated "was" from the Aramaic. You see, flip back a page to John 20.

John 20:22
And when he had said this, he breathed on *them* [breathed in], and saith unto them, Receive ye the Holy Ghost [*pneuma hagion*—no article]:

When he had said this he breathed on them. Those are the same words as "rushing mighty wind." Suddenly there came a sound from heaven as of a "heavy or hard breathing." Suddenly "there was" is a much clearer understanding in our English than "there came." The words "there came" implies something from the outside coming in. While, the words "there was" implies that is was immediately present. Acts 2:2, "*And suddenly there was a sound of heaven [or from heaven] as of a heavy breathing…*"[10] And I have demonstrated this to you in all of the classes from the Gospel of John where Jesus was instructing the apostles as to what to do when the right time came. He breathed on them. The text says "he breathed in." Jesus was instructing the apostles on how to receive the holy spirit when the right time came. Could they have received the holy spirit in the Book of John? No. Why not? It had not yet come. Then what was he doing? He was instructing, teaching, preparing. And what occurred that day in the Temple was that all twelve of these men just breathed in. (All of you here, breathe in, open your mouths and breathe in. Now exhale, inhale, exhale—that's that verse.) They opened their mouth wide, inhaled and exhaled. Acts 2:2b, "*…sound from heaven as of a heavy breathing, and it [the breathing] filled all the house [the Temple] where the twelve apostles were sitting.*"[11]

---

10. A literal translation according to usage of Acts 2:2a.
11. A literal translation according to usage of Acts 2:2b.

FILLED WITH *PNEUMA HAGION* 61

And people, you know how I love that, because people have always thought that in order to get the holy spirit you had to get "all lathered up." Yell and shout and "hoop it up," you know. Now you could be yelling and shouting and "hooping it up" and receive it in manifestation. Because the receiving into manifestation hasn't got anything to do whether you're hooping or hopping or yelping or shouting or what you are doing. Receiving it into manifestation has got everything to do with believing and practicing and operating the principles! But the reason I like this is because they were in the posture of prayer. They were sitting. They were praying. They were as quiet as a church mouse. They were not even audibly praying out loud where everybody else could hear them. They were in the posture of prayer. They were decent and they were in order! All this other stuff is indecent and out of order.

Now that does not mean you have to sit to receive the holy spirit. That means that you must be decent and in order. In our particular culture you might be standing, as many of you have been that receive in my classes. Other times you may have been sitting on chairs. I'm sure you were never sitting like this. Only the youngsters in the front row would be able to get up after they sat that way. The rest of us would have to stay put or get someone to take us by the hand and lift us up because they sat cross-legged. I would like to say that among God's people in this country where many people kneel to pray, this is their custom, their manner. There they would be in order if they were kneeling and receiving the holy spirit. Understand? But I'm sure it's never a custom to run around the church throwing song books or jumping over the top of the seats. Or standing and crying with the loudest voice you've got so everybody's "ear balls" are busted. That is not decent and that is not in order.

This Word of God says that on this day they were all sitting, not hanging from the chandeliers, not shouting. They were decent and they were in order. People, you have got to drive these verses into your brain cells. Because outside of this ministry, I know of no group that sticks dynamically and specifically to the integrity of God's Word. I just came out of meetings off of my itinerary where almost everybody was speaking in tongues, but all they had was an "experiential knowledge." They lacked the knowledge of God's Word as to what they had and how to properly carry it out. Some of those poor people tarried like crazy! Others got into a "hooping and shouting" meeting. Some of them just started talking and saying, "Thank you Jesus, thank you Jesus…," and when they got to going fast enough they couldn't say "thank you Jesus" anymore so they started speaking in tongues! Because the spirit could speak faster than they could or something, I don't know. You see they had the reality of the presence of Christ, but they had worked so hard and the experience was so contrary to the integrity and the accuracy of God's Word! It is God's Word that makes it clear as to *how* men and women are to receive God's wonderful gift and his manifestations.

Now verse 3.

Acts 2:3a
And there appeared unto them [the twelve apostles] cloven tongues like as of fire,…

Was it fire, class? No.

Acts 2:3b
…like as of fire [looked like fire], and it [the cloven tongues] sat upon each of them.

Upon each one of these apostles—this was the phenomenon of Pentecost. It is nowhere promised in God's Word that when people receive the holy spirit (when they're born again, filled with the power of the holy spirit, baptized with it, endued with power from on high, when they speak in tongues for the first time) that there will appear "cloven tongues like as of fire." Phenomenon or phenomena is God's prerogative! You will remember in my Foundational Classes how I teach you about the feast of King Belshazzar and what was written on the wall after they were drinking like fish. Written on the wall that thou art weighed in the balances, and art found wanting.[12] This does not mean that every time a king has a drinking festival, an old drunken brawl, that God writes something on the wall. But for that king He did! And on that occasion it was a phenomenon.

God's prerogative is to give men and women phenomena. This is God's business. But He has not promised that He will give this phenomenon every time the holy spirit is manifested. Therefore, it's phenomenon. That which is promised in the Word of God to every believer when they believe is never phenomenon. But, when God goes beyond what He has promised in His Word to every believer, that is phenomena. Can God then give you a phenomenon or phenomena? Yes. But can that phenomenon or phenomena contradict His revealed Word, the Bible? No. It can simply go beyond that which is guaranteed to every believer. And this is exactly what it is when men have what they call "feelings in their hands."

When men who minister at certain times have different manifestations on their physical body, this is God working with that man giving that man phenomenon or phenomena. This is beyond the line of duty, beyond that which is guaranteed to everybody! If you understand this, then you will never mistake again phenomena and that which is guaranteed in the Word.

---

12. Daniel 5:27.

Then can a man honestly teach phenomena? No! Because phenomena are in whose field? God's. But can a man honestly teach the Word of God? Yes, because God's Word is here today; it will be here tomorrow and this is guaranteed to every believer at the moment they believe. You can guarantee everybody that they will speak in tongues—that I can guarantee, because God's Word says so! But when you speak in tongues, if you should get a certain kind of feeling then that would be phenomenon. That I cannot guarantee.

I would like to say that I could almost guarantee that everybody's going to have something. But what it is, I don't know. But, I'd hate to have to guarantee this right down the line because I couldn't do it biblically. But I've seen very, very, very few people under my ministry who have believed God's Word that when they received into manifestation for the first time and spoke in tongues, that they did not have some type of sign to them. Something happened to them, which was in their particular case phenomenon.

You see, if I told you how God signifies things to me in a phenomenal way then you people would be looking for that same feeling, that same phenomena. And if you didn't get that feeling you would say, "Well, I haven't got it." Don't you see? This is why I do not teach my people this. Sometimes in the Advanced Classes you hear me say how God symbolizes different things to me. But, by that time of course everybody understands the difference between phenomena and that which is guaranteed. I simply show you, just like tonight I'm teaching phenomena, how God for instance "runs up and down my spine" I call it. This is His phenomena to me. When He does this certain thing I always know something is absolutely and most definitely finished, done for! That's right! But now, I can't teach this because I don't know anything about God running up and down spines. I don't even know what it means, except that I know that's the only way I can describe it. But you see, I can't teach it. I wouldn't dare teach it, because suppose He doesn't run up and down yours? Then you would say, "Well I haven't got God!"

On the Day of Pentecost this was the phenomenon, this was their clue that this thing was going to come to pass; it had never come before! And this was God's way of telling them (the twelve apostles) that they should now breathe in and believe.

The word "sat" in verse 3 is remarkably unique, because whenever the word "sat" is used in the Bible it always means something is completely finished. When God had finished His work on the sixth day, it says in Genesis, "And on the seventh day God rested from all his work from which he had made." The word "rested" is the word "sat." Did God sit because He was tired, worn out? No, He "sat" because it is a figure of speech saying, "It's all done," finished, completely complete! It said in Acts, "when the day of Pentecost was fully come" and therefore it sat, it sat! When Jesus Christ ascended up into heaven, on the day of the Ascension, what does the Word of God say Jesus did? He "sat down" at the right hand of God because he had fulfilled and completely, completed everything for our redemption!

Verse 4, "*And, they [the twelve apostles] were all filled with pneuma hagion…*" [13]—no article "the" in the text. In the King James they added the article "the" and capitalized the word "Holy" and the word "Spirit." Therefore, does the text in verse 4 talk about God? Were they all filled with "God"? No! Can't be! The King James Version has it all wrong! See, "The Holy Spirit" (they use the word "Ghost"), but "The Holy Ghost" is God when you

---

13. A literal translation according to usage of Acts 2:4a.

capitalize it. It's always God. And here they took those two Greek words *pneuma* and *hagion*, they added the article "the" and they capitalized the word *pneuma* and the word *hagion*. What happens when you add to the Word of God? You remember Genesis 3? (I covered it in the Foundational Class.) [14] What did Eve do? She added to the Word of God, she deleted it, she changed it around. Whenever you add to the Word of God do you have the Word left? No. It's no longer the Word! "…they were all filled with…" Was it the Giver or the gift? It was the gift! The gift from the Giver. "…they were all filled with *pneuma hagion*."

And what is holy spirit? We learned from Acts 1, it is to be baptized in *pneuma hagion*. We learned from Acts 1, that it is THE promise of THE Father. We learned from Luke 24 that it is to be endued with "power from on high." That's it! They were all filled with—all who? all twelve. Was anybody missed? No. Why not? Not because they were in the Temple. It was because they were in the Temple, yes, but not *just* because they were in the Temple. But they were in the Temple believing and carrying out what Jesus Christ had told them before he had ascended: When you see the sign of the cloven tongues, breathe in, breathe in. Go back to Jerusalem and tarry. Go to the Temple at the hours of prayer.

They had obeyed God right down the line. I've never seen a class of mine where they didn't speak in tongues when they obeyed God! I have seen people in my class not speak in tongues, but they don't believe God! Had they been in Jerusalem that day they'd still be sitting back there. Because today men and women just don't think there are any more "men of God" and they have no reverence for God at all! They just think it's a bunch of

---

14. Dr. Wierwille is referring to the *Foundational Class on Power for Abundant Living*.

baloney! You know what's the greatest time in my class? When I have someone who had been seeking the holy ghost, as he says, for 35 years. When they get it they appreciate my teaching! The rest of the people usually sit around like cold cucumbers on a patch in December. Why? Because we don't appreciate the greatness of the knowledge of God's Word, the power of His holy spirit within us! Because, we haven't been brought up in the churches where they even knew anything about it or never talked about it. So naturally we have no hunger for it. In my classes, I have to build the hunger for the holy spirit in the heart and lives of my people. And of course in two weeks' time they don't get that hungry, because I don't spend that much time getting them hungry.

But these apostles, ten days they had been waiting, tarrying. They never missed a meeting in the Temple in any of the five hours of prayer. They were there expecting all the time! Every time they went to the Temple they went back home because there was no what? no cloven tongues like as of fire. That was the clue they were waiting for. Sure. One day they got there, six bells in the morning (6 am), the first hour of prayer and they were praying. I don't know how long they were praying, but sometime between 6:00am and 9:00am, they were sitting there praying and all at once, *"boom, boom"* there it was! Now how could they have seen the cloven tongues like as of fire with their eyes shut? They couldn't! They had their eyes open while they prayed to watch what was going on.

In the Word of God they kept their eyes open when they prayed! It's remarkable when you watch painted pictures. If the art work was a done by a Protestant artist representing the person praying, the person's eyes in the painting will always be shown with their eyes closed. If the art work was a done by a Roman Catholic artist representing the person praying, the person's eyes in the painting will always be shown with their eyes open. Well, I don't know much about that stuff but this I know, that they were expecting, they were anticipating, they were looking forward to this thing! And they were praying but they had their eyes open, and all at once there it was! Cloven tongues sat upon each one of them. Did anybody get missed? No. Look, nobody gets missed in God's Word by God's rules and regulations when people are at the place they're supposed to be and when they're believing what God Word says. Nobody! Just nobody gets missed!

Now, it says they were all filled. If you are filled, can you get any more filled? If this glass of water is full, can you put any more water into it? Not a bit, not even one drop! It says they were all filled. If they are all filled they're not three-quarters filled. All twelve were filled! Now, you better remember it because somebody's going to tell you later on, when they get you in the old world, they're going to tell you that these men had to get refilled all the time! You know, like when a gas tank is empty so you go back to the gas pump with your old truck or car and get it filled up again. In other words, it leaks out. It gets spent someplace along the line. No, no, no.

With spiritual things, once it's full, it's full and it's never empty. It's always there, and this is remarkable, because on the Day of Pentecost when these twelve men were born again, they received Christ, the fullness of Christ in them. They never had anything more; they never got anything less. They all got the same stuff and the same amount! Wow, that's tremendous people! Because that makes God "no respecter of persons."[15] That makes God's gift to these young boys and girls that same full-

---

15. Acts 10:34—Then Peter opened *his* mouth, and said, Of a truth I perceive that God is no respecter of persons:

ness that He gives to you as an adult! The same God that is in you as an adult is in that child of yours. That same fullness that is in you is in that child!

Well, now they're filled! Now what are they going to do? Well, go to church every morning and sit. Go to Sunday school classes; make the men's brotherhood and the women's guild. Go to the youth meetings, the children's fellowship? No. That's exactly where most people have stopped. In the organized church at best today, right there is where they've stopped, when they've been born again. And that's the only message some ministers have! They would have flunked on the Day of Pentecost because all they can do is get God's people saved.

When they were filled, they were saved. But he didn't pronounce the benediction and God say "go home now." On the Day of Pentecost when they were born again, converted, saved, filled with the holy spirit, they immediately did something in the senses world that was the proof that they had the real power, the real McCoy, the genuine of what God had spoken about within themselves. They didn't give to them the Gospel of John, and say, "Go home and read the Gospel of John." They didn't take them into the prayer tent to pray through a little prayer. Nope. How can you pray through any further if you're already full of the power of God? God's Word says, "and they were all filled with the gift" and right after that they, the twelve apostles, began to do what? to speak. *They* began to speak, not the spirit but the apostles. They began to speak! With other tongues as the *pneuma*, the Spirit (capital "S" is correct) gave them utterance.

There in verse 4 you have both the Giver and the gift. In the first part you have the gift and in the last part you have the Giver. They were all filled with the gift; and once they had the gift they had the God given ability. For the gift is the ability! Suppose I give you the gift of that piece of chalk. Once you have received the gift, you've got what now? the ability that the chalk represents. Class, spiritually the gift is always the ability! They were filled with the gift. The gift is the God given ability. The new birth! The fullness of the holy spirit! And being filled with the gift, that's all God could do.

The next action is man. God had done all He could, now it was up to man to do his part. And man's part was that once God had filled them, now man began to speak with other tongues. They did the speaking in tongues by the gift, the power that was in them, as the spirit gave them utterance.[16] They spoke in tongues, but what they spoke was as the spirit gave it to them. They did the speaking. *What* they spoke was God's business, but *that* they spoke was whose business? Their own. I want to go back and hit this verse some more to bring it to its minutest detail for you.

Now,[17] regarding the time frame of when the Day of Pentecost had come,[18] we had it fifty days after the Feast of the Passover. But in the Old Testament, Leviticus 23:10, 11[19] it gives you "the Feast of the First Fruits," which was a feast that the Jewish people had in the fall of the year after they had gathered in their crop. Then fifty days after, in verse 15,[20] it says fifty days after the offering of the first fruits was the celebration of the

---

16. Acts 2:4b—...and began to speak with other tongues, as the Spirit gave them utterance.
17. Teaching resumes after a five minute intermission and discussion which is explained in the next few paragraphs.
18. Acts 2:1—And when the day of Pentecost was fully come,...
19. Leviticus 23:10b—...then ye shall bring a sheaf of the firstfruits of your harvest unto the priest:
20. Leviticus 23:15—And ye shall count unto you from the morrow after the sabbath, from the day that ye brought the sheaf of the wave offering; seven sabbaths shall be complete:

Feast of the Passover. Now this occurred in the fall of the year.

In the New Testament we find in 1 Corinthians 15:23 [21] that Jesus Christ was the "first fruits" from the dead. He was the "first fruits." In John 20:17, Mary Magdalene met Jesus Christ and he said "Touch me not; for I am not yet ascended to my Father:…" [22] (This line refers back to the "first fruits" offering in the Book of Leviticus.) Then the Day of Pentecost did not fall on the Jewish celebration of Pentecost but the Day of Pentecost, when it was fully come. It fell fifty days after Jesus Christ was the "first fruits" from the dead.

This makes it all fit together. It didn't come after the celebration of the Passover, but it came after the celebration of the "first fruits." And, Jesus Christ being the "first fruits" from the dead, the Day of Pentecost fell fifty days after this. Now if you read these scriptures in the Old Testament and in the New Testament you will see how they all fit together and that is how the Day of Pentecost came fifty days after the resurrection of Jesus Christ!

And the reason Jesus Christ said, "Touch me not; for I am not yet ascended to my Father:" [23] is because the requirement of the "first fruit" was that it had to go to the Temple. And he had not yet gone to the Temple. He went there sometime that morning, because shortly thereafter somebody else touched him on the Resurrection morning. These are the kind of things that we are having this week for, to really dig these things out. If I miss any-

---

21. 1 Corinthians 15:23—But every man in his own order: Christ the firstfruits; afterward they that are Christ's at his coming.
22. John 20:17—Jesus saith unto her, Touch me not; for I am not yet ascended to my Father: but go to my brethren, and say unto them, I ascend unto my Father, and your Father; and *to* my God, and your God.
23. John 20:17.

thing or I say anything that isn't quite where it ought to be, then we stop and take a breath and pick it up.

Now this thing we are talking about in Acts 2:1-4 is the greatest thing that ever happened. It was this occurrence that you and I know looking back to in the Book of Corinthians[24] it said: had Satan known, he would not have crucified the lord of glory. This is so big that it turned the world upside down before the apostle Paul died. And it hasn't done one lousy bit with the world since! Today we have got a "form of godliness" but no power,[25] right? It has done very, very little since that first century. But that first century it took a government which was as devilish as any other government that has ever lived and turned it inside out before the death of the apostle Paul! It took temples that had been dedicated to pagan gods like "Diana of the Ephesians" and it just racked and ruined all that spiritualism and all that paganism! Men and women were soundly converted, filled with the power of the holy spirit. That's why these four verses ought to just set a man's soul on fire! We ought to just thrill at the greatness with which God has set His Word and the greatest experience of all time in the history of the world up until this night, in those four verses! That you could be born again of God's spirit. That people could have lived like the Devil, dead in trespasses and sins, without God and without hope, having no eternal life within them, to get born again of God's spirit, get remission of sins, being a baptism that they could not lose, and they had the testimony in the senses world that they had the real McCoy on the inside because they spoke with tongues!

Don't you see what that speaking in tongues means to

---

24. 1 Corinthians 2:8.
25. 2 Timothy 3:5—Having a form of godliness, but denying the power thereof:...

a believer? It means that it's your proof that Christ is in you and Christ couldn't be in you if God hadn't resurrected him from the dead! *It's the proof* that God raised him! *It's the proof* that he ascended up into heaven and sat down. *It's the proof* that this same Jesus is coming back, it's everything to us people! *It's everything to us!* For without that speaking in tongues you have absolutely no proof, none whatsoever. Either that you are a Christian or that God raised him from the dead, or that he sat down at the right hand of God, or that he's coming back, you have no proof! You have only man's thoughts—that's all.

Acts 2:4 says, "they were all filled with [*pneuma hagion*, the gift]," and when they were filled the first thing they did was to speak with other tongues. Why were they able to speak in tongues when they were born again? Because they had just received the gift! Then can a person speak in tongues who is not born again? No. Can Satan speak in tongues? No. Because to speak in tongues, you've got to get born again! And you can't get born of two seeds! You can only get born of one seed, which is Christ in you.[26]

This is why the gift is the God given ability—the gift is the God given ability. Speaking in tongues is the action.

Acts 2:4a
…they were all filled with the Holy Ghost [the gift], and [they] began to speak with other tongues,…

They did it! They took action! They acted! They acted! The act is the result of the operation of the gift. How many gifts are there? How many? One!—How many? One! And you remember it! Only one gift. They were all what? Filled. When it's full, it's full. They were all

---

26. *Power for Abundant Living*, "The Great Mystery: Christ in You the Hope of Glory", Segment 28.

filled. They had one gift. There it is. That represents the gift. One gift. The gift is the ability. The act is the result of the operation of the gift, by the person who has just received the potential power. This is potential. It becomes kinetic when you use it! *They* spoke with tongues. This ability has nine acts;[27] that's all the ability has available for manifestations. One of those is, which we just saw: they spoke in tongues. Speaking in tongues is the act. The gift is the God given ability. The act is the manifestation, carrying it out. In speaking in tongues, what is the gift? The God-given ability. To do what? speak in tongues. What's the act? the speaking. That's the act.

Once more, let's go over it. In speaking in tongues, what is the gift? It is the God-given ability to speak in tongues. What's the act? The act is speaking in tongues. In interpretation of tongues, what is the gift? It is the God-given ability to interpret. What's the act? The act is interpretation. There you have them; they're all the same now: this speaking in tongues, here is interpretation, here is prophecy, here is word of knowledge, here is word of wisdom, here is the discerning of spirits, here is faith, miracles and here is healings. In healing what's the gift? It is the God-given ability to minister healing. What's the act? The act is healing them! Doing it! Carrying it out. They're all the same! You got it now?

Look, this is God's power line and on the Day of Pentecost they got plugged in! Therefore, this power from God flows into this ability. This is the ability; it's just like an electric motor. Here is your electric line and down here is your motor. So you bring up a little bit of wire in here, it depends on how big the motor is. Let's say you've got 110 volts in here, and you've got only an 8 horse motor. You can only absorb an 8 horse power out of this

---

27. 1 Corinthians 12:8-10.

main line, right? But if you've got a larger horse motor, you still may only have a 110 volts coming in but you absorb more of the power. Got it? Now it's just like that in God. Here's God's unlimited ability, but suppose you never use that. How much power do you draw from God? None!

You know what that is? Just your guarantee you're going to be in heaven. People can be born again and have a "hell of a time" going to heaven! You've seen them. Born again because they've confessed with their mouth the Lord Jesus and believed in their heart, they were saved. And when they got saved they got filled by his presence in here (their heart). They got the ability but they never did what? used it. They never used it, they never used it. And so, some of them went through life and never spoke in tongues, never interpreted, never prophesied. Are they going to be in heaven? Sure, but only because it's grace! And it is seed born inside, else they'd never make it. But what are they laying up for themselves? Nothing! They haven't used anything. They're just like "empties" going through life. You look at them, they might as well not be Christians; they never tapped into anything!

Acts 2, they spoke in tongues. Speaking in tongues. Remember in the last session I said that this was *dunamis* power, inherent power. It becomes kinetic power when I speak in tongues. Then I'm utilizing some of the power! Now, am I going to run out? No. Why? Because I'm plugged in! Don't you see it? Is this little electric motor going to run out? No, because it's plugged in. Well, if you can do it with an electric motor, I have a good idea God can do it with us! Right? So we're constantly plugged in! An electric motor you can unplug, but you can't unplug God! That's because you're plugged in, you're born again of His spirit. But, if you never use the power, God never can put more in. This is why this is called *dunamis* power. And any other word than *dunamis* would be out of order because it's "inherent" power. It's spiritual power! Can you see this? Can you smell it? Can you taste it? Can you touch it? No! It's not senses; it's spirit. But here, when you speak in tongues can you see that? Can you hear that? Yes! That's in the senses realm. This is the kinetic part.

People, I want you to understand this like nobody has ever understood it since the first century! That it just jell in your heart and just fit like a hand in a glove. These are the manifestations: speaking in tongues, interpretation, prophecy, word of knowledge, word of wisdom, discerning of spirits, faith, miracles and healing. This here is *dunamis* power! And the power is the ability. You've got just as much power, just as much ability, as God's Word says you have! This is the righteousness of God, the justification, the sanctification, the redemption, the wisdom, the mercy, the grace. All of that is wrapped up in this spiritual little package! In this package is wrapped up "the works that I do, ye shall do, and greater works than I've done ye shall do, because I go to my Father which is in heaven."[28] This is *dunamis*.

I also shared with you in the last session that there is another word used, which is the Greek word *exousia* translated power. This word *exousia* is the Greek word which is transliterated into the English word "exercise." When I as a believer "exercise" my right, which God has given unto me as His son, I exercise *dunamis*; I bring into manifestation the third word that's used in the Bible, which is the word *energamata*. This word *energamata* is transliterated into our English word of "energy." When I exercise my legal right of this *dunamis*, I will speak in

---

28. John 14:12.

tongues. When I exercise it, I will interpret. When I exercise it, I will prophecy, operate the word of knowledge, the word of wisdom, the discerning of spirits, faith, miracles, and healing. And when I exercise this, these here are the *energamata*, these are the energy! I bring forth speaking in tongues, which is the *energamata*. It's the energy of God in the senses world that I've got the "real McCoy" on the inside and I'm carrying out the job God wants me to do. Now, when I give out, like here, what's God got to do? He's got to pour it in, just like the electric motor. When you turn on the motor the current has to keep coming in or you run out of "poof," or something! Right?

That's why Acts 2:4 said: they spake in tongues as the spirit gave them utterance. Got it now? You see as they spoke in tongues, God kept pouring it in. That's the "in road." God keeps pouring it in. So, all you do is start speaking. Who's got to pour it in? God. Sure. What you speak is whose business? God's! But that you speak is whose business? Yours! That's it! Everybody's waiting on God, and God's sitting in heaven waiting on us! That's right. People are always waiting on God, when God's been waiting on us for 1900 years to do the work of God, to throw the switch, to put the power into manifestation. But you know we get shaky. We wonder if God is really going to do it! We wonder, is it real or not. If you believed Him, you'd know it was in there! How do I know it is in there? His Word says so! And because His Word says so, the only way I can find out if God is a liar is to walk out on it! If it isn't in there, then God is a liar. And the Bible says every man is a liar but God is truth! God doesn't lie like man.[29]

Look, verse 4 is such a tremendous verse—it has both

---

29. Numbers 23:19—God *is* not a man, that he should lie;...

the Giver and the gift in it, and then it has how God feeds this speaking in tongues. All you do is move your lips, your throat, your tongue. You make the sound. You make the words. But the words you make are words which He has already what? given to you. And did He give them to your mind? No! God is what? Spirit! And He can only give it to what He is, that's why you have to have the gift born in you. Listen here![30] Where did I get that word from? God gave it to my spirit (*pneuma*) —to my spirit. Why is it my spirit? Because it's His spirit as a gift to me! There He gave it as a gift. I was born again. I took that gift, now it is my spirit. It is His spirit in me as my spirit because of the gift, do you understand?

Now, God is Spirit and God can only speak to what He is. And this in here is spirit, now God gives it to me. God gives it to me. Did He give it to my mind? No. But part of me is God's spirit all through me. Just like the life of the flesh is in the blood, the soul life is in the blood, and it's in the flesh, so Christ in me is all in me everywhere. He is eyes behind my eyes, he is ears behind my ears, he is heart behind my heart. He is all in all! This is why he is called in the Bible "the inner man."[31] The inner man. And so, God puts this now in His spirit, which He creates within me. That little part up there,[32] that's my brain cells. Now part of me is mind. So, God gives it to my spirit, but the moment I speak it forth, I also have it where? in my mind. That's how you sometimes think you've thought it and made them up yourself, because the moment you hit it you've got part in your mind.

Now this is remarkable when it comes to the operation

---

30. The audio teaching captures Dr. Wierwille speaking in tongues.
31. Ephesians 3:16—That he would grant you, according to the riches of his glory, to be strengthened with might by his Spirit in the inner man;
32. Dr. Wierwille is referring to a diagram on the board.

of the manifestations. Say you want to interpret. Interpretation is in what language in this group? English. And you don't speak English out of your toes! You speak it with your mind, right? Okay. How does He do it? It's very simple. God's spirit feeds to you the inspiration for speaking in tongues and the interpretation. The moment you have spoken in a tongue, *boom*—there's one word in English, then *boom, boom*—four, five, six, seven words. There are the English words in your mind, which He has just given to your spirit, but you are part mind, that's up there in your mind, *boom, boom,* out it comes! Now you interpret.

Prophecy is the same way. Word of knowledge operates the same way. I lay my hands upon people, or I don't, but I have no knowledge at all of what the situation may be. I reach up in "Daddy's Cookie Jar"[33]—*boom, boom.* And the first thing He gives me is always what that person needs because it's God's Spirit speaking to His creation in me, which is now my spirit. My spirit also is a part of me, which is body and soul. And part of the soul and body man is the mind. It brings it to my mind, and I know this is what's wrong with people. They all operate the same way! There is one gift, but there are nine manifestations or evidences in the senses world, of the power of God that's latent in that gift! Acts 2:4.

Acts 2:4a
And they were all filled...

Please remember it. All twelve apostles were filled. Do you understand? Can you get any more when you are

---

33. Dr. Wierwille is using the analogy of going to a cookie jar to see if there are any cookies present as a way of communicating that the believer can go to God to see if He has any revelation for us, but if He doesn't give us any information, it's like there being no cookies in the cookie jar—then you can't have any.

filled? And when they were filled with the gift, the first thing they did was:

Acts 2:4b
...[they] began to speak with other tongues,...

They spoke in tongues, but what they spoke was as the spirit gave them utterance. And remember, what it sounds like is none of your lousy business! But, that it sounds is all of your business. What it sounds like to your senses ears is none of your business. But it is your business, completely yours, to make it sound, to speak it forth. What it sounds like is God's business! *What* you speak is God's business, but *that* you speak is yours.

Now class, that's all there is to Pentecost. This is where they were born again, where they were filled with the power of God. All of this! Could they explain what they had? No. For the revelation of what they received is going to be given many years later, when it was given to the apostle Paul. But, you may not be able to explain something in order to operate it. I cannot explain the operation of a motor and yet I use them. I cannot explain the operation of electricity yet I use it. So in the early church they used the wonderful presence and power of God without being able to explain what they had. Is there any question in anyone's mind in this class, on any segment of these first four verses of the second chapter of the Book of Acts? Do you understand it in minute detail? Do you believe it? I think the believing for our people many times is simpler than to be sure they understand it. Well, aren't they tremendous verses? My oh my, to think God put that whole thing in four verses[34] and I write a book[35] with 300 pages on it. He does the whole thing in four verses. It's a tremendous thing! Well, that's it.

---

34. Acts 2:1-4.
35. Referring to the book, *Receiving the Holy Spirit Today*.

Now verse 5 begins with the results of what occurred that day to those twelve men. On the Day of Pentecost only Jews by religion received. That is important. Only Jews by religion received. Verse 5 says:

Acts 2:5
And there were dwelling at Jerusalem Jews, devout men, out of every nation under heaven.

Someone reiterated this to me at intermission time. This wasn't the Hebrew Pentecost at all that we're concerned about here. But that it is the Pentecost (of the fullness of the Day of Pentecost) when the first fullness of the first fruits of Christ Jesus was made manifest in concretion. These people were *dwelling*, they were living. They didn't come in especially for a feast. They were already there! They lived there—"…there were dwelling at Jerusalem Jews, devout men, out of every nation under heaven."

Acts 2:6a
Now when this was noised abroad,…

What was noised abroad? That these twelve men from Galilee were speaking in tongues, but that wasn't *really* what was noised abroad. That they were speaking in tongues—which were understandable to the hearer. It was tongues to the twelve men from Galilee. They didn't understand one word they spoke. But the people that were present (besides the twelve men at the hour of prayer in the Temple) when they heard these twelve Galileans get up and they heard them speak, which they knew was tongues to the Galileans, they could understand what they said. My oh my, they "hot footed it" out of the Temple so fast, the dust must have been a mile thick. And they ran all over Jerusalem, to the chief priests, to the elders, to the Sanhedrin, everybody in the top echelon, and all the good, religious people they could get a hold of—that's how it got "noised abroad." Had they been in an upper room, with the room insulated, acoustical tile, doors locked, how would it have ever gotten noised abroad?

You could take a dozen of our people and lock these doors, then we could speak in tongues and nobody else would know what was going on. Suppose we were in the midst of Lima, Ohio, or in a public meeting place on the public square, or in Cincinnati or downtown Columbus in an open territory where everybody could come in and where everybody could see. And let's say there were 200-300 people in there and twelve of us who spoke in tongues. And those 200-300 represented different nationalities, men who spoke different languages. And let's say, here I was speaking in Greek. And I didn't know one word of Greek up here, but I was speaking a perfect language in Greek! There was a group of people who had just come over from Greece, and they understood every word I said! I tell you it could get noised around, couldn't it? Even in Columbus or Lima or Wapakoneta or any other place!

Verse 6, "Now when this was noised abroad," and class the only reason it could get noised abroad is because the place was open! And the miracle of Pentecost—I told you what phenomena was, right? The *miracle* of Pentecost was that these men spoke in tongues. It was tongues to them but it was an understandable language to everybody that was coming in to hear. That's the miracle. And miracles are in God's province again. And this is what the scripture meant when it said: "They spake in tongues as the spirit gave them utterance." What they spoke was whose business? God's business. And on that day when they spoke, they spoke in tongues but what they spoke was a known language to the hearers and that's why it was a miracle!

Continuing with verse 6.

FILLED WITH *PNEUMA HAGION*

Acts 2:6a
Now when this was noised abroad, the multitude came together,...

...in the upper room? No! No! No! There was only one place the multitude could have come together, and that was in an area big enough to accommodate them and that was the Temple.

Acts 2:6b
...the multitude came together, and [they] were confounded,...

The word "confounded" is "flabbergasted"; they were shook, their eyeballs flipped. Why?

Acts 2:6c
...because that every man heard them speak in his own [what?] language.

Peter and James and John, those twelve apostles, they were speaking in tongues. The only language those men knew was northern Aramaic. That's all they could speak, sense knowledge wise. And here they were speaking other languages. It was tongues to the speaker but a known language to the hearers! And this is what shook them. This is what confounded them. This is what flabbergasted them! That these men who could speak nothing but northern Galilean (Aramaic), were there speaking in a number of different languages, which we will see a little later on they're named.

Verse 7 says,

Acts 2:7
And they were all [all] amazed and marvelled, saying one to another, Behold, are not all these which speak [what?] Galilaeans?

Didn't I tell you—they were all Galileans. Not *all* of

the "about 120" were Galileans. And not *all* of the "about 500 brethren," unto whom Jesus Christ appeared after his resurrection were Galileans, but the twelve apostles were all Galileans! It's another proof that there were only twelve that originally received.

Verses 8-11, "[Then] how hear we..."—they are all Galileans who can only speak northern Aramaic.

> **Acts 2:8-11 (not KJV)**
> [Then] how hear we every man in our own tongue [our own language], wherein we were born?
> [They heard them speak in] the Parthian language, in the language of the Medes, the Elamites, dwellers in Mesopotamia, and in Judaea, and Cappadocia, in Pontus, and Asia,
> Phrygia, and Pamphylia, in Egypt, and in the parts of Libya about Cyrene, and strangers of Rome, Jews and [what?] proselytes,
> Cretes and Arabians, we do hear them speak in our tongues [our languages] the wonderful works of [what?] God.

Then speaking in tongues is to speak what? the wonderful works of God! These men spoke in tongues; they didn't understand one thing. But the people out there heard them and understood every word they said. And they said, "My God! They are only Galileans and they're speaking the wonderful works of God in our language." Isn't that something? And you know those Jews from Judea that it mentioned, they hated the Galileans.

When the Galileans came down for the festivals of the Jews in Jerusalem, they did not even allow them to stay in the city of Jerusalem. They had segregation. That's right. They had to stay outside of the city of Jerusalem in an area on the Mount of Olives, which to this day is called the Galilean Hill. When Joseph and Mary and Jesus came down for the Passover every year as the Word of God says, they never were allowed to stay in the city of Jerusalem. They always had to stay out on the Galilean Hill, because the Judeans hated the Galileans. They despised them.

Isn't it interesting how God many times takes the most despised sense knowledge wise and sets them on their high places when He needs somebody? These were the Galileans. They were the ones who'd been born again of God's spirit. Look at "old cussing" Peter for instance. Sure. These were the men who got their lives changed! These were the men in whom God lived. And these were the men who spoke in tongues. What they spoke was God's business, but they spoke like a house of fire! They didn't stand around and say, "Well, I wonder if I'm saying the right word now. I wonder if God's got any more to give me today? I wonder if I can speak even three words in tongues?" No! Those men just moved their lips, their throats, their tongues; they made the sounds like a house of fire! And it *shook* every hearer! It shook every hearer right down to their foundation! And these men who hated the Galileans had to say that speaking in tongues (that these men were speaking) was "the wonderful works of God." Shouldn't every Christian want to speak the wonderful works of God? You bet your life!

Then why should you ever be afraid of, or ashamed of your speaking in tongues? My goodness sakes, we ought to be ashamed of ourselves that we hadn't done it. In the early days (when we opened here about 1961 or 1962), on two or three occasions in my early ministry, some of the people would come to me on some occasion and they'd say, "I heard so and so was going to be in here tonight. Maybe it would be good if we didn't speak in tongues. They might be offended!"

What the "H" is the matter with them? This place is dedicated to the accuracy of God's Word! And when we can't speak in tongues at this place you'd better close this joint down! Burn her up! Do something with it. When speaking in tongues offends you, you better go get saved and filled with the power of God! Let me tell you something, you're offending *me* when you don't speak in tongues. That's because I represent God, and the Bible says you offend God when you don't do the works of God. So they're the ones that ought to be ashamed, not old V.P. Wierwille or my group of people who believe God's Word!

We're not ashamed of God's Word, what's the matter with them? If it turns somebody away, good riddance. He never had anything to begin with anyway. But, when men of God, women of God, really hear the Word of God, it rings a bell in your soul! The Word of God says that speaking in tongues is for the unbelieving believer. It shakes him up a little bit. And he needs to get shook up, because he's living worthlessly for God. He isn't doing a lousy thing for Him!

"Speak in tongues the wonderful works of God"—I didn't write the Book. Therefore, when I speak in tongues I don't care what I feel like. The Word of God says that I'm speaking what? the wonderful works of God. Amen. And I'll go by the Word and not my feelings or yours or anybody else's.

Verse 12 says:

Acts 2:12a
And they were all amazed, and were in doubt,…

We got them amazed so often they're running out of amazement in this chapter. They were *all* amazed. And then there's the next one: they were in, what? doubt. Why do people get in doubt? It's because they don't understand, that's why. They didn't understand it, that's why they were in doubt.

Acts 2:12b
...saying one to another, What meaneth this?

What's the meaning of it? What's the meaning? Then you've got to have a few "birds" like in verse 13 around all the time. A few little old mockers, you know. They should have been mocking birds! They were just in the wrong category. They're human beings, but should have been birds.

Acts 2:13
Others mocking said, These men are full of new wine.

And you will notice in my holy spirit book, I've got a footnote a page long on that verse. It's the longest footnote you ever read in your life, a whole page long. Why should it be "new"? And why should anybody have wine this early because they never drink wine early in the morning. You've got to be an American to do that, to be an "old wino"! But, in the Bible lands they never had their wine until the day's work was over with. Then they'd have wine. I think maybe verse 12 explains it. They were all amazed. Those fellows, the mockers were so shook they didn't know whether it was morning, afternoon or night! Verse 14.

Acts 2:14
But Peter, standing up with the [what?] eleven,...

And eleven and one make how many? twelve. Look, when they received they were sitting. But when they "get to cracking" for the Lord over here, they stood up. And when they stood up, all the eleven backed themselves up behind Peter saying, if you want to fight here we are! The Army of the Lord, spiritually. Peter was the one who spoke, but all eleven stood up behind him. And Peter, "lifted up his voice." Class, did Peter have time to consult his commentaries? No sir! Did he have time to go into his office and make out his notes for his Sunday morning service? No? Are you sure?

How in the world is a preacher going to preach unless he has his little black book to write his sermon out longhand. Or type it out? Sure. Did you ever see them? They got to take that little old book in the pulpit every Sunday or they are stuck. They tell the story about the fellow who always made his notes on eight and a half by eleven. He laid them up there on the pulpit and one morning he was preaching on that text, where it says, "Lord, I come unto you" or something like that, I forget where that is. And just about that time he was really getting to cracking on that coming unto the Lord business, his sermon paper fell off the pulpit onto the floor. He reached over and his pulpit was loose, and he went all the way down with it coming unto him!

You know why we have to write out so much of our sermon? It's because we haven't got a connection! We're not plugged in. We're not alive, we're not vital! We're not studying the Word during the week. If you study the Word during the week, you don't have to write it all out for Sunday! But the average minister is better cocktail shaker than he knows the Word of God! He can shake more out of a cocktail than he can out of the Word, because he doesn't study the Word. I'll tell you it is pitiful that you and I have had to sit under that stuff! And that we were stupid enough to sit. We must have been as dumb above our ears as we were on what we were sitting! How we could sit so long and listen to nothing! It's pitiful that intelligent people like us can be "hood-winked," "hog-tied," or "blinded" by old Satan for years. That we can sit and listen to absolutely nothing! And walk away poverty stricken having a little ticklish sensation in the heart because we like the poor fellow. Maybe we like the girl or the man or the neighbor we sat next to—something's wrong! I always loved this. I never get to teach it except to you, so you are going to get it![36]

When I was in the University of Chicago Divinity School, the absolute requirement for anyone to speak at the John Rockefeller Memorial Chapel was that he had to read his manuscript line by line and word by word. He even had to submit his manuscript ahead of time so the intellectual brains could go over it! To see if what he said agreed with what they thought ought to be said. And they did not allow anybody to speak extemporaneously because he might say "ain't" when he should have said something else. He might use a word which was not quite apropos to the intellectual society, of the adherence of the Rockefeller Memorial Chapel. And it was the deadest place I ever went to! There were beautiful intellectually stimulating sermons, English that was topnotch, but no "power of God." Nobody ever got saved in that lousy outfit! And yet they had it all written out, line by line, word by word. I never heard anybody speak in tongues! Most likely if I had, the place would have fallen down. That's right.

I never saw anybody come out of that fellowship praising the Lord and saying, "Well, it was good to be in God's house this morning. Man, I can go out in the world this week and lick'em!" I never saw anyone come out of that place who didn't have to go see a psychiatrist or a psychologist later. No answers! Everything else perfect, but lacking one thing, the perfection of God's Word, ladies and gentlemen. That's it. And I tell you, today I'd rather be with men and women who know God and the power of God, and the resurrection of our Lord Jesus Christ, even if they say "ain't" than to be with all the people in the world who speak the best English but have no connec-

---

36. Audience laughs at Dr. Wierwille's comment.

tion with God! I'm not degrading good English, but I'm upgrading the greatness of God's Word and the power of God. That's right.

So we write them all out, you know. Then we go into the pulpit on a Sunday morning and we read it line by line and word by word. And it's the most invigorating and inspiring session you could ever attend.

Dr. Wierwille reads in a mocking voice of a formal preacher, "Dearly beloved brethren, this morning I wish to bring you the inspirational message from God's Word dealing with the text from Saint John, chapter 33 and one-third...33, verse 3, sorry!"

Now isn't that inspiring? No! And then you see every once in a while I'm supposed to read this manuscript at least three times before I step into the pulpit! And so, I'm supposed to be able to read it, "Yea, verily I say unto thee, thou should'est enjoy this message this morning." I'm supposed to look at my audience every once and a while. Great! Inspirational, right? Man, you walk out of that service and you're just inspired to the gills, right? No!

How would you like to have an emergency operation, an appendectomy, by a doctor who has to read the operation from the text book? How would you like it, sir? How would you like to have a hernia operation by some doctor who is a specialist, you know? He's has been trained four years of college and three years of medical work. He's got to operate on you but he's got to write it all out and read it. He knows you're coming in at 7:30 in the morning, so tonight he goes into his office; he takes out the big book and he writes it down.

This is his concordance: appendectomy, 7:30 a.m., Mrs. Baloko, yes. "Nurse gives shot of morphine"— writes it all out. Now I got it done, I'm the doctor, and you're the patient. You're going to get it this morning! Now they wheel you in with a severe case of appendicitis.

Filled with *Pneuma Hagion*

And I'm supposed to perform the appendectomy, and I have it all written out. I bring the book in and here I am reading. And I say, "Nurse, scalpel…, cut one." My goodness, something's wrong here. I thought this was supposed to be an appendectomy? But I look down in there and I see a baby! Just got it from the wrong department, out of the wrong book. Last night, while I was going through the commentaries, I picked up the book for what I thought was "appendicitis" but when I got it written out here, I had that other thing. Where do you go to have a baby? What department? obstetrics. I got a hold of the obstetrics book instead of the appendicitis book!

Well, when you go in to have an emergency operation you want a doctor who has read the book before, at the right page, right? And you want that fellow to know exactly what to do. You wouldn't trust your physical life to lie on an operating table, by a stupid doctor who had to confer to his text book and read it line by line! But, somehow or other with our spiritual eternal verity (our eternal life) we've trusted those to men! But you wouldn't do it with your physical life! Is your physical life worth more than your spiritual or eternal life? No.

I'd rather have a man operate on me for appendicitis, even if he was reading the obstetrics book, than to have someone try to tell me about the eternal verities of my soul, who didn't know one hill of beans or hailstorm about it and had to read it from the Book! It's pitiful, but in the spiritual field that's exactly what we've done! And the remarkable thing is that we've done it so long, that we think they're right, and everybody else who goes by the inspiration of the Word of God is wrong! Remember the bicycle story from the Foundational Class? The boy was riding the bicycle with the crooked handlebars so long that when somebody takes a crack at it like I do, we think he's all wrong and they're all right! How stupid can you be!

People, when you read the Word it just becomes so remarkable, because how in the world could Peter have given this great sermon, and I tell you this is a sermon whatever a sermon is (that I've always said). This sermon is so tremendous, and he never read it from a commentary, he never went in his office and made notes, he never went out and wrote them all down and read them to his congregation! Then how in the world was he able to give it? Because he had a connection, ladies and gentlemen! He had spoken in tongues. He had heard himself and that ol' Peter was bold! He didn't fear man or the Devil! And that's the first thing you have to get into your heart and life if you're really going to walk for God! As long as you are afraid of your neighbor, or as long as you are afraid of the Devil in any capacity working in any person, you're never going to walk for God! And speaking in tongues ought to get rid of that fear for you!

For when you speak in tongues, you got the external manifestation that you've got the real McCoy on the inside. That God is in you! And if God is in you, you make a majority! When God is in us we are more than conquerors! And Peter knew that! He had a connection with God. And he just got up and just opened his heart and he just poured out his soul! That's why he stood up with the eleven. And he lifted up his voice and he said to them:

Acts 2:14b, 15
...Ye men of Judaea, [you fellows listen to me], and all...that dwell at Jerusalem, be this known unto you, and hearken to my words:
For these [fellows] are not drunken, as ye suppose, [why?] seeing it is *but* the third hour of the day.

It was only nine o'clock in the morning. And you don't drink at that time, you drink after supper.

Then verse 16.

Acts 2:16
But this is that [this is *"like"* that] which was spoken by the prophet Joel;

This experience of Pentecost is NOT that prophecy of Joel fulfilled. The prophecy of Joel is addressed to whom? to Israel; and it will be fulfilled to Israel in due time. But like that prophecy in Joel is addressed to Israel, and the things will come to pass, so this (today) is like that prophecy and it has come to pass.

Quoting from that record in Joel:[37]

Acts 2:17-19
And it shall come to pass in the last days, saith God, I will pour out of my Spirit upon all flesh; and your sons [talking to Israel] and your daughters shall prophesy, and your young men shall see visions, and your old men shall dream dreams:
And on my servants [Israel] and on my handmaidens I will pour out in those days of my Spirit; and they shall [what?] prophesy:
And [in those days of Joel] I will shew wonders in heaven above, and signs in the earth beneath; blood, and fire, and vapour of smoke:

The sun, in the days of Joel's prophecy—this is like that, but it isn't that. But in Joel's days, in that day when that prophecy comes to pass:

Acts 2:20
The sun shall be turned into darkness [Has this occurred yet? No!], and the moon into blood, [Has this occurred yet? No!] before [that] great and notable day of the Lord come:

This is his coming when he comes back to the earth, with his saints that he is talking about.

---

37. Joel 2:28-32.

Acts 2:21
And it shall come to pass, *that* whosoever [in that day] shall call on the name of the Lord shall be [what?] saved.

Whosoever calleth on the name of the Lord at this time—this is like that!

Verse 22, "Ye men of Israel,...." You listen to the Lord now, and you're going to get saved! Just like in the days of Joel, those people that listened and called upon the name of the Lord, they're going to be saved.

Acts 2:22
Ye men of Israel, hear these words; Jesus of Nazareth, [a "God"?—No!] a man...

That's what the Word of God says, that's what it means! Was Jesus God? No! Was God Jesus? No! But God was *in* Jesus Christ, reconciling the world unto Himself. Jesus was a man—a man! But, he was approved of God.

Acts 2:22b, 23
...approved of God among you [the people of Israel] by miracles and wonders and signs, which God did by him in the midst of you, as ye yourselves also know:
Him, being delivered by the determinate counsel and foreknowledge of God [there's your foreknowledge, understand it?], ye have taken,...

Look at Peter. He's bold, isn't he? Fifty days before this, where was he? Behind closed doors for fear of these same fellows, for fear of the Jews, remember? What took the fear out of him? Being born again of God's spirit and speaking in tongues, that convinced him.

Acts 22:23b
...ye have taken, and by wicked hands have crucified and [you] slain [him]:

FILLED WITH *PNEUMA HAGION*

Last year, the Vatican Council said he didn't do it. The Word of God said he did. Somebody's wrong.

> **Acts 22:24-27**
> Whom God hath raised up, having loosed the pains [or the bonds] of death: because it was not possible that he should be holden of it [of death because God raised him].
> For David speaketh concerning him, I foresaw the Lord always before my face, for he is on my right hand, that I should not be moved:
> Therefore did my heart rejoice, and my tongue was glad; moreover also my flesh shall rest in hope:
> Because thou wilt not leave my soul [Jesus Christ] in hell [the grave], neither wilt thou suffer thine Holy One [Jesus Christ] to see corruption.

When Jesus Christ died, he started to corrupt. Had he stayed in the grave, over any long period of time, what would have happened to his body? It would have corrupted, because Jesus of Nazareth was a what? a man! But God raised him.

Therefore, Verse 28:

> **Acts 2:28**
> Thou hast made known to me the ways of life; thou shalt make me full of joy with thy countenance.

Remember I read that God raised Jesus Christ from the dead?[38] Now nobody can get saved except that they believe that God raised him from the dead. Did Peter preach the Resurrection? We're going to have somebody getting saved after Peter gets through, and he couldn't get saved unless he believed in what? the Resurrection. And faith cometh by hearing and hearing cometh by the Word of God. That Peter must have been right on the ball!

---

38. Acts 2:24—Whom God hath raised up...

Verse 29.

Acts 2:29
Men *and* brethren; let me freely speak unto you of the patriarch David, that he is both dead and [what?] buried, and his sepulcher is with us until this day.

Then how in the world can he be alive if the Bible says he's dead? He isn't alive! David is dead! The sepulcher is even with him.

Acts 2:30-32
Therefore being a prophet, and knowing that God had sworn with an oath to him, that of the fruit of his loins, according to the flesh, he would raise up Christ to sit on his throne [the throne of David];
He [David] seeing this before [it ever came to pass] spake of the resurrection of Christ [So David must have gotten it by word of knowledge or word of wisdom, right?], that his soul [that he, Jesus Christ] was not left in hell [the grave], neither his flesh did see corruption.
This Jesus hath God raised up, whereof we all are [what?] witnesses.

How were they witnesses? By their speaking in tongues! That's what we read a little while ago. That was why they were witnesses! That's the only reason they knew he had got up and was in them, because they spoke in tongues. That's why Peter stood up with the eleven. That's why the people were all shocked when they heard them speak. They were witnesses, witnesses, witnesses! They didn't argue about it they just spoke in tongues, that's all.

Acts 2:33a
Therefore being by the right hand of God exalted, and having received [here it is] of the Father the promise of the Holy Ghost,...

The promise of the *pneuma*, the *hagion*. The article added to emphasis that it was the same thing they had just received.

Acts 2:33b
...he hath shed forth this, which ye now see and hear.

What did they see and hear? the speaking in tongues. That was the witness.

Acts 2:34a
For David is not ascended into the heavens:...

David hasn't ascended into the heavens—what did verse 34 say? David is what? He's not ascended. Before we read that he was dead. So he ain't gone up yet, has he? So he's still what? Dead. And his little ol' spirit ain't gone up there either.

Acts 2:34-36
For David is not ascended into the heavens [because he is still dead]: but he saith himself, The LORD said unto my Lord, Sit thou on my right hand,
Until I make thy foes they footstool.
Therefore let all the house of Israel [Jews only, Israel] know assuredly, that God hath made that same Jesus, whom ye have crucified, both Lord and Christ.

How did he make him both Lord and Christ? By God raising him from the dead!

Acts 2:37
Now when they heard *this*, they were pricked in their heart, and said unto Peter and to the rest of the apostles, Men *and* brethren, what shall we do?

We'll save it for the next section. Now it's time for a word of prayer. You've been wonderful.

YE SHALL RECEIVE

I do not know how many of you people have missed this drawing[1] in the new holy spirit book. How we ever forgot it, I don't know, but we sure did. I was just sick when someone told me that we neglected to put it into

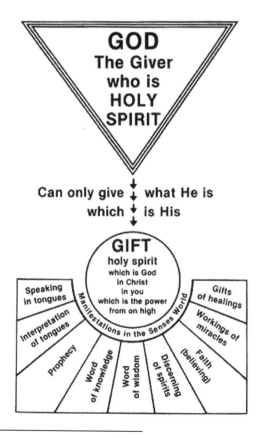

---

1. Illustration included in other editions of *Receiving the Holy Spirit Today* book, as well as in the *Power for Abundant Living* class, 1967.

the new holy spirit book. Why it's not in there I haven't got the slightest idea, because it was supposed to be in there but it isn't. It is a tremendous drawing outlining the whole thing.

Last time, we did what we call a "pure translation from Aramaic." Just literally taking the words in Aramaic on one of the verses that I was teaching and driving home to you people, and it's really wonderful how the purity of the text literally substantiates the reality of the greatness of His Word.

Acts 2:2
And suddenly there came a sound from heaven as of a rushing mighty wind, and it filled all the house where they were sitting.

The pure translation from Aramaic may sound a little rough, because it's a raw translation since it is word by word, but it reads in the Aramaic with the first usage in every word: "*Was from the stillness from heaven, sound like intense breathing.*"

See it, that's pure Aramaic: sound like intense breathing. "Sound as of a heavy breathing," I gave to you from the critical texts. Well that's wonderful. We really gratefully appreciate the work on these. I'm glad all you students that are here are working some of these things as we go along, it's wonderful! And if you have any light, like this particular thing or any added information, that's what we're here for—to share it so we can really understand the greatness of this Word.

I think also you ought to not only transfer this information on *dechomai* and *lambanō* and the *pneuma* and *hagion* scriptures into your Bibles, but I think this is a good time for you to learn and to go through Appendix 3 and 4 of the holy spirit book[2] that deal with the holy

---

2. Referring to *Receiving the Holy Spirit Today* book.

spirit field, its usages and so forth. For instance, in the appendix dealing with the use and usage of the word *pneuma*, it talks about how it's first used as *pneuma* (spirit) with the article "the," "the spirit." It's used with pronouns: "my spirit" or "the spirit of me." It is also used with prepositions: "with," "by" or "through" the spirit. Used adverbially: spiritually. And so forth—these are 11 different usages.

Now, under the usage of the word *pneuma* or *hagion*: 1. Meaning God; 2. Meaning God's gifts. All of God's gifts are God given spiritual abilities: the ministries, His *pneuma* upon certain believers, etc. And as you follow those numbers through (I have given them in that appendix where you have been transferring from "The Spirit," and so forth, the *hagion* the *pneuma*), I give you the usage in there. In the old holy spirit book (fourth edition), for instance, it would be on page 260. In the fifth edition of the holy spirit book, the new one, it will be on page 240.

In Matthew 1:18, *pneuma hagion*: ...she was found with child of [by] *pneuma hagion*.[3] The usage is "1b." So, if you can remember what "1b" is you are in business. If you can't, you go back a few places. And I think all of us will be going back a few times until we've worked this thing sufficiently to under-stand it.

"1b" is the Giver, and this appears on page 232 in the new (fifth) edition, and it will appear on page 252 in the old (fourth) edition.[4] The Giver. God, as the giver of gifts by his divine grace and will. It is God to man.

Then back to that Matthew 1:18, the usage is "1b." "...she was found with child of [or by] *pneuma hagion*." God's gift to man. It was God's doing there, *pneuma*

---

3. Appendix III (page numbers and usage labels vary by editions).
4. Labels may vary in later editions; eg. Seventh Edition, Fifth printing Matthew 1:18 appears as "1a"—God, the Giver (p.246).

hagion. The preposition *ek* (translated "of" or "by"), governs only the genitive case and it's "from the interior out" answering the question "with what"? She was found with child "of" or "by" what? *pneuma hagion*—by God's operation of the creation of soul life, as I teach you in the Foundational Class.

"…with child." The preposition *en* (with), governs the dative case answering the question, by who? God, who is Holy Spirit.

So, I've given you all the usages and where they are not absolute, I have given you the choices to make up your own mind on which one you might think it is. Because some of them will have two usages, I have listed them there. And so, if you work this thing in your mind, you'll become very versatile in the field.

Well now, we were through Acts 2 last session, Peter's tremendous sermon. We finished with verse 36 of Acts 2.

Acts 2:37
Now when they heard *this*, they were pricked in their heart,…

Whenever you read the word "heart" you've got to ask yourself the question: Is it the seat of the spirit, or is it the seat of the personal life? The seat of the personal life is referred to in the Bible as "heart" because this is where the decisions are made; this is where "the will" is in operation. It's the seat of your personal life. You and I would refer to it as "mind." And so, you must always decide whether it's the seat of the spirit or the seat of the personal life. If it's the seat of the personal life, it's where the decisions are made. The real innermost decisions, and this of course you make within your mind. Now remember, whenever you get into the word "heart," every time you read that you can always tell from the context whether it's the "seat of the spirit" or whether it's the "seat of the personal life."

Now here in verse 37, "…when they heard this, they were pricked in their heart,…" What must this be? Is it the seat of the personal life or the seat of the spirit? The personal life, why? Because they didn't have holy spirit. They were not yet born again, as of yet. Therefore it would definitely have to be the seat of the personal life.

> **Acts 2:37**
> Now when they heard *this*, they were pricked in their heart, and said unto Peter and to the rest of the apostles, Men *and* brethren, what shall we do?

Verse 38.

> **Acts 2:38**
> Then Peter said unto them, Repent,…

When we repent we do not confess our sin, we confess the savior from sin, the Lord Jesus Christ. To repent is to get saved. And you know faith cometh by hearing, and hearing cometh by the Word of God. And we must confess with our mouth the Lord Jesus (Romans 10:9, 10) and believe God raised him from the dead, thou shalt be saved. To repent is a one-time deal. You can only repent once! And when you repent you do not confess your sin, you confess the Savior from sin, the Lord Jesus Christ.

And this is what Peter said to them, and repentance gives you remission of sin. This is in the Foundational Class. Remember the little diagram in the Foundational Class? You can look it up if you want to. I'll find it for you; it's on page 17. At the bottom of the page on the right hand side it says, "Repentance is not a confession of sin, but a confession of Jesus Christ as Lord and Savior, believing that God raised Him from the dead. This action gives the confessor remission of sins, and makes him a born-again son of God, and puts him into perfect fellowship with the Father as his son."[5]

So, Peter said unto them "repent"—repent. And when a man repents he is baptized in the name of Jesus Christ.

Acts 2:38b
...be baptized every one of you in the name of Jesus Christ...

The baptism is not water. If you put water in here you're all wet to begin with, and you cannot add to the Word of God any more than anybody else can subtract from it. But remembering our work from Acts chapter 1 and from Luke, where it said they were to be baptized "in" or "with" *pneuma hagion*, the gift. And the reason it's a baptism is because there's nothing in here, and when you get born again, when you repent, Christ comes in! You are baptized with his presence. It's a one-time deal! If you could repent a second time then you could lose your salvation and get born of another seed! But you can no more get born of another seed than you can get born of another physical seed. If you're once born, you're born! And you will be that seed forever, physically as well as spiritually!

Therefore, this baptism here has nothing to do with water, but has everything to do with Christ in you.

Acts 2:38
...Peter said,...Repent, and [when you repent you will] be baptized every one of you in the name of Jesus Christ...

Now you see, they have water baptism in the name of Jesus Christ. This has nothing to do with water baptism. They take this verse and they water baptize it "in

---

5. Quoted from the Extended Syllabus of the *Power for Abundant Living* class (page 41 in later versions).

the name of Jesus" only, they call it or something else. But the name of Jesus Christ, the reason this wording is used—it's like in the Old Testament when someone had a real severe situation and he pleaded for leniency in the name of "such and such" a leader or "such and such" a man. Let's say I had a very precarious situation and the governor of the state of Ohio was my wonderful intimate friend. And so I would say to you, I have this tremendous need, but I appeal to you to be lenient and loving to me and help me in the name of the governor of the state of Ohio, because the governor would back up what I would say. This is what this means.

Baptized in the name, well how much is in that name? The Word of God says that God raised him up and gave him a name which is above all names; that at the name of Jesus every knee must bow in heaven above, in the earth beneath and the waters underneath the earth.[6] All of this is in us because it's "Christ in you," that's why it's:

Acts 2:38b
...in the name of Jesus Christ, for the remission of sins,...

So when you repent, Christ comes in and you get remission of sins. All the sins that have been committed up until that time are remitted. They're wiped out! They're washed away! And as the scripture says in the Old Testament, God has put our sins behind us like He put His hand behind His back.[7] I hardly ever give you that scripture in the Foundational Class but it's in there. How He has put our sins away like He puts His hand behind His back. Well, if you have your hand behind your back can you see it? No! So, in remission of sin, He puts our sin like His hand behind His back. He can't see them anymore.

---

6. Philippians 2:10.
7. Isaiah 38:17c—...for thou hast cast all my sins behind thy back.

Verse 38 continued, "...and ye shall" absolutely, ye shall, not ye will.

Acts 2:38c
...ye shall [*lambanō*] receive...

Receive is the Greek word *lambanō*. You all have this marked, right? Alright now look at that. This is to the church. Right here is the first message to the church after the Day of Pentecost when men asked the question: "What must we do to get saved in the age which you and I live?" And it's remarkable the answer Peter gave. It's truly remarkable, because here it is written so plainly and yet 1900 years later hardly anybody ever gives it accurately! And yet it's written here just as plain as day. And it means what it says, and it says what it means. In other words, when you are baptized, when you repent, confess with your mouth the Lord Jesus, you get baptized with the presence of Christ, which gives you what? remission of sins. Now are you full? When the Day of Pentecost was *fully* come, they were all filled. Are you full? Yes. Alright, now since you are full, what's the first thing you do? Speak in tongues! That's what it says, "and ye shall receive," *lambanō*—manifest. You've already received spiritually, right? Now you are to receive something into the senses realm. Now you're supposed to do something. And it says:

Acts 2:38c
...ye shall receive the gift [*lambanō* the gift],...

Lambanō the gift, manifest the gift. And there is only one manifestation of the gift, in its initial evidence, and that is on the Day of Pentecost when they were all filled they spoke in tongues (Acts 2:4), remember?

So here you have got the same thing, manifest the gift of "the *hagion pneuma*" is the text. I believe it's in error. I believe the original text must have had "*pneuma hagion*" but in the process of translation they got the word *hagion* in front of the word *pneuma*, that's all. It would read literally "the spirit holy." I believe it's an error in the critical Greek text. But either way it wouldn't make any difference because you shall *lambanō*, shall manifest the gift, manifest the gift, "the gift of." And I believe, I think it's in my book also in the fifth edition, that if you're going to say it's "the gift of," then it must be a small "h" and a small "s." The gift *of* holy spirit. If the preposition "of"—which is by the way the same Greek preposition as the word "from." If that word is to be "manifest the gift *from* the *pneuma hagion*" then it will have to be the Giver, which would have to be a capital "H" and a capital "S." Understand? So it could be either one or the other, that's one of those two usages.

You'll have to make up your own mind as to what you feel the Word really says. I believe it says "from." I believe that the original read as follows: "...*And ye shall [lambanō] the gift from God [the Holy Spirit]*..."[8] The Holy Spirit—with a capital "H" and a capital "S." My reason for thinking this is because why should it say the word "gift" twice? If you have a small "h" and a small "s," in essence it would mean: And ye shall [*lambanō*] the gift of the gift. Right? However, I believe it's the Giver. The first is the "*lambanōing*" of the gift from the Giver which you have just received, because you repented and were baptized in the name of Jesus, and you received remission, now *lambanō* the gift which you have just received from the Giver, who is The Holy Spirit. This is what I believe the original text must have said. Isn't that a wonderful verse of scripture? One verse of scripture has everything for the church age in it.

And yet today among the sincere Bible believing people who are seeking after the holy spirit (as they call it)

---

8. A literal translation according to usage of Acts 2:38c.

they always talk about it as being "baptized in the holy ghost." Are you baptized with the holy ghost? Like it's a second experience, or a third, or a fourth. To be baptized with the holy spirit was explained in Acts 1 and in Luke that it is to "be endued with power from on high" which is the new birth—which is the new birth! Peter didn't say, "Repent and be baptized with the name of Jesus and ye shall receive 'something added.' " He said, "Ye shall receive something in manifestation"! You've already got it. Now you're going to manifest it. He didn't say, "Are you baptized with the holy ghost?" He didn't say, "You will be baptized with the holy ghost." He said, "You will receive"—*lambanō*. It's a tremendous verse of scripture and you've got to drive this into your brain cells! Because, this is the accuracy of the church age in which you and I live.

Verse 39.

> **Acts 2:39**
> For the promise is unto you [talking to Israel], and to your children [Israel], and to all that are afar off, *even* as many as the Lord our God shall call.

And in the last phrase you and I got in! Before that we were not in it! It was addressed to Israel. But then it says, "as many as the Lord our God shall call." Well, has He called you? Have you accepted Him? Alright then the promise is to you.

Verses 40, 41.

> **Acts 2:40, 41a**
> And with many other words did he testify and exhort, saying, Save yourselves from this untoward [lousy] generation.
> Then they that gladly received...

And what is that word received? *Dechomai*. Isn't that something! Those words are just fantastic! "Then they who gladly received,"—subjectively received. In other words they believed the Word of God. They had asked the question, "Men and brethren, what shall we do?" Peter laid it out on the line and they believed. And when they believed, they received it subjectively, *dechomai*.

Acts 2:41a
Then they that gladly received his word were baptized:...

In water? It doesn't say water. If you put water in there you're all wet again! Because they were baptized in the name, he had just told them in verse 38 what they would get, right? And they just carried it out. They were baptized, not in water, but in the name of Jesus Christ with the fullness of the power of God.

Acts 2:41b
...and the same day [on the Day of Pentecost] there were added *unto them* about three thousand souls.

About three thousand persons, alive persons. I said to you that this never could have occurred in the upper room. Do you see why? Because there were about 3,000 people converted. And if the proportion in that day was as bad as it is today, they must have had 30,000 people present to get 3,000 converted (and that's still a good percentage). So I don't know how many people they had, but I know about 3,000 were converted that day.

Now, verse 42.

Acts 2:42
And they continued steadfastly in the apostles' doctrine [the teaching of the apostles]...

Doctrine is for right believing—do you remember that from the Foundational Class? The apostles taught them right believing. These 3,000 were just converted. And when they were converted, what do you think happened to them? It does not say they spoke in tongues, does it? But they must have, because he had told them in Acts 2:38 that when they were baptized in the name of Jesus Christ for the remission of sins, "ye shall [absolutely] receive [*lambanō*] the gift." So they must have all spoken in tongues. Sure! It's as plain as day, if you have any spiritual understanding, any light. Now, this is the end of the story as far as the original outpouring. And let's just remember that on this day only Jews, by religion, received. Nobody else!

Now, the next record is in Acts, chapter 8. There are only five records on the receiving of the holy spirit; they graduate, they evolve, they add light. And all that can be known about the holy spirit is written in the Word of God. Everything else is guess work.

We've got to tell our people to get rid of calling God a person. There is not one record in the Bible that says, "God is a person." This is theology, this is teaching, these are the doctrines and commandments of men! It says in the Word of God that God is spirit.[9] Then if I'd say God is a person, I could be right or I could be wrong. And 99 times out of 100 I will be wrong! Therefore, God is not a person! God is Spirit, God is Spirit! And if we'd just come back to the Word and speak the Word, we'd know we're always right. Otherwise, we're not quite sure.

Acts 8 occurred some ten, twelve, or fifteen years later; I do not know exactly nor does anybody else know. But it occurred some years after the original outpouring in Acts 2. Because, by the time Acts 8 occurs, persecution had set into Jerusalem. Now in order to instigate persecution against a Christian cause, that Christian cause has to make a tremendous indentation in a community, in an

---

9. John 4:24—God *is* a Spirit: and they that worship him must worship *him* in spirit and in truth.

area over a period of time. You cannot only reach the lower strata of society; you have to reach the intermediate strata, as well as the top strata of society. Because, the average leader doesn't give a "hoot" if you reach the lower strata in a society. He becomes involved when you reach the top strata, when you get among the governors, the men in authority, the men who make the rules and regulations. When you start winning them, that's when persecution sets in!

Now, Acts chapter 8 occurred after the persecution had set in. For it says in verse 1:

> **Acts 8:1a**
> And Saul was consenting unto his death. [This is Stephen's death.] And at that time there was a great persecution…

When the Word of God says "great" it means what? Great! It doesn't mean "a persecution"; it means a "great persecution"!

> **Acts 8:1b**
> …against the church which was at Jerusalem; and they were all scattered abroad throughout the regions of Judaea and Samaria, except the apostles.

In other words the apostles stayed in Jerusalem. But the rest of the leaders of the church in Jerusalem were scattered abroad, all over the area, because of the persecution.

> **Acts 8:2, 3**
> And devout men carried Stephen *to his burial*, and make great lamentation over him.
> As for Saul [Saul was his Hebrew name; Paul was his Greek name.], he made havock of the church, entering into every house, and haling men and women committed *them* to [what?] prison.

Was Saul sincere? Yes. He was absolutely convinced that he was working for God and doing God a favor by taking the Christians and binding them, putting them in prison, even voting against them that they would be executed. People, this is why I teach you that sincerity is no guarantee for truth. Paul was just as sincere then, as he was later when he got converted! You can be as sincere for evil as you can be for truth! Sincerity is no guarantee for truth! Truth is truth, sincerity or no sincerity.

Now, Verse 4.

Acts 8:4a
Therefore they that were scattered abroad went every where preaching the...

Reader's Digest? Experience? Oh, that's great—experience, right? No!

Acts 8:4b
...preaching [one thing, what?] the word.

As I told you on my itinerary last week I ran into a lot of these things, the usual stuff. Nothing is ever new. I've been through this mill so often. If I ever got anything new, I'd most likely be shocked! But, every person they bring into these fellowships, you know what they talk about? Experience. So they bring in Doctor "D" and he talks about his experience, they bring in Doctor "P" and he talks about his experience, they bring in Reverend "K" and he tells them how he has experienced it. The early church didn't have to talk about experience. They talked about the Word and experiences came!

For many, many years when I had to preach every Sunday two or three times, usually three different sermons, I always endeavored to document, illustrate my teaching by the things which were currently happening that week. If it was over a week old, I wouldn't use an illustration. It had to say that God had done it today or yesterday. It had to be "hotter than a firecracker" right then. Because if God isn't doing anything today what difference does it make that He did it five years ago? That's over with. We want to know what He's doing today! And people, this is really tremendous. I know that everybody likes to hear experiences. But experiences just "tickle your ear balls" and when you go home you're as stupid as you were when you came! You had a good time. You put an extra two dollars in the collection because it just thrilled you while you were there! But when you go home, what have you got? You haven't got a thing you can live on! Because you can't live on V.P.'s experience.[10] I can't live on your experience, but both of us can live on the Word of God! It is the Word of God which is our food! It is our meat! It is our sustenance!

And these men (verse 4) who were scattered abroad went everywhere with the Word. They preached only one thing and that was the Word! They went everywhere preaching the Word, because faith cometh by hearing, not by experience! It comes by hearing the Word, class! Look, you've got to drive some of this stuff into your brain cells, because we have grads all over the United States. They love the Word, but they sure love to be in fellowships where somebody gives his experience! They just get so blessed. Look, I love experience too! I get blessed too but never blessed like when I hear somebody unfold the Word! When someone unfolds the Word, nothing thrills my soul like the unfolding of the Word! Nothing! They went everywhere preaching what? The Word!

Verse 5.

Acts 8:5
Then Philip went down to the city of [what?] Samaria, and preached Christ unto them.

---

10. Dr. Victor Paul Wierwille is referring to himself which stands for Victor Paul.

Now in Samaria the people were "half" Jews. They were despised by the "pure-blooded" Jews, so to speak. The Jews in Jerusalem hated the Samaritans. Remember the story of "The Good Samaritan"? Nobody would do anything for him—neither the Levites, nor the priests. They were all too good, but a poor little old Samaritan, whom everybody reviled. They would rather feed the dogs, than they would the Samaritan. Now, the Word of God moved out from Jerusalem to these people. They were not Jews, but technically you could refer to them as "half Jews." On the Day of Pentecost, Jews only. Now you're going to see Samaritans, who were "half Jews," "half Gentiles," so to speak. Philip went down to the city of Samaria and he preached what unto them? Christ. And Christ is the Word!

Verse 6 is tremendous!

Acts 8:6
And the people with one accord [unity of purpose] gave heed [they listened] unto those things which Philip spake, hearing and seeing the miracles which he did.

They didn't believe Philip's preaching because it sounded good to their ears, because he used a fluent language—no, no! Because he was a graduate of the proper theological school—nope! They believed what Philip said, because he had some proof in the senses world. If this were the criteria today we'd empty the pulpits because a man can talk. Talk is cheap, but can he produce anything? Those fellows weren't going to get "hoodwinked" by a man who just talked! They believed what he said. They believed Philip's words (the preaching of the Word), because of the miracles which he did!

That's tremendous, isn't it? Had there been no miracles, those fellows would have said, "You're nuts Philip!

Go on home." No, No, No! Why? We are going to see that they were used to having something happen in that community. And when Philip got down there with the Word of God, he had to have some proof or they never would have believed him! And the proof he had to have, had to be bigger than what they had before! They believed Philip's preaching because of the miracles which *he* did! Who did them? Philip. It doesn't say God did them. Philip did them. If there are going to be any miracles done today, you and I are going to have to do them! How was Philip able to do them? Because he was filled with a power from where? on high! He had the God-given ability but Philip had to carry out the action! He had to carry out the job. This is why that verse of scripture just hits all the teaching in the healing field right between the eyeballs of the healings that are going on today. Because they always say, "I'm not doing it; it is God doing it." Well, what does that verse say? Does it say "God" is doing it? No, it said, Philip did it! Verse 6, "…miracles which he did."

While I'm thinking about these matters here, it will appear again later on in verse 13, where it said:

Acts 8:13c
…wondered, beholding the miracles and signs which were done.

I'm going to straighten out for you tonight, the word "signs," "miracles," and "wonders" in the Word of God. You should take your Bible, as the days and weeks go by now, and mark some of these in your Bible, so that you will be able to get a greater understanding of their usage in the Word.

This word here in verse 6, "and seeing the miracles" —miracles is the word *sēmeion*. In verse 13, the word "miracles" is *dunamis*, and the word "sign" is the word *sēmeion*. Now, I have things like this marked in my Bible so that when I'm reading along I can spot this, like when I teach you tonight or any other time. It's in my Bible because you can't just remember everything all the time. So when I have a few of these things that I don't teach every week written down in my Bible, when I come to them I can share them with people. By the way, we better look up Hebrews 2:4 before I go to the board.

> **Hebrews 2:4**
> God also bearing *them* witness, both with signs and wonders, and with divers miracles, and gifts of the Holy Ghost, according to his own will?

Signs, wonders and divers miracles. All three words that I want to give you are used in Hebrews 2:4. All three of them.

The first word I want to give you is a familiar Greek word, *dunamis*. Now, I'm going to add to what I taught you last session of this word. Last session I was talking to you about its usage in the singular. In the singular the word *dunamis* is "power." What kind of power? Inherent power. That's it! Now, here in the text it's in the plural. Whenever the word *dunamis* is in the plural usage, it is always "mighty works." The phrase "divers miracles" in Hebrews 2:4 is the word *dunamis*, mighty works. The other word I want you to make a note of is the Greek word *teras*, which is a "wonder." That's the best translation of that word, and it is the effect produced on those who witness the *dunamis*, mighty works. The word *teras* is a "wonder"; the people "wondered" because of what the men of God did. The word "wonder" is the word *teras* and this is the effect produced on those who witness the mighty power! A man operates the mighty power and it produces the effect of a wonder. "Signs," is the word *sēmeion*, "wonders" is *teras* and "miracles" is *dunamis*, plural, mighty works. All three in one verse! Now, let's go back to Acts 8.

Acts 8:6
And the people with one accord gave heed unto those things which Philip spake, hearing and seeing the miracles [*sēmeion*] which he did.

Got it? The signs which he did, that which is signified by the work accomplished. In other words, they saw something which was in concretion before them. The next verse tells you what they saw. Verse 7, "For unclean spirits," unclean spirits are devil spirits. The reason they're called "unclean" is because no man should have them, and if you got the wrong kind of spirit, it's always an "unclean" or devil spirit. Because it's a devil spirit, it's unclean.

Acts 8:7
For unclean spirits, crying with loud voice, came out of many that were [what?] possessed...

There's the key, my oh my! The true spirit of God. How do you get the true spirit of God? By confessing with your mouth, right? Believing God did what? Raised him from the dead.[11] This you have freedom of will to do, right? You make up your own mind whether you are going to confess him or whether you're not, right?

But in unclean spirits, devil spirits, you have no freedom of will. You don't control them. They come and they control you. That's the difference between the genuine and the counterfeit. My oh my, and that's a tremendous difference! Do you see why class, I keep driving in the Foundational Class all the time to our people that the greatest thing you have is freedom of will? Don't let anybody touch it! Nobody! Under no condition! Because that is the difference between the genuine and the counterfeit. The genuine is always received from God by freedom of

---

11. Romans 10:9, 10.

will. The counterfeit may produce great results, but it's always because they are possessed!

Now you take a person who is possessed, he can do a lot of good (looks good), but he has no freedom of will to carry it out! What kind of glory is that kind of a person to the Father? None whatsoever! No more so than my son here. If I would possess him, then every time I wanted something done I'd just say, "Do it"! He would just walk out and do it. Would that be a great thing? No, it wouldn't! The greatness of a son is that he knows the father's will, and he knows what makes the heart of the father happy. So instead of my saying to him, "Do it," he already goes out and does it before I ever ask him to do it by the freedom of his will. That's what makes the heart of a father happy! And that is why God is happy because He has sons who have freedom of will. And when we, by our freedom of our will, so walk to bring glory to His name, so doing His will without Him possessing us, this makes the heart of the Father happy! And that's the only kind of son that's worth having! One who is possessed is "no deal"!

But in the devil spirit field, it's always possession! You see why I hate people's usage of terms, not people, but I hate their usage of terms like when they say, "Well, I gave myself over to the holy spirit," "I allowed God to possess me," "I am fully his channel." You see why I hit the ceiling every time those kinds of things are said? Because I understand the counterfeit! The counterfeit possesses. Never the true God!

Acts 8:7, "For unclean spirits, crying with loud voice," they yelled like hell when Philip was in there doing the mighty works. Why? Because they liked where they were, and old Philip was getting in there disturbing them. He was taking out devil spirits, out of people and they didn't like it, so on the way out they would yell their fool head off!

Acts 8:7, 8
...[devil spirits, because they can talk] crying with [a] loud voice, came out of many [many—that town was loaded with them]...: and many taken with palsies [paralysis—this is physical], and that were lame, were healed.
And there was great joy in that city [of Samaria].

Samaria was the capital of the province of Samaria. It was the capital city. You wonder how so many people can get possessed in a community? in a city, in an area? The only way they could get so possessed is because there were people living there that were possessed. The next verse tells you about it.

Acts 8:9
But there was a certain man, called Simon, which beforetime [before the time of the coming of Philip] in the same city used sorcery,...

Sorcery is spiritualism, black arts, "hooky pookism," I call it. Sorcery is divination. Sorcery is the usage of amulets and other kind of things. Little things they wear around their neck; you know, the St. Christopher's and all that baloney! That's all spiritualism. The rabbit's feet are all spiritualism. All the extrasensory perception stuff.

Acts 8:9
...there was a certain man, called Simon, which beforetime [the time of the coming of Philip] in the same city...

The word "same" is not in any of the critical Greek texts, because if it's in the city of Samaria it's got to be the same city. I have the word "same" scratched out in my Bible because it's not in the text. I'm after the word, I want the word and nothing but the word!

Verse 9 continued.

Acts 8:9b
...in the same city [the city of Samaria] used sorcery, and bewitched [hoodwinked] the people of Samaria,...

Now there it's remarkable. The word "people" is the Greek word *ethnos* meaning "nation." That's really something! It doesn't register yet, huh? Look at it.

Acts 8:9a
But there was a certain man called Simon, which beforetime in the...city [the city of Samaria, also the capital of Samaria] used sorcery and bewitched the people [the whole nation] of Samaria,...

That's what it says! That's what it means! That Simon must have been really operating something, huh? Alright, what about Jeane Dixon?[12] Where is she located? Washington. "...and bewitched the whole nation." You see how devil spirits get in control? How they hoodwink people? How they control a whole city, and a whole nation? Exactly! The word "people" is the word *ethnos*, meaning "nation" of Samaria.

Acts 8:9c
...giving out that himself was some great one:

The word "some" is the word "certain" and you must put it in your Bible: "...giving out that himself was [a certain] great one." He was top echelon! He was "big boy"! He was the one that really was loaded. He was not just some spirit possessed man, he was a definite, certain one! That's the essence of it. That's a tremendous enlightening verse isn't it, this verse 9. I don't know if I have

---

12. Jeane L. Dixon was one of the best-known American self-proclaimed psychics and astrologers of the 20th century, due to her syndicated newspaper astrology column, some well-publicized predictions, and a best-selling biography. (Wikipedia)

ever given this to some of you or not. I don't think I have, because I never get a chance to teach a lot of this in the Foundational Classes.

Alright, verse 10.

Acts 8:10a
To whom they all gave heed, from the least to the greatest,...

Look, the least person in the nation of Samaria as well as the greatest, the top leaders all the way down.

Acts 8:10b
...saying, This man is the great power of God.

This man is the great "power of God"? They were right! He was the great "power of God"! He was not just "some man"; he was a "certain great one"! He had bewitched the whole nation of Samaria, and the people said, "He is the great one. He's got the true prophecy, every first of January we'll consult him and put it in our newspaper so we'll all know what's going to happen"—that's exactly what they did, "...saying, This man is the great power of God." They just forgot to understand or say one thing, which god? That's all. He was the great power of god, but which god? Satan! As the Bible says, there are two gods: One is the God and Father of our Lord Jesus Christ, the other is the god who possesses people,[13] called "Satan." He *was* the great power of god, but which god? Satan! But did the people believe that? They thought he was the power of the "true God"—the right God.

Verse 11.

Acts 8:11a
And to him [Simon] they had regard,...

---

13. 2 Corinthians 4:4—In whom the god of this world hath blinded the minds of them which believe not, lest the light of the glorious gospel of Christ, who is the image of God, should shine unto them.

They had respect, they listened to him. The words "had regard" are the same words as the word "heed" in verse 6. "Gave heed." And verse 10, "To whom they all gave heed." This "had regard" are the same words. To him they gave heed, they had regard. They gave heed. Why?

Acts 8:11b
...because that of long [long] time he had bewitched them with sorceries.

He had bewitched them with his spiritualism, with his extra sensory perception, with his predictions, with the signs, the miracles and the wonders that he had wrought. Satan does do signs, miracles and wonders but the Word of God says, they are *lying* signs, miracles and wonders.[14] Why? Because they are done with the power of Satan, and they are so designed that they will lead people away from the true God, to the power of Satan, so that man will not be born again, so that Satan has them hooked. And then when life is all over with, they have had no eternal life, so they have none in the future!

Acts 8:11b, 12a
...because...of [a long] long time he had bewitched them with sorceries.
But when they [the people] believed Philip preaching the things...

The words "the things" is not in any critical Greek texts. The word "concerning" is a remarkable word also. The word "concerning" means in essence "the whole deal." The complete deal. It's a circle, concerning, it's a complete rounded in, everything in it!

Acts 8:12a
But when they believed Philip preaching...concerning [the whole deal]...

---

14. 2 Thessalonians 2:9—*Even him*, whose coming is after the working of Satan with all power and signs and lying wonders.

Understand? Isn't that something? These usages of words are just terrific!

Acts 8:12b
...the kingdom of God, and the name of Jesus Christ, they were baptized [in water? No, no, no—baptized in the name of Jesus Christ], both men and women.

What happened to them? They got saved. That's right! They got converted and praised God! You know there's an indication that a community, a nation, can be "hoodwinked" for a very long time by spiritualism, but when The Word of God is really preached, and really taught, and men hear it and listen to it, that those men and those women can get saved! This is because the true God is bigger than Satan! Remarkable! But how are they going to get saved except they hear the Word? How are they going to get saved except people like you rise up with the accuracy and knowledge of God's Word, else they'll never have it! They're not going to learn it from any seminary in the United States today, or in any Bible College. It says, "they were baptized, both men and women!" —they got saved! That's what happened to them. Born again! Well praise the Lord, right? You bet your life!

Verse 13.

Acts 8:13
Then Simon himself believed also:...

What happened to that ol' Simon? He got saved! Well praise the Lord! After having "hoodwinked" the whole nation of Samaria, and having operated devil spirits for years, low and behold Philip gets down there preaching the Word, and Simon believes what he hears. And when you believe, what do you get? Born again. Amen! A tremendous thing! And verse 13 says "he was baptized,..." in water? No—in the name of Jesus Christ.

And you know I love this verse because it has so much in it. You see, ordinarily people teach in the fundamental churches that when you're really born again, God takes desires away from you, right? They say He takes your sin from you, out of your mind. Like if before you liked to chew tobacco, now you don't chew any more. If you like to take "snuff" you've had enough of that "snuff" now since you got saved, so you no longer take "snuff." He cleans up your mind, your life. You had a desire to do evil before, now you no longer have that desire. You see, they don't understand body, soul and spirit. And this is why they've taught that.

Now suppose you're taught that. Let's say these children up here in the front row were taught this for 8, 9, or 10 years. Then, they would never be able to get saved, until they would carry out what laws we had set up. And therefore they would say, when they got saved at 16, 18 or 20 years old, "Well, God took the desire of smoking away from me!" God never did anything like it! Never did anything like it! And this verse teaches that truth. It said, "Simon…believed also" and "he was baptized," he got saved. But, he did something!

Acts 8:13b
>…he continued with Philip [he followed Philip around], and wondered [he wondered], beholding the miracles [*dunamis*, the mighty works] and signs [*sēmeion*, the signs] which were done.

By the way, there is a word added in all critical Greek texts which is not in here. It should read: "…and wondered, beholding the GREAT mighty works"—the word "great" is not in the King James Version, but it is in every critical Greek text. "…*and wondered, beholding the great mighty works and the significance of that which was wrought, the signs which were done.*"[15] What was Simon

---

15. A literal translation according to usage of Acts 8:13b.

trying to figure out? How can Philip do those mighty signs, those mighty works and have the significance of the work wrought? Simon knew what he had operated before. He knew the signs, miracles, and wonders he had done. But here was a fellow that was doing more than he was able to do! Simon followed Peter around. He believed on the Lord Jesus Christ and got saved, but he had no renewed mind. So he followed him around, scratched his head and said, "Well, I wonder if I could learn how to do this?"; "I wonder if I can do that?"; "Maybe I could buy that from him and then I can go out here and do it." See, that's the attitude.

In Acts 8 comes up the greatest usage of the Greek words *dechomai* and *lambanō*. Words that have just never been understood, and they are real simple and real easy. And of course now, here in the class it will all make sense to you. You see, in verse 12 it told us that the people believed. In verse 13 it told us Simon believed. And when you believe you receive, because all believing equals receiving. So they were born again. They were baptized in the name of Jesus. With the presence, they were filled with the power of God. But this now is the first time in the history of the Christian church, since the Day of Pentecost, when somebody was born again that he did not immediately manifest in the senses realm. This has never happened before, and this is why this record is in the Word of God to educate us, to bring us up, to tell us about the holy spirit field.

These people were born again but they hadn't "*lambanō'd*" anything. They hadn't manifested anything. They had just confessed with their mouth the Lord Jesus and believed in their heart that God had raised him from the dead, but they had no evidence. And this was the first time in the history of the Christian Church that it ever happened, that when somebody was born again they didn't immediately afterwards speak in tongues! This is the first time.

Now verse 14.

Acts 8:14
Now when the apostles which were at Jerusalem heard that Samaria had received [*dechomai*] the word of God [they had received spiritually the Word of God], they sent unto them Peter and John:

The top brass! Peter and John, who stood above all the apostles in Jerusalem. They sent the top men down to Samaria. Why? Because something had happened in the Church which had never happened before! And God sent down the best that He had to take care of the situation. Because you just can't let the Church "go off." If the Church is off at one place it becomes a disgrace to God! And so immediately after they had *"dechomai'd"* they should have spoken in tongues, everybody else did, but they didn't in Samaria. So Peter and John "hot footed" from Jerusalem down to Samaria. They got there in a hurry because they heard that Samaria had *"dechomai'd"* (subjectively received the Word of God).

Acts 8:14b, 15
…they sent unto them Peter and John:
Who, when they were come down, prayed for them, that they might receive [*lambanō*, manifest, receive into manifestation *pneuma hagion*—no article; receive into manifestation the gift, holy spirit]…:

The gift. They had received it spiritually, do you see it? But they had never received anything out there in the senses realm. They hadn't done anything with it! So Peter and John come down and pray for them that they might receive (manifest). To pray is to believe! To carry out the ministry. To get the job done!

Verse 16 is a parenthesis. Do you see it? Remember it. Because you can read on from verse 15 to verse 17.

Acts 8:15, 17
…that they might receive the Holy Ghost [*pneuma hagion*]:
[Then verse 17] Then laid they *their* hands on them, and they received [*lambanō*] the Holy Ghost [*pneuma hagion*].

But verse 16 is a parenthesis set in for explanation, and this I want to give to you accurately. Verse 16, we shall read, "For as yet he was fallen upon none of them:…" Now that cannot mean literally what they say it means, because the verses above have told us that they were already born again, right?

Acts 8:16
(For as yet he was fallen upon none of them: only they were baptized in the name of the Lord Jesus.)

They were born again, baptized in the name of Jesus, but "for as yet he was fallen upon none of them:…" I believe that every place where it talks about the gift, it should always have been the word "it," because it's in the third person singular where you have "he, she, or it." So they chose the word "he" when it should have been the word "it." The "gift" should not be referred to as a "he" or a "she," but always as an "it." The holy spirit—it. The gift—it.

Now, keep your finger here and I'll show you one usage that I'd like for you to remember. And the next time somebody jumps you about the holy spirit being a "he" all the time, a "person," then ask them to explain Romans 8:16: "The Spirit itself.…" What's it called? It's called an "it." So let them chew on that one for a while! Okay?

Back to Acts 8:16. "(For as yet, he was fallen upon none of them:….)." They were born again, but they had never manifested anything. And the usage of the word "upon" is remarkable! This word "upon" is the Greek word *epi*, which equals "drawing unto themselves" knowledge. This is its one usage. I would like to say that literally it means: "drawing unto themselves from God" which not only includes knowledge but everything that God has available. It will illustrate itself in the picture diagram I gave you in the last session. This is Christ in you with its nine manifestations. (See Diagram below).

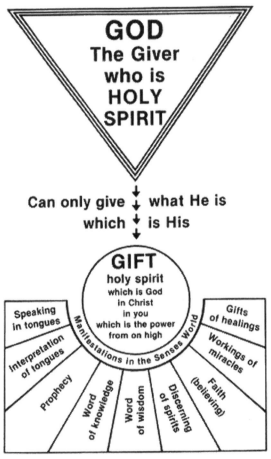

The Greek word *epi* always means "super position." It is used in the genitive, in the dative, and in the accusative case in the Bible. That's all, three ways. Now, in Acts 8:16, it's in the genitive case. And it's this kind of "drawing unto themselves." They hadn't drawn anything. "For as yet it was fallen upon none of them." See it? It's still superimposed. They were born again. They had this connection to God (see diagram). But they had not drawn on any of that power. Why? Because, they had not yet spoken in tongues. That's why it's used in this *genitive case* and that's the word *epi*. Any other word than the word *epi* would knock the Word of God to pieces here. Isn't that remarkable! They were born again, but they weren't drawing any power. Remember how I said electricity was like a motor? If the switch is thrown on, then the power will enter. So these people weren't using any of this power, because they were not speaking in tongues. For as yet, it had fallen upon none of them. That's remarkable!

Now, in the *dative case* the word *epi* means "drawn closer" to the end of actual superposition. It has actually come down where they are "tapped" in there. Now, remember the nine? Have you ever heard about people who spoke in tongues once, then never did afterwards? That's this usage. Well, in the Pentecostal fields you find them all the time. They spoke once but haven't spoken since. Sometimes we find them in this Ministry and that's a disgrace to my teaching, because I'm a better teacher than that. When they speak the night that I minister the holy spirit to them, then they don't speak for a year or two! They had been "drawn closer" than this, but they have just operated once! That's its actual superposition.

The third usage of the word *epi* is in the *accusative case*. It is as follows where the *epi* is here (top of the chart) and comes down in there (bottom of the chart). That's the word *epi* and it's in the *accusative case*, which means to "pull in." They've pulled it in. Why are the pulling it in? Because, they are giving out here, they're giving out there. They are operating all nine manifestations! And operating all nine, they are constantly "pulling it in." Pulling it in, that's what it means. And literally this is its definition: "Active motion to the point to be reached." Wow, that's a tremendous definition! Active—active. I speak in tongues. Active motion to the point to be reached. To be reached is speaking in tongues, interpretation, prophecy, word of knowledge—it's active motion, I'm pulling in. I'm pulling in from God who gives it to me in here. That's what it is! This is it's usage in Acts 19:6.[16] It was actually superimposed upon the grace. Actually touching it, touching it. Actually touching it. Isn't that tremendous? The usage of that is just remarkable!

Here's a man who is born again, but he has never spoken in tongues. Never received word of knowledge, never operates anything. He never uses any of the manifestations. Other people who have at one time maybe operated just once or twice, it's drawn closer to them. It's actually been pulled down to them, but they've never done anything with it. But this is where you really go all out, active motion to the point to be reached, and operate all nine manifestations. That's where it's "upon," to the end where it's pulled in. It's like pulling in electricity into the motor. Acts 8, that's verse 16.

Acts 8:16
(For as yet he was fallen upon none of them:...).

To the end that they had never actively engaged it. Do you understand? Now isn't that wonderful? Just tremendous!

---

16. Acts 19:6—And when Paul had laid *his* hands upon them, the Holy Ghost came on them; and they spake with tongues, and prophesied.

Verse 17.

Acts 8:17
Then laid they [Peter and John] *their* hands on them,...

Why did they lay hands on them? Simply because God told them to do it. Number one, revelation (lay hands on), and the laying on of hands identified them with the people to whom they were ministering. And then revelation manifestations in operation: word of knowledge, word of wisdom and discerning of spirits. Which one do you think they must have really used in Samaria? Discerning of spirits! Because of a very long time Simon had bewitched them with "hooky pookism"—devil spirits. Now Peter and John come down. The people are born again of God's spirit but they have never manifested anything, and Peter and John want to find out what's holding up the works; why are they not manifesting? So they lay hands on them.

You don't get anything by the laying on of hands. That's just like pouring water on them. Water wouldn't cleanse someone on the inside. The laying on of hands doesn't communicate anything. The laying on of hands is only to identify you with the person to whom you are ministering. Because you can't give anybody anything with the laying on of hands (not the laying on of hands we are talking about here).

The laying on of hands is used in the Bible whenever manifestations go into operation. They laid hands on them before they sent Paul and Barnabas away from Antioch. The laying on of hands was for revelation to come and it was the laying on of hands when revelation came which said, "Separate me Barnabas and Saul for the work whereunto I have called them."[17] And they sent Paul one way

---

17. Acts 13:2.

and Barnabas another. Not because of the laying on of hands but because of the revelation that came. Do you understand? You can't communicate anything with the laying on of hands! My laying on of hands does not bless you. But, my laying on of hands may make the blessing available because of revelation. You got it? Well you remember it, okay? Because Simon had the same opinion most people had. We are going to see it after a bit.

Verse 17.

> **Acts 8:17**
> Then laid they *their* hands on them, and they received [*lambanō*] the Holy Ghost.

They received into manifestation *pneuma hagion*, the gift. What was blocking them? I don't know. It doesn't say what was blocking them, but something must have been blocking them from manifesting. So Peter and John come down and lay hands on them. Revelation goes into operation: word of knowledge, word of wisdom, and discerning of spirits. Peter and John operated faith, miracles and healing. They must have taken care of the situation for the Word of God says, they *lambanō'd*. They *lambanō'd*, they manifested the gift. Now it doesn't say they spoke in tongues, does it? It just says they *lambanō'd*, right? That's all it says. Just leave it set.

Verse 18.

> **Acts 8:18**
> And when Simon saw [saw with his sense knowledge] that through [or by way of] the laying on of the apostles hands the Holy Ghost [the *pneuma* the *hagion*] was given,...

The reason the article is there is to emphasize both of them (the *pneuma*, the *hagion*), to emphasize that it's the same gift they're talking about. The gift was given, not spiritually but in manifestation because Simon saw something. Simon *saw* something. Well what did Simon see? He could not see spirit, right? He must have seen what? Manifestation. That's the answer. Whatever it was he *saw*. He saw, right? You can't see spirit, right class? Therefore, he must have seen what? the manifestation of the spirit. And how many manifestations of the spirit are there? Nine! Therefore he must have seen at least one of the manifestations.

Now, by sheer logic, even though the Word does not say it, Simon saw them speak in tongues. That's what he saw! Because, prophecy would not have been the real "clincher." To do miracles and wonders would not have been the real clincher, because Philip had already done that and Simon had done that, right? What did Simon see that so shook him, that ol' Simon would have paid anything for it, to have it? I know the Bible doesn't say they spoke in tongues, and in my book I say that. And I don't tell them in my book[18] what I'm telling you. But I'm telling you that when you have any spiritual understanding and rightly divide the Word, you will have to know and have to admit that what Simon saw was that they spoke with tongues! That's what he saw, but it doesn't say it, therefore I don't teach it in my book. I just leave it set, because we get misunderstood enough when I just stick straight to the Word. But when I get a group of advanced students like you, then I can take you a little deeper and show you the greatness of it!

But, whatever it was I know one thing, he wasn't pedaling peanuts! That isn't what Simon saw. Simon saw a manifestation, an evidence. He couldn't see the spirit. That's why when it says, "...when Simon saw that through the laying on of...hands..." Simon thought it was the laying on of hands that did the job. It wasn't the laying on

---

18. Referring to *Receiving the Holy Spirit Today* book.

of hands at all! He offered them money. It says so in verse 18.

> **Acts 8:18**
> And when Simon saw that through the laying on of the apostles' hands the Holy Ghost was given, he offered them money,

Cash in fist! He'd have paid them off right then and there.

Verse 19.

> **Acts 8:19**
> Saying, Give me also this power,...

And the word "power" is the Greek word *exousia*. Give me also this ability to exercise, that I can do this. That I can put my hands on people and "*boom, boom, boom*" something happens. That's what he wanted, the "Midas touch."[19] He thought that every time they laid hands on them, Simon saw something. Laid hands on them what? Simon saw something. It's that old Midas touch! Why don't we "Midas touch" anymore? Every time, it turned gold didn't it? That's how they feel about healing. They used to just drive me sick with these healing campaigns, especially when they had old Billy Branham there. They would sometimes get him with two fellows and hold him up, you know, so he could still put his hands on a few more people. They'd run them through, sometimes 1,500 or 2,000 people in one night! His hands would get so tired, and he'd get so tired that they put two men behind him. One on each side to hold him up, so he could still put his hand on them. You know, the old Midas touch.

That's what old Simon wanted to buy. "Just give me

---

19. Dr. Wierwille is referring to the Greek myth in which everything King Midas touched, turned to gold.

that ability. I can just lay my old hands on that girl and '*boom, boom*' " Lay it on that girl, "*boom, boom*"; lay it on that fellow, "*boom, boom.*" The old Midas touch! No, no, no, no, no! It isn't in the laying on of hands, it's in the revelation and believing, understand? But what did Simon think? Had he renewed his mind? No. Was he born again? Sure. But he was as crooked as a dog's hind leg. That's right! Because he wanted to buy it and he wanted to make money out of it. That's what he wanted to do with it. Utilize it for his own aggrandizement, his own benefit! For his own glory. He certainly didn't have the renewed mind!

> **Acts 8:19, 20**
> ...Give me also this power, that on whomsoever I lay hands, he may receive [*lambanō*—may manifest] the Holy Ghost [*pneuma hagion*—holy spirit].
> But Peter said unto him, thy money perish [rot], with thee,

Could Simon lose his salvation? Could he perish? No. No. What part of Simon could yet perish? the body. That's why the original text gives the word "rot" for perish. Peter said unto him, thy money rot with you!

> **Acts 8:20b**
> ...because thou hast thought...

Where are thoughts? in the mind. He thought that the gift of God was the ministry of an apostle. That's what he wanted to buy! He thought Philip was great, but these apostles when they came down from Jerusalem were able to do something Philip couldn't do. And that's what Simon wanted to buy. He wanted to buy the ministry of an apostle. And you do not buy the ministry of an apostle! The ministry of an apostle is a gift from who? God, in a perpendicular way.

Verse 20 continued.

Acts 8:20c, 21a
...because thou hast thought that the gift of God may be purchased with [what?] money.
Thou hast neither part nor lot [a place] in this matter [ministry]:...

The word "matter" is the word "ministry." Peter said to Simon, he neither had part nor a place in this ministry of an apostle. Why?

Acts 8:21b
...for thy heart is not right in the sight of God.

The word "heart," is it the seat of the spirit or the seat of the mind? Mind. Why? Because his heart was okay, because he was born again of God's spirit. So the seat of his spiritual heart was "top echelon" for it was eternal life! But what about the seat of his personal life? His thoughts were still out in left field! He had not been transformed by the renewing of his mind. He had not allowed this mind to live in him which was in Christ Jesus. He had not put on the Lord Jesus Christ. He had not been transformed in his mind according to the image that was created!

Acts 8:21b, 22a
...for thy heart is not right in the sight of [whom?] God.
[Then verse 22] Repent...

Could he repent? No. Why not? He had already repented back in verse 13, and how many times can a man repent? Once. How many times can he get saved? Once. That's why he can only repent once. The word that is used here is the word "forsake" in the text. Not repent. Forsake. And that's exactly it if you're born again of God's spirit, you repented, now what do you do with your evil thoughts and your evil ways when you learned the Word of God? You forsake them! You give them up! Get rid of them.

Acts 8:22

[Forsake] therefore of this thy wickedness, and pray God, if perhaps [that] the [thoughts] of thine heart may be forgiven thee.

"…if perhaps" is the word "that." It couldn't be "if perhaps," do you know why? It's contrary to the Word. That verse in the King James says, "maybe" God will do. The Word says, "if we confess our sins he is faithful and just to forgive," and no "if" or "perhaps" about it! King James has sure got this all messed up, haven't they? Really. They got their theology in the way when they translated it.

Acts 8:22b

…pray God, [that] the [thoughts—the text is plural] of thine heart [mind]…

Is this the seat of the personal life, or the seat of the spirit? Personal life. The text reads, "that the thoughts of your mind." The thoughts of your mind—where do you have thoughts? in your mind. Why sure. The thoughts of your mind may be…remission? No!

Acts 8:22c

…may be [what?] forgiven thee.

Because he got remission of sins when he got saved, but now he had not renewed his mind. He thought he could buy a ministry and he brought his money out to buy it, and Peter said, "Your money rot with you!" You can't buy this ministry. "*…and pray God, that the thoughts of your mind may be forgiven thee.*" [20] Isn't that a marvelous usage of the word?

Acts 8:23

For I perceive that thou art in the gall of bitterness, and *in* the bond of iniquity.

---

20. A literal translation according to usage of Acts 8:22b.

Simon was saved, but he was still in the gall of bitterness, and he was in the bond of iniquity. Who is the bond of iniquity? Satan. Bond means enslaved by Satan. He was born again, but still enslaved by Satan. I think there are lots of people like that, born again of God's spirit and yet they are enslaved by Satan in their mind.

Verse 24.

> **Acts 8:24**
> Then answered Simon, and said, Pray ye to the Lord for me, that none of these things which ye have spoken come upon me.

It doesn't say that Peter prayed for him, but do you think he did? It doesn't say but I bet he did. Would you do it?

Now, that's the end of the story. What a story! Samaritans. Half Jews. Philip comes down to preach and they get saved but no manifestations. This is the first time in the history of the Christian church that they didn't speak in tongues when somebody got saved. And so, Peter and John come down to find out what in the world is going on here. They lay hands on them, *"Boom, boom, boom"*—oh, devil spirit, huh? GET OUT! They then start speaking in tongues like a house of fire! That's what happened. Then Simon saw through laying on of hands (verse 18)—Now we've got the church back in alignment and harmony. We're back on the ball for God because now in the church everybody is speaking in tongues! We need some Peters and Johns and a few of these, don't we?

The next record is Acts 9. It's the third record in the Word of God. Acts, chapter 9.

> **Acts 9:1, 2**
> And Saul, yet breathing out threatenings and slaughter against the disciples of the Lord, went unto the high priest [in Jerusalem],

And [he] desired of him letters [of introduction to the top brass]…[in] Damascus to the synagogues, that if he found any of this way [the way—I told you they were called "followers of the way" before they were called Christians], whether they were men or women, he might bring them bound unto Jerusalem.

Wasn't Paul (or Saul) zealous? Man, he had them in Jerusalem, had them close in Samaria, but he just wasn't satisfied with getting them out of Jerusalem and Samaria, he wanted to go to the city of Damascus, that great commercial city, and get the Christians even from there! He was really sold on his product, wasn't he? And look, he got himself letters of introduction from the top brass! Got all of his handcuffs together and his chains and he headed out toward Damascus.

Acts 9:3, 4
And as he journeyed, he came near Damascus: and suddenly there shined round about him a light from heaven:
And he fell to the [ground], and heard a voice saying unto him, Saul, Saul, why persecutest thou me?

Wow, what a shocker that was! Did you think Saul thought he was persecuting God? He thought he was doing God a favor! But he was really persecuting God's people! Do you see how sometimes we can think we're right and we're all wrong? Sincerity is no guarantee for truth.

Verse 5.

Acts 9:5
And he said, Who art thou, Lord? And the Lord said, I am Jesus whom thou persecutest: *it is* hard for thee to kick against the pricks.

You know, this was an illustration that they understood, but very few of us understand that a "prick" is a "goad." When they drove the oxen in front of the plows, they had a stick that was pointed like a pencil. They didn't use a whip, it was a stick. It's called a "goad" translated "prick" here. And when this old ox doesn't move fast enough they give him a little poke! They push him along a little. Now when this farmer drives this ox, when he gives him a little push, the tendency of the ox is to kick. So instead of pulling this stick back, he holds it right in place. He gives him one and then he holds it right there. Then when that ox kicks, the harder he kicks, the harder he kicks into the goad. So he does this two or three times and the oxen quits kicking. He gets a little poke and he starts heading the other way!

Now that's the picture you have in mind, where the Lord said to him, "...*it is* hard for thee to kick against the pricks." The harder he kicked, the more he injured himself! Because the goad was there, the Word of God is there. The harder you kick against the Word of God, the more you hurt yourself! Because, it's that Word of God which stands as the prick, the goad.

Acts 9:6
And he trembling and astonished said, Lord, what will thou have me to do?...

Isn't that something? Sounds like Acts 2:38. When you get to the place and you say Lord what do you want me to do? When you reach that place, you no longer say, "I've got to do what the neighbors say or the head elders, or my denomination." When you come to the place where you say, "Lord, what do you want me to do?" You're going to get some answers.

Acts 9:6b-10a
...And the Lord *said* unto him, Arise, and go into the city, and it shall be told thee what thou must do. And the men which journeyed with him stood speechless, hearing a voice, but seeing no man.

> And Saul arose from the earth; and when his eyes were opened, he saw no man: but they led him by the hand, and brought *him* into Damascus.
> And he was three days without sight, and neither did eat nor drink.
> And [But] there was a certain disciple at Damascus, named Ananias;...

A certain what? Disciple. Was he an apostle? No. He was just a disciple. That I love! Here's the next step.

You see, the teaching has been in the churches that only the bishops can minister the holy spirit. They get that from Acts 8 where Peter and John had to come down from Jerusalem to minister the holy spirit because they say: Philip couldn't do it because Philip was just a preacher, he was not an apostle! And an apostle was a bishop. And therefore they had to send back to the headquarters to get the bishops of the church over to lay hands on them so they could get the holy ghost. My oh my! That's why in the Anglican church, in the Roman Catholic church, and a few of your other denominations, at the time of confirmation who comes to lay hands on the children? the bishop. However Ananias wasn't a bishop! Well, that knocks that theory, doesn't it? Ananias was just a what? a disciple, just like you and I. Just like many of God's people are today, they are just disciples. They have no ministry of apostles, prophets, evangelists, teachers or pastors, but they are disciples; they're followers of the Lord Jesus Christ! And Ananias was just a disciple! Look, write that in your mind. He was just a disciple. I don't want to belittle "just a disciple" but I want to show you the greatness of a disciple. He didn't have to be a Peter or a John. He didn't have to be a bishop or a head elder. The word "bishop" is the Greek word for which the word "elder" is the Hebrew word in the Old Testament. Same word. Whenever you talk about the "elders" of the Old

Testament, it's the same word as the Greek word "bishop" in the New Testament. It means rulership.

> **Acts 9:10a**
> ...there was a certain disciple named Ananias; and to him said the Lord in a [what?] vision,...

And the word "vision" means vision. He showed it to him in a picture, a vision—a picture. Just like Moses and Elijah appeared in a vision to Jesus on the mount of transfiguration. If you understand TV or picture, you understand the word "vision." It was shown to him in a vision. Like Peter's vision when he was on housetop and the sheet was let down from heaven in which there were all kinds of animals. Remember? That's it! a picture. The Lord said to Ananias in a vision:

> **Acts 9:10**
> ...Ananias. And he said, Behold I *am here*, Lord.

I love this, because if the Lord ever spoke to a lot of church people we'd have oodles of funerals. They'd die of fright because they've never heard from heaven in a lifetime! And if God would ever dare talk to them, their old heart would just stop beating! But, here was Ananias, just a disciple, but he must have been in tune, right? He must have been tapped in! The *epi* must have been in the accusative case! Sure. And the first thing when the Lord said, "Ananias," Ananias said, "Here I am Lord!"

> **Acts 9:11a**
> And the Lord *said* unto him, Arise [arise], and go...

Do you say, "But Lord I don't like to arise and go. Lord, I love it so much where I am that I can just sit." Every Sunday night when I say, "Will someone please speak in tongues," only a few of you ever get up. The rest of you just sit. What's the matter with you? Not all of you, but most of you. Why? Because you haven't got to the place yet that you know you ought to "arise and go." You think "let somebody else rise and go."

You love to hear me teach the Word. It oils your palette but then you don't do what I tell you. You still sit, why? Because you are more scared of the Devil or people than you are loving of God's Word.

I love this in Ananias. You know sense knowledge wise what Ananias should have said? "Lord, I don't want to rise and I don't want to go. Lord, I love it here in Damascus. And I tell you, I've just been enjoying these services so much meeting with the brethren and having this other fella teaching the Word to me. If you don't mind Lord, I'd just love to sit around and enjoy this the rest of my life."

Now listen class. There's a time that comes when you either arise and go, or you never do anything! If the Word of God is right and speaking in tongues is so wonderful, shouldn't every one of our people want to be the first person up? (When the resurrection of the Lord comes, you don't want to drag your feet, do you?) Well now look, why don't we? Well do it! Do it! Now suppose three others stand? So what! Stay standing! If somebody else starts speaking and they get one word in ahead of you and you hear it, shut up! Wait until they're through then you give yours. Sure! And after we've had 3 or 4, or 5 or 6, I'll run the show, we'll set you down. Don't worry about it! But isn't that tremendous?

Acts 9:11a
And the Lord *said* unto him, [the Lord said unto him] Arise, and go [arise, go],...

But isn't it true that it's a lot easier many times to sit and hatch? It's what we may think, but then we miss the blessing too! Imagine what a joy it's going to be for you when you can get up in this meeting on a Sunday night, or any night and YOU can boldly speak in tongues and interpret! Look, you're going to thrill like you've never thrilled before, because you just know that you and God make a majority! Arise! Go! Go where?

Acts 9:11b
...into the street which is called Straight,...

And that's remarkable! This is the only way that he could get into that street because the street called "Straight" runs through Damascus east and west. I've walked this whole area. I just walked it for the joy, the thrill, and the experience of the accuracy of the Word.

When you come down from where Ananias lived, there is only one way to get into the street called "Straight." You've got to go into it because it's a dead end. The street called "Straight" goes east and west all the way through the center of Damascus. And coming down from the territory where Ananias lived, there is only one way you can get into the street, and that's to walk straight into it because this street dead ends right into the street called "Straight." Remarkable. It's called "the street called Straight" but it doesn't go straight! It goes straight through town. I guess that's what they meant, straight through Damascus. It goes straight through from east to west. And he said:

Acts 9:11c
...and enquire in the house of [what?] Judas for *one* called Saul, of Tarsus: for, behold, he [what?] prayeth,

You talk about information; the Lord gave it to him, didn't he? Ananias didn't know what house he had gone to, but the Lord knew! And the Lord said to Ananias, you go to the house of Judas and enquire for one called Saul of Tarsus, for behold, he what? prayeth. What do you think Saul of Tarsus will be doing when Ananias gets there? Not peeling potatoes! Not singing glory halleluiah or "Standing on the Promises." He's going to be one man who's going to be doing what? Praying! There may be a hundred men in that house doing something else, but there's going to be one man who's going to be praying.

Now class, what difference does it make if you get revelation by vision or just by that still small voice. What difference does it make if you get revelation, as long as you get what? revelation! Get the information! That's what you're after. The Lord in a vision showed Ananias the house of Judas. He said go to the house of Judas and enquire for a man named Saul of Tarsus. He's praying —showed him a picture!

Acts 9:12a
And hath seen in a vision a man named Ananias…

In other words God had given a vision to who? Saul. And told him:

Acts 9:12b
…coming in, and putting *his* hands on him, that he might receive his sight.

The word "receive" is not *dechomai* or *lambanō*, it's *anablepsē*. It means to get your sight back that you've lost.

I love verse 13.

Acts 9:13, 14
Then Ananias answered, Lord, I have heard by many of this man, how much evil he hath done to thy saints at Jerusalem:
And here he hath authority from the chief priests to bind all that call on thy name.

Ananias didn't like it when the Lord said, Get up and go! Like maybe some of you didn't like it when I said, "Get up and speak in tongues and interpret!" Well still do it! Ananias didn't like it so he complained to who? the management. He didn't run all over town among the church body and say, "Hey, the Lord talked to me this morning, before breakfast, and the Lord said I ought to go the house of Judas, but fellows don't you think I'm right not going?" No! He didn't run all over town! God told him to go. He didn't like what he heard so he said to God, "Lord I don't like the job!" I told you, he just complained to management. If you don't like the Word of God, tell God you don't like it! Don't argue with me.

Verse 15 says:

> **Acts 9:15a**
> But the Lord said unto him, Go…

Now that must have shook the shoes off of him! That word "go" is doubly emphasized. He shouted it from heaven, louder than I shouted it to you! That's that word "go." He didn't say arise any more, he shouted, "Go!" Not even get up, just go!

> **Acts 9:15b**
> …Go thy way: for he is a chosen [what?] vessel unto me,…

Oh, how I like that! Who would have ever chosen Saul? Not me! If Saul would have come to Headquarters we'd have locked the door! Kept him out. Well look at his record! He killed the Christians, persecuted them, beat them up. Now he's over here in Damascus to get some more prisoners. Who would have ever thought that he was a chosen vessel? Let that thing jell in you sometime!

It's not up to us to make the decisions. It's up to us to teach the Word and whosoever will, may come! Open the door and keep it open. Because how do you know if that man out there doesn't amount to a hill of beans in a hail storm? He hasn't done anything worth ever looking at. How do you know that tomorrow that man may become saved and do ten times as much for the Lord, than you and I have done? How do you know? You don't! Therefore, we're not responsible for letting people in or out, we're responsible to preach the Word! We're responsible to hold the Word forth! I tell you this is tremendous.

The Lord said, "He is a chosen vessel." My oh my! When you look at it sense knowledge wise, he's the most unlikely fellow that would ever be a chosen vessel for the Lord, right? He had committed murder. When God saved him he must have remitted those sins too, right? Just think it through sometime. He stood at the stoning of Stephen, consented to it and said, "Go on and kill him!" And Stephen was a man of God! He literally committed murder. And yet God saved him. And God said, "He is a chosen vessel unto me." Isn't that something?

Verse 15, continued.

Acts 9:15c, 16
...to bear my name before the Gentiles, and kings, and the children of Israel:
For I will shew him how great things he must suffer for my name's sake.

How much great things he will have to go through, because of his believing, because of my name. The word "suffer" is not the negative sense like "you suffer your way to heaven," that's not it!

Verse 17.

Acts 9:17a
And Ananias went his way,...

The Lord had told him which way to go. Ananias talked to the Lord. The Lord talked back to Ananias and said "go" and Ananias went!

Acts 9:17b
...and [he] entered into the house;...

Of Herman? No! The Word of God was "the house of Judas." The Word of God is the will of God. It means what it says, and says what it means, so he went to the house of Judas.

Acts 9:17c
...and putting his hands on him said, Brother [Brother! Brother!] Saul,...

Was he converted? Sure, otherwise he couldn't have been a brother. That's right. Converted on the road to Damascus. Saved! Born again of God's spirit! This is why I know God gave him a little more revelation than just what's written here in the Book. Because by the time Ananias got there he knew Paul was a brother. And they didn't haphazardly call them brothers like they do today! You know, you go in some churches and it's "brother this" and "sister this" and "brother in that" and "sister in that." It all depends on how empty they are! But, this "brother" meant that he was born again of God's spirit!

Acts 9:17d
...Brother Saul, the Lord, *even* Jesus, that appeared unto thee in the way as thou camest, hath sent me, that thou mightest receive [*anablepsē*] thy sight, and [and, and] be filled with...Holy Ghost [*pneuma hagion*].

Not filled with spiritually, but full in manifestation to the end of the accusative case, "pull in," active motion to the point to be pushed at.

Verse 18.

Acts 9:18
And immediately there fell from his eyes as it had been scales: and he received sight forthwith, and arose, and was baptized.

In water? No! I believe it says, "and was baptized." It's simply to wrap it up, to tell us that he was born again of God's spirit and received the fullness of God, the whole deal. That's all. Does it say he spoke in tongues? No. But back in those verses before, he said the Lord had told him, "thou mightest receive thy sight, and be filled with the Holy Ghost [*pneuma hagion*]." If he got his sight back, he must have been also filled in manifestation with the holy spirit. That's why in 1 Corinthians 14:18, if you have to have it, Paul states, "I thank my God, I speak with tongues more than ye all:" Did the apostle Paul speak in tongues? Definitely! This is the third record in the Word of God.

The first one is the Day of Pentecost, Acts 2, when the twelve received. And twelve only! And they were all Jews by religion. That same day there were about 3,000 added to the church, they all received! That's the first record.

The second record is in Acts 8 with Samaritan or "half Jews," where Philip ministered the Word of God. They got born again but they manifested nothing! Peter and John arrived on the scene, ministered to them, and they manifested something (for Simon saw).[21]

Now the third record is the record of the meanest man that ever lived: Saul. One individual gets born again of God's spirit and not only speaks in tongues, but gets healed physically. So, this is a story of an individual, and I tell you it's a tremendous story. A story of a man who is dedicated, who is committed to the wrong thing! He is sincere. He goes all out for the Devil. God saves him! God fills him, and he becomes a chosen vessel. And as you and I know from the Word of God, it was to this man that the abundance of the revelation of what it was that

---

21. Acts 8:18—And when Simon saw that through laying on of the apostle's hands the Holy Ghost was given, he offered them money.

came on the Day of Pentecost was later given. It was to him, that there was given the abundance of the revelation, which nobody else had ever had before to that extent! And when Paul received the power of the holy spirit, he spoke in tongues!

That's why we've had three records. On the Day of Pentecost, when they received they spoke in tongues. In Acts 8, when those Samaritans received, it doesn't say they spoke in tongues but it says that Simon did what? Saw something! In Acts 9 when Paul received, it doesn't say in Chapter 9 he spoke in tongues, but in 1 Corinthians 14 it says, "…I speak in tongues more than ye all:"

Those are the first three records; we have only two left! We'll cover those next. Let's stand for a word of prayer.

FREED FROM THE LAW

And in Him is no what? Darkness.[1] And God does not send evil. If God would send evil He would have to be a fiend. He would have to be Satan. Then what do you do about the story where Jesus said, "A kingdom divided against itself cannot stand..." Therefore, the true God can't have any bad in Him, and the Devil can't have any good in him. It's that sharply cut.

Now, in the Word of God, God's laws are like that. God had for instance told Pharaoh to let His people go. Pharaoh knew the Word, he knew the law. But Pharaoh decided not to let them go so Pharaoh bumped his head (as I call it) up against the law. And this is why the Bible says, God brought it on him. Because, God had set the law. That's why the Word of God says, and God did "so and so" to Pharaoh, or God did "so and so" to somebody else. It's because these people ran up against God's law. The old English and Oriental way of expressing it is by saying, God did it! Understand? God never did it actively. He only permitted it to happen to people because He had placed this law.

Now, here is a man. One man chooses the Lord Jesus Christ, therefore he gets saved. Another man chooses not to choose the Lord Jesus Christ, therefore he goes on unsaved. This person is referred to in the Bible as predestinated. Once again, this person is referred to as being predestinated. And the guy that racked and ruined this understanding was my old buddy, John Calvin. He

---

1. 1 John 1:5—This then is the message which we have heard of him, and declare unto you, that God is light, and in him is no darkness at all.

really hashed that to pieces, because John Calvin taught that predestination meant: God takes one man by the nap of the neck and sends him to heaven; He takes another fellow by the nap of the neck and says, I think you'd do better in hell! So He sends him to hell. That's why John Calvin said that you can't do anything about it. In reality John Calvin taught fatalism. If you can't do anything about it, it's fatalism! And since you have no choice whether you're going to go to heaven or hell, God takes you and sends one to heaven; He sends the other to hell. Then God is as responsible for those in hell as He is in heaven, by sheer logic!

This teaching is all through the reform churches. And the reason John Calvin propagated this is because they didn't understand predestination. The reason God can predestinate one to heaven and the other to hell is not because God actively does this, but because God permits man to have freedom of choice. And by His foreknowledge (God's foreknowledge) He knows even before this person is born that there will come a day in his life when this person will accept the Lord Jesus Christ! There will never come a day when this other man will accept. God knows this by His foreknowledge. Thus knowing it by His foreknowledge, the Word says He predestinates this man for heaven, and this man for hell.

> **Romans 8:29**
> For whom he did [what?] foreknow, he also did predestinate *to be* conformed to the image of his Son,...

The key is in the word "foreknowledge." To "foreknow" is to know everything ahead of time.

Verse 30.

> **Romans 8:30**
> Moreover whom he did predestinate [in His foreknowledge those when they came along], them he

[did what to?]…called: and whom he called, them he also justified: and whom he justified, them he [God] also glorified.

Isn't that tremendous? Therefore, for us who are born again of God's spirit He called, right? He called us! How did He call us? by His Word. Faith cometh how? hearing. And hearing cometh by the Word. So He called us by His Word. He knew that when you heard the Word, you would believe. That's how He calls you. Then when He calls you, and He knew you would believe, then when you believe you got justified. And when you got justified He also did what with you? glorified you! Isn't that a tremendous thing? These great truths of God's Word are so frequently misunderstood, because they do not understand foreknowledge or predestination. So, do you understand it now? It's like this all through the Bible, all through the Word.

We have covered three records in the Book of Acts. Acts 2, the original outpouring when the 12 apostles received. After Peter preached that day about 3,000 were converted and they were all Jews by religion. And when they received they all spoke in tongues. That was the external manifestation of the internal reality and presence of the holy spirit. There is only one basic evidence that people have received the holy spirit in the Bible and that is speaking in tongues. That is the basic. That is the initial external evidence in the senses world which you can see and hear of the internal reality and presence of His holy spirit which you cannot see, or smell, or taste, or touch.

The second record was in Acts 8, some ten to fifteen years after the experience of the Day of Pentecost. And it does not say they spoke in tongues but Simon saw something. It doesn't say what he saw, but he couldn't see spirit therefore he had to see what? manifestation. It doesn't say they spoke in tongues, but I am sure that you know from the accuracy of God's Word that he had to do something in the senses realm so they would know he had the spirit, right? And in its least common denominator if you really want to know the Word of God, you'll have to admit that they spoke in tongues. That's what he saw but it doesn't say it.

The third record which we covered last session was to show you a man who was absolutely devilish in everything he did. He thought he was right. He did everything according to God's plan as he saw it, but he was all wrong. All wrong! And he got saved on the road to Damascus. And being saved on the road to Damascus he was led into the city and he was blinded. And a simple little disciple named Ananias went to the house of Judas and ministered the holy spirit to him and healing. It doesn't say in Acts 9 that Paul spoke in tongues, but in 1 Corinthians 14 we read last session that Paul said, "...I speak with tongues more than ye all:"

Now we go to the fourth record in the Book of Acts, which is Chapter 10. Again, here I do not know the exact number of years that transpired between Acts 2 and Acts 10. But I do know it was fifteen to twenty years after the original outpouring, many years, when Acts 10 occurred. And now here, for the first time you have the record of the Gentiles coming into the church, the Body of Christ, without becoming proselytes, without becoming Jews by religion. All up until this time, Acts 2 they were what? Jews. Acts 8, Samaritans—half Jews. Acts 9, an individual Jew—Paul. Now Acts 10 is the first time in the history of the Christian church that the Gentiles come into the Body of Christ without becoming proselytes. Now there were other Gentiles who had already come into the fellowship before this, but they had been proselytes of Judaism. Now we're going to read the record of pure Gentiles coming into the church for the first time.

Before I read this chapter with you, let me bring you up historically a little bit on the Gentiles. I told you that the Jews hated the Samaritans. They did. But when it came to Gentiles, they multiplied their hate! To them a Gentile was worse than a dog! They had the oracles of God and the Gentiles didn't have enough sense to get circumcised to become Jews by religion, so they really hated them. And tonight you're going to read the story of how God prepared a man who was a Jew by religion, to bring the Word of God to the Gentiles whom he wouldn't touch with a ten foot pole! You will see those Gentiles getting born again of God's spirit, filled with the holy spirit, and it's one of the greatest records in the Word of God on the holy spirit, outside of Acts 2.

Now Chapter 10.

Acts 10:1
There was a certain man in Caesarea called Cornelius, a centurion of the band called the Italian *band*,

A centurion is one who was head of a hundred soldiers, of the Italian band from Rome. He was:

Acts 10:2, 3a
A devout *man*, and one that feared God [loved God, respected, had awe, reverence for God] with all his house [his wife, and kids, and servants],...[he] gave much alms to the people, and prayed to God alway. He saw in a vision [a vision] evidently [clearly, openly] about the ninth hour of the day...

The ninth hour of the day is what time our time? Three o'clock in the afternoon.

Acts 10:3b, 4
...an angel of God coming into him, and saying unto him, Cornelius.

And when he looked on him, he was afraid, and said, What is it, Lord? And he said unto him, Thy prayers and thine alms are come up for a memorial before God.

This in here is phenomenon. He was not yet born again, therefore he could not have been operating manifestations of the spirit, right? Therefore, it's in the category of phenomena. Which again is whose business? God's business.

Acts 10:5, 6a
And now send men to Joppa, and call for *one* Simon, whose surname is Peter:
He lodgeth...

Look at the information God gives him right down the line, straight revelation.

Acts 10:6
He lodgeth with one Simon a tanner, whose house is by the sea side:...

And that is real enlightening because they had zoning in those days as well as today. If you were a tanner because you stunk up the place by tanning the hides, you were never allowed to build in the city limits. You had to build outside of the city limits. Not only did your place of business have to be outside of the city limits, it had to be downwind of the prevailing winds. It's a remarkable little insight, isn't it? For he dwelleth by the sea side. Because that way the stink could blow right over the Sea of Galilee, and by the time it got on the other side the stink would be gone.

Acts 10:6b
...[call for] Simon a tanner, whose house is by the sea side: he shall tell thee what thou oughtest to do.

Isn't that remarkable? God has aligned Himself with men who know the Word to teach the Word so that others can get saved.

God could have gotten him saved, I suppose, some other way if He decided to. But, since Peter knew the Word of God and Peter was down there in Joppa, he said, Go get Peter and bring him over here and he will tell you what to do! That's remarkable, because the average person would have said, "Well after all, I'm the centurion, I'm the head of a hundred soldiers of the great state of Rome! You want me to get some little fellow down from the stinking place of a tanner? Have him come in here and stink up all my house? Walk all over my rug? Oh, no! Lord, if you want me I've been good! I've been giving much alms." You know, it said that. He had given much alms to the people. He built hospitals. He had told him how to raise chickens. He had done all these wonderful things for them. And yet the Lord said to him, all of those good things are wonderful, but Cornelius still was unsaved. You know this is why a man can build hospitals, give all his money to the poor, does all of this stuff and still have no eternal life abiding within him!

This man shall tell thee what to do. And I'll bet you a dollar to a doughnut, he's going to have to carry out literally what that man says to do! When he says, open your mouth wide and breathe in, he doesn't mean open your mouth a tiny bit. He said wide, he meant wide!

Acts 10:6c, 7
…he shall tell thee what thou oughtest to do.
And when the angel which spake unto Cornelius was departed,…

You see God showed him a vision, a picture, and the voice of the angel spoke to him and interpreted the vision to him, told him the score.

Acts 10:7, 8
And when the angel which spake unto Cornelius was departed, he called two of his household servants, and a devout soldier of them that waited on him continually;
And when he had declared all *these* things unto them, he sent them to [where?] Joppa.

Why? Because that was where Peter was, that's where God had said to go, right? Class, let me ask you something again. Was the Word of God literally the will of God for Cornelius? Don't you see it every time in the Word of God, when men get something they always literally obey God's Word! Always! Literally!

Now, verse 9.

Acts 10:9
On the morrow, as they went on their journey, and drew nigh unto the city, Peter went up upon the housetop to pray about the sixth hour:

What time? Twelve, noon. And Peter was real human.

Acts 10:10
And he became very hungry, and would have eaten: [and] while they made ready [for the dinner], he fell into a trance,

The spiritualists like this verse because they use it to prove that Peter had a "trance" like they go into a trance —no, no! The word "trance" here simply means a vision, which has with it what I refer to as a dormant state of mental activity. It's like you people when you daydream. Ever done this? It's about like it is—not quite. You're wide awake and you're looking out there; you're not seeing anything, but you're maybe seeing with your mind-eyes some other thing. That's this dormant state of mental activity! The trance. I defined this "trance" in a book recently or in an article that was written. Now, the reason I know this is because verse 17 says what this vision which he had seen should mean.

Go back to verse 10, "but while they made ready, he fell into a trance," he had a vision, which was a dormant state of mental activity. He just had his mind renewed, had it in neutral, and there was the vision. And what did he see? Verse 11.

> **Acts 10:11**
> ...[he] saw heaven opened, and a certain vessel descending unto him, as it had been a great sheet knit at the four corners, and let down to the earth:

You know, a fellow holding on each corner. Four corners. Holding on.

> **Acts 10:12**
> Wherein [inside of it] were all manner of four-footed beasts of the earth, and wild beasts, and creeping things, and fowls of the air.

The whole thing that Peter just wasn't allowed to even eat or think about was because he had been legalistic and still in his eating methods a legalistic Jew.

Verse 13.

> **Acts 10:13**
> And there came a voice to him, Rise, Peter; kill, and [what?] eat.

You know what the psychiatrist would say about this? Oh, that was just normal because it was dinner time and he was hungry, therefore he just had a picture of meat coming down. They've always got answers for everything. But, this is what God did. And it wasn't because Peter was hungry.

Verses 14-16.

Acts 10:14-16
But Peter said, Not so, Lord [not me]; for [you know Lord] I have never eaten any thing that is common or unclean.
And the voice *spake* unto him again the second time, What God hath cleansed, *that* call not thou common [defiled].
This was done thrice [three times]: and the vessel was received up again into heaven.

Three times. Verse 17.

Acts 10:17
Now while Peter doubted [the word is "considered deeply"] in himself what this vision which he had seen should mean, behold, the men which were sent from Cornelius had made inquiry for Simon's house, and stood before the gate.

Isn't that a wonderful synchronization of God's perfect timing? To start those fellows out from Cornelius's place and get them up to Joppa, to the house where Simon Peter was dwelling with Simon the tanner, and that those fellows got there just at the time when that sheet was going up! That's something on synchronization, isn't it? And they were right outside of the gate. Verse 18 says, they knocked—nope! It says, they "called." They called because that's the oriental way, the eastern way, the biblical way of contacting people. You have to know them by name, and you call them by name. You never knock on the door, or ring the doorbell. You walk outside the house and say, "Hey Herman!" Then old Herman comes. You have to know their names. It's really a wonderful orientalism in here.

Verses 18-20.

Acts 10:18, 19a
...[They] called, and asked whether Simon, which was surnamed Peter, were lodged there.
While Peter thought on the vision,...

While Peter was still considering that three times he had seen this thing, now look what it says, "the Spirit" —the Spirit, the Spirit. God by revelation (word of knowledge and word of wisdom and discerning of spirits—one of those three or a combination thereof), by the Spirit "said to him." The first vision was not said by the spirit, it was a picture in Technicolor. This was the Spirit speaking to Peter's spirit, which was in Peter, God's spirit in Peter.

Acts 10:19b, 20
...[and] the Spirit said unto him, Behold, three men [what?] seek thee.
Arise therefore, and get thee down, and go with them, doubting nothing: for I have [what?] sent them.

Isn't it marvelous and wonderful how God prepares men to meet situations by doing this so lovingly and so graciously? He had to have somebody to send. Nobody was better than Peter! But to get Peter and to prepare him to make this trip, He doesn't tell him a lot of things. He shows him just a little picture and He says to him, "Pete, I want you to remember that which I have cleansed don't you ever dare call unclean." That's it. And not only did He prepare him that way, but He goes lovingly further and by the spirit said to him, "Peter, there are three men outside." And at that very moment when He told him, they were calling his name! And then the Lord said, I want you to go with those three men and don't you doubt at all! Isn't that loving?

All revelation is loving and wonderful. Revelation, when it's given by God to us men and women of God, when this revelation is given to us, it's always within the ability of what we are able to understand. It's always loving, it's always kind, it's always gentle, it's always God dealing with us according to the ability that we are able to receive.

> **Acts 10:21-23**
> Then Peter went down to the men which were sent unto him from Cornelius; and said, Behold, I am he [Peter] whom ye seek: what *is* the cause wherefore you are come?
> And they said, Cornelius the centurion, a just man, and one that feareth God, and of good report among all the nation of the Jews, was warned from God by an holy angel to send for thee into his house, and to hear words of thee.
> Then called he them in, and lodged *them*. And on the morrow [the next day] Peter went away with them, and certain brethren from Joppa accompanied him.

Peter took six witnesses with him from Joppa. Six Christian Jews who had been born again, who were also still zealous for the law, but at least they were Christian. They were born again of God's spirit. He took these men with him. The reason I know it was six is because the Word of God says so in Acts 11:12.[2] Do you wonder why he took these six men along? Because, I believe that God by revelation told him. Before he ever left town, God said to him, Hey, you'd better get John and Joe and Bill and Herman and the rest. You'd better get those six men, and let them go with you!

---

2. Acts 11:12—And the Spirit bade me go with them, nothing doubting. Moreover these six brethren accompanied me…

Acts 10:24a
And [on] the morrow after they entered into Caesarea. And Cornelius waited for them,...

Isn't that something? How did Cornelius know that Peter would come? God had told him to send for Peter, but the point I want you to see is that Cornelius believed all along Peter would come because God had said. He believed he would come. And you know what he did? He swept the rug, got the house ready, got the chairs set, put the hymnals out, put their pencils and pieces of paper there for them and said let's go to work! He waited for them. This is remarkable, class!

Acts 10:24b
...and [he] had called together his kinsmen and near friends.

Did Peter have to conduct a newspaper campaign of advertising to get the people in? Did he have to run to the radio station and have a radio broadcast for 15 minutes to tell the people they were going to have a meeting at Cornelius's house tonight for the Lord? No! The man who wanted the Word of God, he had seen to it that the meeting was promoted! And he had gone out and got his kinsman, near friends and the rest of the people in the area. He got them, and he brought them all in!

Acts 10:25a
And as Peter was coming in,...

I marvel at this, because how did Cornelius know Peter was going to get there at that time? He didn't. They could have been sitting there for four, five or six hours. They were there expecting and ready when Peter got there. They didn't wait for Peter to come first and then send out to everybody and say, "Well now Pete come on in, let's get the meeting rolling." They were sitting there waiting for the meeting to start! They were hungry for the Word, and if you're hungry you're there.

> **Acts 10:25**
> And as Peter was coming in, Cornelius met him, and fell down at his feet, and worshiped *him*.

The word "worshiped" is like the word "adoration." He adored him. This is an eastern orientalism, it's a custom. This is the way they show homage to people, respect. To worship him does not mean that he prayed to him like we worship God. That's not the word at all! It was that he bowed to him. He *salaam'd* him. He gave him a special courtesy, the way he treated him.

> **Acts 10:26, 27a**
> But Peter took him up, saying, Stand up; I myself also am a man.
> And as he talked with him,...

He talked with him, talked with Cornelius. He asked Cornelius a few questions. They talked things over a little bit. Because what you can know by your sense knowledge, God expects you to know! Revelation begins where the information which you can accurately gain by your senses, ceases. Generally speaking, that's why no man has revelation if he can know it by his senses, God won't give him revelation. Then all these people I hear all the time they say, well God told me this. The heck God told him that! Bunch of baloney![3] God's revelation begins where the senses terminate. What you and I can know by our senses God expects us to know. That's right!

I suppose God could take us and teach us the whole Word of God in one night if He wanted to. He could knock our heads against the stone wall and we'd have a big hole in it. He could just pour it in if He wanted to.

---

3. A bunch of baloney" means something is nonsense.

He could do this, He's God Almighty, but the reason He will not do it is because He has limited himself to His Word where He said, we are to: study to show ourselves approved of God.[4] And that's why if you want to do God's Word you'd better study it! And for people who do not study God's Word and they tell me, God's telling them so and so, they're lying every time! Every blessed time, class, never get fooled by it! They're just pulling your fool leg and you're stupid enough to enjoy it. I tell you don't go down the drain on it. If they haven't got enough courage or enough guts or enough drive, to work the Word of God, God's not going to be talking to them (generally speaking). He could still do it if it was what? phenomenon. But that's few and far between!

Peter talked with old Cornelius and said: Okay, now what's going on here? I've got the Word down in Joppa, you wanted me over here. Now what's the score? Where do we go from here? And as they talked together, verse 27.

> **Acts 10:27**
> And as he talked with him, he went in, and found many that were come together.

A whole gang! A whole household.

> **Acts 10:28**
> And he said unto them, Ye know how that it is an unlawful thing for a man that is a Jew to keep company, or come unto one of another nation; but God hath shewed me that I should not call any man common [defiled] or unclean.

Do you think Peter would have ever gone to Cornelius's house had he not had the vision of the sheet from

---

4. 2 Timothy 2:15—Study to shew thyself approved unto God, a workman that needeth not to be ashamed, rightly dividing the word of truth.

heaven? And had the spirit not told him to go? Peter still would be sitting back in Joppa. God had to talk to him! It wasn't the three men that came to Joppa that made Peter go. No, no, no. The reason Peter went was because of the information God had given him, via the vision and by way of the spirit. That's the only reason. That's why when he gets there and he gets this information from Cornelius, the first thing he said to the people: it's most unusual that I'm here. Because no Jew was allowed to go into the place of a Gentile or they would be contaminated! (He'd feel he hadn't had a bath for six years!) But, God has showed me that I should not call any man common or unclean.

> **Acts 10:29**
> Therefore came I *unto you* without gainsaying [without hesitation], as soon as I was sent for: I ask therefore for what intent ye have sent for me?

What do you want me over here for?

> **Acts 10:30-33**
> And Cornelius said, Four days ago I was fasting until this hour; and at the ninth hour I prayed in my house, and, behold, a man stood before me in bright clothing,
> And said, Cornelius, thy prayer is heard, and thine alms are had in remembrance in the sight of God.
> Send therefore to Joppa, and call hither Simon, whose surname is Peter; he is lodged in the house of *one* Simon a tanner by the sea side: who, when he cometh, shall speak unto thee.
> Immediately…

Verse 33, "immediately…"; I like that. Did he act on the Word of God after six months? He acted when? Immediately!

In my classes you'll hear me say different things at times, and then you'll see what sense knowledge wise people say: well V.P. is getting mad at them! I'm not mad at them at all! I'm mad at the Devil because the people don't obey God's Word! Like when I minister the holy spirit. I say to them, "Open your mouth wide" and somebody doesn't, and I say, "Well open it wide!" They think it's my fault! It's not my fault at all, they're just not immediately doing what? Obeying. And if they all immediately obey, they always get it! Nobody ever misses. And when they don't, they never get it. Never. Because you can't get it from God if you don't obey the Word of God, right? That's the key to it!

Cornelius didn't wait five weeks. Immediately, after he'd had the revelation, he called the three men in, told them what he wanted, got them ready, got the old mules packed, and the next morning he sent them out. Real pronto!

Acts 10:33
Immediately therefore I sent to thee; and thou hast well done that thou are come. Now therefore are we all here present before God, to hear all things that are commanded thee of [who?] God.

Wow, isn't that a statement! Old Cornelius didn't want to hear about Peter's experiences with his wife. He didn't want to hear about how he'd given up a drunkard's grave. How he'd quit smoking cigarettes, chewing tobacco and taking snuff. He didn't want to hear how he used to dance and didn't dance any more. He wanted to hear one thing —What's God got to say? He didn't give a hoot about experience; he wanted to know what God has to say. What a tremendous revelation. Look at what would happen in our churches today if the people that go there simply say, "Don't be a late news reporter, don't tell us what happened in Vietnam and the rest of the places. Tell us what God's got to say!" We wouldn't have any services on Sunday in the United States anymore. You talk about a Gentile, a dog, worse than a dog. Only interested in one thing, "What's God got to say!" And people, that ought to be the heart cry from all of us. When we go to our churches, when we go to our religious meetings, we ought to be interested in one thing. What's God got to say! Hear the commandment of the Lord, the commands that God has! That's right.

Acts 10:34
Then Peter opened *his* mouth [he started his sermon], and said, Of a truth I perceive that God is no respecter of persons:

Now this is something for Peter to say. I tell you without the vision, without the revelation from the spirit, Peter wouldn't have touched this with a ten foot pole! First thing he said, I see God is no respecter of persons, and that is a tremendous revelation! This is true for us too. God is no respecter of persons.

"But in every nation"—nation is Gentile. The nations are not listed among the Jews. This refers to all Gentile nations.

Acts 10:35-38a
But in every nation [Gentile nations] he that feareth him [have respect, awe, reverence God], and worketh righteousness, is accepted with him.
The word which *God* sent unto the children of Israel, preaching peace by Jesus Christ: (he is Lord of all.) That word, *I say*, ye know, which was published throughout all Judaea and began from Galilee, after the baptism which John preached;
How God anointed Jesus of Nazareth with… [*pneuma hagion*] holy spirit [no article "the"; he anointed him with the gift] and with power:…

This is two nouns used, one thing meant. It's a figure of speech. Two nouns are used but only one thing meant:

"holy spirit and with power." Power is holy spirit, holy spirit is power.

Acts 10:38b
…who went about doing good, and healing all that were oppressed…

Is that all without exception or all without distinction? Without distinction, not everybody was healed. But all that believed, and all that came under his ministry had believed, all without any distinction.

And they were oppressed by God? NO!

Acts 10:38c
…[and they were oppressed] of the devil; for God was with him.

Why should God have to be with him, if Jesus Christ was God?

Verse 39.

Acts 10:39, 40
And we are witnesses of all things which he did both in the land of the Jews, and in Jerusalem; whom they slew and hanged on a tree:
Him God raised up the third day, and shewed him openly;

There's the Resurrection teaching.

Acts 10:41-44a
Not to all people, but unto witnesses chosen before of God, *even* to us, who did eat and drink with him after he rose from the dead.
And he commanded us to preach unto the people, and to testify that it is he which was ordained of God *to be* the Judge of quick [the living] and dead.
To him give all the prophets witness, that through his

name whosoever believeth in him shall receive remission of sins.
While Peter yet spake...

While Peter was yet preaching—you are going to see here this one time a man preaching never gets a chance to say amen, pronounce the benediction and go to the back of the church. He never gets that far along.

Acts 10:44
While Peter yet spake [while he's preaching] these words, the Holy Ghost [the Holy, the Spirit] fell on all them which heard the word.

They heard to the end that they believed. Here was Peter preaching his heart out! Here's Cornelius and that whole gang. And while Peter is yet preaching, these people are believing, and as they are believing they are receiving. While Peter yet spake, something happened for "the holy," "the ghost" (the spirit), fell on them which heard the word. It fell on them to the same extent that it fell back in Acts 8, that it came into manifestation. In Acts 8 it hadn't fallen, here it fell. They made the contact and they were bringing it into evidence. They were bringing the spirit into evidence! You can't see spirit but you could see what? Evidence. While Peter is yet preaching these people are getting saved and they're doing something!

Verse 45.

Acts 10:45a
And they of the circumcision which believed...

That is those six brethren that Peter brought along, remember? They of the circumcision, Jews who were born again, they believed.

Acts 10:45b
...[they] were astonished [they were flabbergasted],

as many as came with Peter, because that on the Gentiles also…

That on the Gentiles *also*—The key word is the word "also"! The word "also" implies that somebody else had it before, right? Now the Gentiles, what? Also. On the Day of Pentecost some 18, 20, 25 years before in Jerusalem, Peter and eleven other apostles had received the power of the holy spirit. And when they were born again, the first thing they did was what? Spoke in tongues! And here Peter some years later has six brethren with him who are born again of God's spirit, but they are of the circumcision of the Jews, and Peter's preaching and he's in a Gentile home. And while he's preaching:

Acts 10:45c
…on the Gentiles also…

Those Jews were so flabbergasted that had they been wearing dentures that stuff they put on to keep them in wouldn't have held them! They'd have fallen right off. I tell you it took more than Poligrip[5] to hold their teeth in! Because the word "astonished" is "shook," "flabbergasted"! I tell you these Jews were so rocked, these Jews were so shaken, that there are not words for me to describe how they were shook! It was terrific! And you know what shook them?

Acts 10:45c
…[Because] that on the Gentiles also was poured out the gift of [*pneuma hagion* (holy spirit—no article)].

That's what shook them. Now while Peter was preaching, if Cornelius got up and said, "Hey Peter, I think we had better go out and have a circumcision ceremony. All of us fellows will come out behind the barn and you can circumcise us a little bit. And we'll all become Jews!"

---

5. A brand of denture adhesive.

That would not have shook those brethren, would it? No! Because then they would have become proselytes of Judaism. That wouldn't have shook them at all! But I tell you, this shook them, this really shook them! "...that on the Gentiles also was poured out the gift..." without them becoming proselytes! Those people who like water, we pour it to them over here. Do you know why? You could have taken those Gentiles to the creek and you could have put them under, forward in the name of the Father, backwards in the name of the son and straight up in the name of the spirit. That never would have convinced those Jews who came with Peter, or Peter, that on the Gentiles *also* was poured out the gift! You could have taken them to the creek and drowned them with baptism water! That would have never convinced Peter and those six brethren who accompanied him that the Gentiles also had received! You could have washed them in "Lux" and "Ivory" and it wouldn't have convinced them! That's right.

Class, there has to be one evidence of being a Christian. There has to be one evidence which is indisputable and undeniable. An evidence which cannot be contradicted, and which when once manifested you've got the proof in the senses world of the real McCoy on the inside! And this has to be so iron clad that nobody can fool anybody on it. The Scripture says, "For they heard them speak with tongues, and magnify God..."[6] Wow, isn't that something! Nothing else would have convinced Peter that these Gentiles *also*, because Peter some 15, 18, 20 years before in Jerusalem, they had received and when they received, what did they do? Spoke in tongues!

Verse 45, "...that on the Gentiles also..." Also! For the Gentiles were speaking in tongues! That's the only undisputable proof in the world. That's right. Look, nothing else would have convinced Peter and you know it!

---

6. Acts 10:46.

That's why speaking in tongues is the greatest manifestation in the senses realm, which is the proof to you that you're a Christian! And it's the proof to me that you are born again of God's spirit! Then I know, and you know! On the Gentiles *also* was poured out the gift—that's the only proof you've got! That's the only proof a Christian has—what a proof, huh?

You see, Peter would never had gone, had God not sent down the sheet and given him the Word, and then telling him by the spirit to go and having those three men there at the same time. Peter never would have gone to begin with. Now he went. What he was really expecting nobody knows. I'm going to show you in a minute that this really shook Peter. It really shook him, but Peter goes and Peter carries out God's orders! He simply starts preaching the Word, that's all. That's Peter's responsibility. Preach the Word. So he preached the Word. We want to hear what's commanded to you of God! So Peter preaches the Word. And while he's preaching the Word, Cornelius believes and the rest of the people believe. And when they start believing they don't head towards the nearest bathtub, they simply open their mouth and they what? Speak in tongues. And this is that on the Gentiles *also* was poured out the gift!

> **Acts 10:46**
> For they heard them speak with [in] tongues, and magnify God....

And they knew that when people spoke in tongues, they were speaking the wonderful works of God, and the wonderful works of God magnify God! Every time you speak in tongues you magnify God! It's a witness to the God who saved you and who lives within you. That's how it magnifies! They were speaking the wonderful works of God on the Day of Pentecost. Here it says that when they spoke in tongues they magnified God! All speaking in tongues is the magnification of God, for it's the testimony in the senses world that you have Christ within!

Now the last three words of verse 46:

Acts 10:46b, 47
…Then answered Peter,
Can any man forbid water, that these should not be baptized, which have received [*lambanō'd*] the Holy Ghost [the *pneuma* the *hagion* like we did, by speaking in tongues] as well as we?

This is the first time that water comes into the Book of Acts, first time. It's the first time water comes in. You know why water comes in? The reason water comes in is because old Peter was just all broken up! He was all shook! He didn't mind—after he saw the sheet, after he had the spirit tell him to go, he didn't mind to go and preach the Word. That was not too bad but he never got to say amen! And here was Cornelius speaking in tongues, here was his woman speaking in tongues, here were all the family speaking in tongues, all—everybody speaking! My oh my! Peter says, "Hey, we better just make sure this is real, we better give them a little water extra."

I wonder why Peter wanted to give them water? Because Peter in his background was a Jew, and the Jews were all zealous for what? the law. And Peter had been under John's baptism and John baptized with water. And so Peter, real frustrated said, "Well now, that's good. They speak just like we do, but man I've been hearing this Jew and Gentile…we better be sure this is kosher and take them down and dip them!" That's the first thought he had. But you know something? He never took them down and water baptized them. He never took them down to drink. Because about the time Peter got to thinking about this thing, the spirit witnessed to him and said, "Hold off a minute Peter!" Hold off. No use of water drowning that outfit! Because you heard them speak in tongues! They got the real McCoy.

The reason I know that is because the Word of God says so. Because after this experience and word gets back to Jerusalem that Peter's been down to a household of Cornelius, what do you think those Jews who were still zealous for the law, even though they were born again, what do you think they would do with old Peter? We're going to have a little third degree in Jerusalem when Peter gets back. We're going to call Peter in and put him on the carpet! And say, alright Peter, why did you do it? That's it, that's exactly what happened! Just exactly.

Because in Acts, chapter 11, it says:

Acts 11:1-7
And the apostles and brethren that were in Judaea heard that the Gentiles [also] had received [*dechomai'd*] the word of God.
And when Peter was come up to Jerusalem, they that were of the circumcision contended with him [an argument, fight],
Saying, Thou [went] in to men uncircumcised, and didst eat with them.
But Peter rehearsed *the matter* [means he told them all about it] from the beginning, and expounded *it* by order unto them, saying,
I was in the city of Joppa praying: and in a trance I saw a vision, A certain vessel descend, as it had been a great sheet, let down from heaven by four corners; and it came even unto me:
Upon the which when I had fastened mine eyes, I considered, and saw fourfooted beasts of the earth, and wild beasts, and creeping things, and fowls of the air.

And I heard a voice saying unto me, Arise, Peter; slay and eat.

You see he's telling them exactly what he had done, what he was told.

Acts 11:8-12a
But I said, Not so, Lord: for nothing common or unclean hath at any time entered into my mouth.
But the voice answered me again from heaven, What God hath cleansed, *that* call not thou common [defiled].
And this was done three times: and all were drawn up again into heaven.
And, behold, immediately there were three men already come unto the house where I was, sent from Caesarea unto me.
And the spirit bade me go with them nothing doubting,...

Has he reported it accurately? Yes, right down the line. "...moreover these six brethren..."—he's got all six of them with him sitting right down there before the Sanhedrin, all six of his testimonies, his witnesses you know, he's got them all there. They are Jews that have been born again, who accompanied him to Joppa. He took them along to Jerusalem, paid for their transportation and bought them their suit, had them there.

Acts 11:12b-14
...these six brethren accompanied me, and we entered into the man's house:
And he shewed us how he had seen an angel in his house, which stood and said unto him, Send men to Joppa, and call for Simon, whose surname is Peter;
Who shall tell thee words, whereby thou and all thy house shall be [what?] saved.

That's not what we learned in verse 10, did we? But it's just as much because we learned in there that Cornelius said to him, "I want to hear whatever God has commanded." And if a man is unsaved, the first thing God wants for that man is to get saved. That's right! So this is what happened. "Thou and all thy house shall be saved."

Acts 11:15
And as I began to speak, the Holy Ghost [the *pneuma* the *hagion*] fell on them, as on us [just like it did on us] at the beginning.

Now, in Acts chapter 10, back to verse 47, "Can any man forbid water, that these should not be baptized…?" Peter said. Now you're back to Chapter 11, Acts 11:16.

Acts 11:16, 17
Then remembered I the word of the Lord, how that he said, John [who] indeed baptized with [what?] water; but ye shall be baptized with [*pneuma hagion*] the Holy Ghost.
Forasmuch then as God gave them the like gift as *he did* unto us, who believed on the Lord Jesus Christ; [who] was I, that I could withstand God?

You know what he said? He wanted to water baptize them but the moment he got to thinking about it, the Lord said, Hey! Water baptism was whose baptism? John's. And this is not John's baptism. This is the baptism of the Holy Spirit. Christ in you the hope of glory! They've spoken in tongues. "Then who was I, that I could withstand God?" So he never water baptized them. Didn't have to because God told him not to. Isn't that wonderful?

And it says:

Acts 11:18
When they heard these things, they held their peace,

and glorified God, saying, Then hath God also to the Gentiles granted repentance unto life.

Isn't that wonderful? Back to Chapter 10.

Acts 10: 47, 48a
Can any man forbid water, that these should not be baptized, which have received the Holy Ghost as well as we?
And he commanded them to be baptized in the name of the Lord….

You see he never baptized them. He simply commanded them and said, Well all of you just get saved. That's all that is necessary. Just get born again and speak in tongues. That's all.

Acts 10:48b
…Then prayed they him to tarry certain days.

I suppose they had a great big feast! This is the forth record in the Bible, and it's how the Gentiles got in. And class, there was only one proof that the Gentiles had received the same thing that they had received in Jerusalem many years before. And that one proof in the senses world which is undeniable and indisputable was that they heard them speak in tongues. How do you like that? That's the Word of God people. I didn't write the Book! But it's as simple as day, isn't it?

Speaking in tongues is the external manifestation in the senses realm, of the internal reality and presence of His holy spirit. Whenever anybody is born again of God's spirit they can speak in tongues! And when they speak in a tongue, that's the proof that they are born again! God knows whether you're born again, but you don't know. I don't know if you're born again! But when you speak in tongues, you know it. When you speak in tongues, I know it if I hear you speak. That's why speaking in tongues is the only manifestation that you can't fool people on. That's right. Speaking in tongues is the only manifestation that is audible, it's distinctive. It has a certain type of rhythm to it that languages have to them. It has a certain type of enunciation. That's why nobody can ever fool you. Now if she went, "Beep, beep, beep, beep, beep, beep, beep," that wouldn't be speaking in tongues; that would be a squirrel barking or something! That's right.

I've been through that mill you know. I've been at meetings where people said were speaking in tongues, but it sounded just like what I was saying (beep, beep, beep…). It sounded like some old squirrel up in a tree that I'm getting ready to shoot in September. They go beep, beep, beep, beep! No speaking in tongues in that!

People, look at the greatness of this speaking in tongues and how little we've really loved *God* for it. How little we've really loved God for it. How *little* we've really *loved* God for it. Man, we should just love Him forever because we can speak in tongues! For speaking in tongues, if it didn't do anything else, it does a lot of other things but if it didn't do anything else, it's your proof in the senses world that you've got eternal life. And you're heaven bound and all hell can't stop you from going! Isn't that tremendous?

The fifth and final record in the Word of God regarding any one or any group receiving the holy spirit, and completing all that can be known about the receiving of the holy spirit is in Acts 19. People, you have to settle it in your mind that all that can be known about anybody receiving the holy spirit is in those five records.

And I've taught them as detailed as I know them in this session. That's one reason why we're here, so that I can teach what I know about these chapters. This is all that can be known. I didn't say that there could not be more things known from the chapters I've taught. I don't know if I know it all, but I've taught you all I know! There may be more things we can work out in more detail, but the essence I'm positive is absolutely as I give it! Therefore, somebody else comes along and has a little different experience; you've got to make up your mind whether the Word of God is right or whether their experience is right. As for me and for those of us who are in this class I hope that you get to the place that the Word of God settles it! That this is all that can be known, this is all that's in the Word, that's all there is. There is no more! And you can't go by man's opinion; you've got to go by the Word of God.

In order to understand Acts 19, you have to go back to Acts 18.

Acts 18, verse 24.

Acts 18:24a
And a certain Jew named Apollos,…

Apollos is called the golden tongued orator in the Bible because he was so well educated, had a very fluent speech and he was one of the great orators of the time.

Acts 18:24b
…born at Alexandria,…

Alexandria was the seat of the Diaspora Jews, as they are called in the Bible. "Diaspora" means dispersion. Those who had been dispersed because of persecution and had settled in Alexandria in Egypt. They were a Greek speaking Jew in Alexandria, in Egypt.

Acts 18:24, 25
A certain Jew named Apollos, born in Alexandria, an eloquent man, *and* mighty in the scriptures [mighty in the Scriptures], came to Ephesus.
This man was instructed in the way of the Lord; and being fervent in the spirit [spiritually enthused, spiri-

tually fervent, spiritually dynamic], he spake and taught diligently the things of the Lord, knowing only the baptism of John.

But he knew only as far as what? "...knowing only the baptism of John." And that's the key—that's the key! He didn't know about speaking in tongues. Says he didn't know anything about it—all he knew was as far as what? the baptism of John. So he was a Jew and only knowing water baptism, how far could he go? You can't go beyond what you know. You can't teach beyond what you know. You can't lead people beyond what you know. The man was instructed in things of the Lord, but only to the degree that he understood the new birth, and being a Jew that had been zealous for the law. All he knew was to get them born again and water baptize them, the baptism of John. Every baptism to this day in water is nothing but the baptism of John! That's all he knew.

Verse 26.

Acts 18:26
And he began to speak boldly in the synagogue: whom when Aquila and Priscilla had heard, they took him unto *them*, and expounded unto him the way of God more [what?] perfectly.

I love that! That's tremendous! Aquila and Priscilla were lay people. Christians who had left Rome because of the persecution against the Christians in Rome and came to Ephesus. They were "lay" or "common" people and they took this great preacher home with them, this Apollos who was eloquent in the scripture. A mighty man of God but all he knew was the baptism of John. Aquila and Priscilla knew more than he did! They heard him in the synagogue. And when he was in the synagogue Aquila and Priscilla got up and said, "Hey, Apollos, listen to us a little bit." No they didn't. Why didn't they? You talk about culture, that's it! A wonderful culture, isn't it? Because they knew that Apollos had been called of God, and even though he didn't know it all and they knew more even than he did, they didn't disgrace this man of God publicly.

Man there's a lesson to the American people there! Because the American people yack any time they feel like it! They stand up, they yell, they shout, they say what they got to say. It got me into all kind of trouble too because we had some woman who couldn't keep her mouth shut. That's right. She had been a Bible teacher, graduated from Moody Bible College, took courses at Moody and all the rest. And here I was teaching the greatness of God's Word and there she was sitting back there and she said, "Why, I don't believe that! That can't be right, I believe it means this." I finally said loudly, "Shut up!" And I just lost 25 people out of a class that quickly. You know what they said about me? I've been on the phone and spent $20 dollars of your money today trying to smooth over things and give them an understanding of God's Word. They said, "Dr. Wierwille hasn't got any love." I think some of my people know I got more love in my little finger, than that woman has in her whole lousy body when it comes right down to it, but she was way out of order! And she's out of order for two reasons.

First of all, she was indecent as an individual. If she had anything to say, she ought to wait until I'm through then she can yack all night! (I can go home and go to sleep while she's yacking!) But, there is a lot more involved. I've never told hardly anybody this in my life, because really in many respects it's none of your lousy business! No more than theirs. But I told them on the phone, why I am like I am sometimes. When God originally told me He'd teach me the Word if I taught it, God meant what He said, and He said what He meant! When

He told me He'd teach me the Word like they hadn't known it since the first century, He meant it! But then, He put me across the barrel a few places.

The first one was God said, "If you teach it..." If I learned something new or if something comes up, like last night you had a good illustration but you didn't know it, but when we had dug this word *epi* which was as new to me as it was to you, last night's the first time in my life I taught it! When did I learn it? Dee, didn't you teach it to me in the morning? Didn't we go over it then? Or the night before or sometime? It was right there. The next time a group meets, I've got to teach it! If it's one person, or two or three, if it's a Thursday night I teach it, if it's a Sunday night I teach it, if it's a Monday night I teach it! Any time I'm with a group where I am teaching, the moment God has shown me something, or something has unfolded that really fits, I have to teach it. That's where He's got me across the barrel.

Number two is when He talked to me He said, "While I'm teaching the Word, NOBODY talks!" Nobody asks questions, nobody sticks up their head and contradicts the Word! He said, "The moment anybody sticks up their head and says that which is contrary to My Word, you just teach My Word in total command!" That's what happened with that woman, but people don't know, they don't understand, and they don't care. All they're still concerned about is to have the Word of God in a pattern they like to have it. That's right.

But you see, having this ministry drive you, whether you like it or whether you don't, is none of my business or yours. God gave me the ministry. God's responsible for giving it to me, I'm responsible for carrying it out! If I have no friends, that's God's responsibility, if I carry out His Word. But, I'd rather have God as my friend than all the people in the world! Because my life's pretty short, even if I live as old as Methuselah, at the rate I'm going, I'm not believing that big! And if the Lord doesn't return, I tell you my life is short. And when I'm gone this knowledge of God's Word that's within my soul, is gone too! Unless some of you people learn it, like I'm teaching my heart out here again. Then if you learn it, it can live! If you don't learn it, you're going to either have to go to God directly and God's going to have to favor you and give it to you or it's not going to be in the world again! It's as simple as all that!

Look, Aquila and Priscilla I love them and I love Apollos, because Aquila and Priscilla didn't yack! I know everybody always wonders in the Foundational Classes why they can't sit around and ask questions. And every once and a while somebody will stick their head up and ask a question and I'll say, "Honey, just wait." Or sometimes you know me well enough or you don't know me well enough, you've heard me say, "Shut up!" Does that mean that I'm angry? Not one lousy bit! It only means that I'm doing what God said I had to do. Because the most precious thing I have in my soul is the knowledge of God's Word.

Now there's a lot of our people, and I love our people who can really work the Word. And a lot of others of you, that love to work the Word. You're a real blessing! You're a real enthusiasm, you're a real love to my soul and I love you beyond anything words can express. But when it still comes down to really putting that Word together, and in the final details when God called me, He set that within my soul and nobody pulls my leg. I may get fooled for 15 minutes or a half hour, maybe an hour; maybe I let it go a day. But from the time I hear it, it doesn't sit right. And if it doesn't sit right I may say "yes" with my mouth, but in my heart I know that there's something wrong, and I just say "yes" to get the people to go home, or to do something. And when I finally get spiritually "sobered up," as I call it, I finally get to that place we could put it together, it "fits like a hand in a glove" and we can teach it to kids!

One of the greatest indications of this ministry is that we can take these children on the front row and teach them the Word of God. That's great! If you can teach it to a little child, then an adult can understand it if he wants to. But as to be able to teach a little child, you've got to use the language they understand. You've got to use words that they understand. You've got to have the type of presentation that fits into the thinking of those boys and those girls, else you couldn't reach them! And I think it's the greatness of the power of God that the ministry rests in our people who are able to take the children to children's fellowship and teach them. I marvel every Sunday night! To let our wonderful teachers teach them the greatness of God's Word. Man, that they can do it is the greatest testimony to the ministry. And you know, we do it here without a commentary. Nobody brings a Sunday school quarterly! Nobody is reading it out of a church magazine to them! They just take God's Word and teach it to them like I have taught it to you! It's a tremendous thing.

Well, that Apollos, all he knew was water baptism. And there sits Aquila and Priscilla[7] and they hear him preach. They see souls get saved and they praise the Lord for it, but they know he needs a little more light. So they say to Apollos, why don't you come home for chicken with us on Sunday? So they take him home, give him mashed potatoes and gravy and chicken and peas, or corn that goes together. Then I suppose Aquila finally said, "Say Apollos, Priscilla and I would just like to share

---

7. Acts 18:2—And found a certain Jew named Aquila, born in Pontus, lately come from Italy, with his wife Priscilla;...

something with you which we learned in Rome, about the receiving of the holy spirit and speaking in tongues." And they must have talked all afternoon and all evening and all the next day, and brought him right up to date. And, then what did they do? They said, now since we have taught you, you better go back in the church at Ephesus and tell them who told you some more truth, and you better straighten those people out that you got born again—no! I love that too!

Don't you see how when you really walk in the spirit of God, it doesn't disgrace people, it doesn't belittle them, it doesn't make fools out of them. Instead of sending Apollos back to straighten those people up and give them more light, the Lord said, "Hey Apollos, I think you better go over to Achaia, over here now." Never lets him go back into Ephesus at all. That's right, because it says so in the next verse, 27.

> **Acts 18:27**
> And when he was disposed [ready, desirous, guided] to pass into Achaia, the brethren wrote, exhorting the disciples [Aquila and Priscilla and the rest of them exhorted the disciples at Achaia] to receive him [Apollos]: who, when he was come [to Achaia], helped them much which had believed through [what?] grace:

Isn't that wonderful?

> **Acts 18:28**
> For he mightily convinced the Jews, *and that* publickly, shewing by the scriptures that Jesus was [the] Christ.

> **Acts 19:1**
> And it came to pass, that, while Apollos was at Corinth [the capital city in Achaia], Paul having passed through the upper coasts came to Ephesus: and finding certain [what?] disciples,

FREED FROM THE LAW 187

Who had discipled them to the Lord? Apollos. Right! In his ministry there he had won these to the Lord. They were born again! And what do you think he had done to them after they got born again? Water baptized them. Why? Because that's all that he what? that he knew. That's all Apollos knew, until Aquila and Priscilla were guided by the Lord to take him home for dinner and teach him the Word of God more perfectly. Wonderful.

Paul comes to Ephesus and he finds those disciples who are born again.

> **Acts 19:2a**
> He said unto them [he said to them], Have ye received [*lambanō'd*, manifested]…[holy spirit, *pneuma hagion*; no article, the gift] since [when] you believed?…

The word "since" is the same word as the word "when" and there it should be "when." "…*Have you lambanō'd the gift when you believed?*…"[8] Did you manifest anything when you believed?

> **Acts 19:2b**
> …And they said unto him, We have not so much as heard whether there be any Holy Ghost [*pneuma hagion*].

Any manifestation of the gift is what it's talking about. They had heard about "The Holy Ghost," who is God because they were saved, right? But what had they not heard about? The gift in manifestation; the gift in manifestation. They hadn't heard anything about the gift and how it operates, why? Apollos didn't know it. It's what the Word says! And you can't teach beyond what you know, right? Apollos didn't know it so he didn't teach it. He couldn't! So when Paul comes down he said, Did you

---

8. A literal translation according to usage of Acts 19:2a.

lambanō anything? They said, We've not so much as heard.

> **Acts 19:3**
> And he said unto them, Unto what then were you baptized? And they said, Unto John's baptism.

Who baptized them? Apollos had baptized them. That's all he knew!

> **Acts 19:4, 5**
> Then said Paul, John verily baptized with the baptism of repentance, saying unto the people, that they should believe on him which should come after him, that is, on Christ Jesus.
> When they heard *this*, they were baptized in the name of the Lord Jesus.

When they heard this they were baptized in the name of the Lord Jesus! By whom were they baptized? Apollos! By Apollos! Paul is reporting; Paul is reporting what Apollos did. He is simply saying what Apollos did. He's talking about John's baptism in verse 3. Then he describes John's baptism and how they believed. And says, "When they heard this [that Apollos preached regarding John's baptism and that Jesus should come, believe on him] they were baptized in the name of the Lord Jesus." That's what Apollos had done. Now people the commentaries all say exactly what some of you said a little while ago, that Paul baptized them in water. He didn't either! That's when you go back to Chapter 18, verse 24, to start reading to get the whole story. To get it all put together. Paul did not baptize them in water! Apollos baptized them in water, and water baptism is John the Baptist's baptism.

> **Acts 19:6a**
> And when Paul....

Now it's going to tell you what Paul did. Because he asked them back in verse 2, "Have you received [*lam-*

banō'd]? They said we have not so much as heard." Then after he goes through telling them what John did, then Paul does something in verse 6:

> **Acts 19:6b**
> ...Paul...laid *his* hands upon them,...

For what purpose? for revelation, word of knowledge, word of wisdom, discerning of spirits. What he can do to help them to *lambanō*.

> **Acts 19:6c**
> ...laid *his* hands upon them, the Holy Ghost [the *pneuma*, the *hagion*] came on them; and they spake with tongues,...

It came on them to the end that it settled—that's the word *epi* again there, isn't it?—upon them, where it made the contact to the point that they were drawing it out and they spake with tongues, and then for the first time it mentions—and what?

> **Acts 19:6d**
> ...and prophesied.

This is the fifth and final record. This is the record of people who have been born again under the ministry of a man who knew nothing but water baptism. And so he water baptized them, that's all he could do. But, there was something more they ought to have in manifestation. And when Paul comes, he lays hands on them, finds out what it is, takes it out or helps them and it says "they spake with tongues." Speaking in tongues again is the external manifestation in the senses realm that they have Jesus Christ within! Five records in the Book of Acts, that's all there are, no more!

In Acts, chapter 2, Jews only, twelve apostles who received on the original outpouring, and it specifically says, when they were born again when they received, they did one thing what? Spoke in tongues.

In Acts, chapter 8, it does not say they spoke in tongues, but it says Simon what? saw. He had to see a manifestation.

In Acts, chapter 9, when Paul received it doesn't say he spoke in tongues. Yet in 1 Corinthians 14:18, the Word of God says, Paul spoke in tongues more than anyone else in the church in Corinth.

In Acts, chapter 10, the household of Cornelius. The fourth record. When they were born again what did they do? Spoke in tongues.

Acts 19, when they *lambanō'd* and the power of Christ within them, what did they do? Spoke in tongues.

All five records either specifically said they spoke in tongues or it is implied so dynamically that you've got to be stupider than stupid to miss it! And if you've got a baseball game, and at the end of the ninth inning the score is five to nothing in your favor, I'll bet you won the ball game! It seems to me when the Word of God is five to nothing that the Word of God ought to win the ballgame! Doesn't it to you? Doesn't it seem to you that every Christian ought to be speaking in tongues? Boldly! And if they're not, they are not living up to the Word of God. They're only "short changing" themselves! They're defeating themselves. They're hurting themselves and they're hurting the cause of Christ here upon earth.

This thing here in Ephesus was so tremendous, that when Paul had finished this ministering, there were only about twelve men in verse 7.[9] That wasn't a very big congregation was it? And yet after this occurred, verse 8.

Acts 19:8, 9
...he [Paul] went into the synagogue, and spake boldly for the space of three months, disputing and persuading the things concerning the kingdom of God.

---

9. Acts 19:7—And all the men were about twelve.

> But when divers [many] were hardened, and believed not, but spake evil of that way before the multitude, he [Paul] departed from them, and separated the disciples [the believers],...

Did he break up the church? Right down the line! Right down the line! And if you did it today in your community, they'd call you "nice" names I'll tell you. Paul did it. He taught them the Word of God. And when many of them were hardened in their hearts (and that means they refused to believe the Word of God) and they spoke evil of the way, he said alright fellows if that's the way you want to act, you people inside of this fellowship who really want to believe God's Word, go with me! The rest of you can stay, you can pay the mortgage on the brick and stone and whatever else there is. You can have the building, we don't want the building.

Today, we've got church splits too! But the fight is always over who gets the building. We go to court, you know. We've got a half a dozen of them rolling now, that I just read in a magazine a week or two ago, where they have split up a church because of a certain merger. I think it's EUB and somebody else.[10] They don't want to merge, and therefore they've got the fights in the high courts. Who's going to get the property? You see, when you join a Methodist church you pay and pray the rest of the days of your life! But you have no control! Because when you join, there's already a little signed paper that no matter if you build the church with your Grandpa's money, that church does not belong to you or to the people; it belongs to the denomination! The United Church of Christ is like this too you know, and the Evangelical Reform. This way

---

10. The Evangelical United Brethren subsequently merged with The Methodist Church in 1968, to form the new larger United Methodist Church.
(https://en.wikipedia.org/wiki/Evangelical_United_Brethren_Church)

the people in a community can build the building but they in New York and Washington control it. When you walk out they say, "Okay, go ahead and walk, it belongs to us!" And that sort of keeps you in, you know. You got your money there, now you don't like to leave.

The Apostle Paul said keep the blooming money! Keep your mortgages, keep your stone and mortar and your baloney. We're going out to the school of a fellow by the name of Tyrannus. He's already paying the electric bill and taking care of the heat, we'll just use his property! That's right. So they went the school of one Tyrannus.[11]

And it says in verse 10:

> **Acts 19:10**
> And this continued for the space of two years [and three months]; so that all they which dwelt in Asia heard the word of the Lord Jesus, both Jews and Greeks.

Wow, I tell you that's something! Two years and three months, all Asia heard the Word of God! It started out with Apollos getting a few of them saved, and Paul coming in there getting the job culminated, to where they were speaking in tongues, prophesying, operating the manifestations! And there were only about twelve men! And after it started two years, and three months later, all Asia Minor had heard the Word of God!

Somebody got to be moving for the Lord! Somebody got on the move! Somebody raised a heck of a stink in every community and every town with the greatness of God's Word! It got to be a "sweet savor" because of the knowledge that dwelt in those men. But just imagine what happened in Asia Minor the next two years and three months! How many synagogues were broken up? How many times they had to move into new homes, into the

---

11. Acts 19:9b—...disputing daily in the school of one Tyrannus.

areas to keep the Word. But, all Asia Minor heard the Word of God in two years, and three months. A feat which has not been duplicated since that day! Even with our multi-millions for missions, our great theological seminaries, all of our great educational institutions, our millions of dollars in publications, not once has all Asia Minor heard the Word of God in one generation since! And they did it in two years and three months!

Either God has changed or people. It's because God has not changed but because people have. The greatness of the Word doesn't live within us, it doesn't thrill us! It doesn't make us bold enough to be a separated people. It doesn't make us bold enough to come out from among them as the Word of God says. We still want to horse around with everybody else and ride the fence. I said to somebody, we're pretty lucky it isn't charged with electricity because you would get one leg on one side, and one on the other. Maybe if we got charged with electricity we'd have to rise up (like someone sitting on a tack)! But you see, I'm not responsible for that. Neither was the apostle Paul. We are responsible for rightly dividing the Word and making it living and real! Then the people, who this Word lives in, are responsible for teaching it to someone else and carrying it on. If they don't do it, the job won't get done! The reason the job isn't done today, is not because the Word is not in our midst, but because we're still straddling the fence! We haven't come to the place that we're absolutely convinced that someday we've got to appear before God and stand in judgment before Him, for how have we handled the Word of God and what have we done with it! We will be rewarded for what we do with the greatness of God's Word!

We still feel that it's important how we are rewarded in the "here and now" by the way the neighbors like us, or the local church people, or the head bishop or the head preacher. We're not! Only before God! And ladies and gentlemen, I didn't write the Book. But I know that Paul, they could only stand him in the synagogue for three months. By that time he had caused so much trouble because he was preaching the Word of God, that they hated him. They despised him. They talked evil of that way. They said, "That's a bunch of baloney! This speaking in tongues business is of the Devil. And you better get circumcised," and all this other stuff. And Paul said, "Alright, if that's the way you feel about the wonderfulness of God's Word that I'm teaching you, nuts to you! I'll go to the school of Tyrannus!" And he took the boys out and headed toward old Tyrannus's little old school house. Why? Because there he was free to teach the Word of God. There he was free for people to come.

When I read this story I always think of this place. Only God could put this place here. Only God! That's right! Through the believing of some people. That's all. Because, do you know something? Here's one place where we can still today teach the Word as God gives us understanding. Where else can you do it? You can't take this Word of God into any church in the United States accurately, and be allowed to teach it the way I teach it here, with the same enthusiasm and yelling at people, you just can't do this in any church over a period of longer than three months today. By that time they'll have your hide! They'll skin you alive, boil you in oil, give you your hat and a boot on the way out! Why? Because you can't put the greatness of God's Word in the old fossilized, wine skins of organization and institutionalism and denominationalism!

It is the Word of God which is alive and vital! It is enthusiasm, it's dynamite, and this thing just effervesces. You get to be the kind of person that even your "myrtles" can't hold your girdles in! Spiritually speaking. Because you're just bubbling out all over! Because of the greatness of the Word in your heart. Isn't that true? When that Word is in your heart you just expand! You just can't sit in those little straight jackets. You may sit there some of you, but even while you're sitting there you're miserable and you know it. Maybe you don't have enough sense to get out of them, but you still know it. Why? Because that Word of God is life! It is always effervescing, it is always wonderful!

And so Paul taught two years and three months and all Asia heard the Word of God. And it produced the biggest revival the world has ever seen, in that area, at that time! It's a tremendous revival! And you know it says in verse 11:

> **Acts 19:11, 12**
> And God wrought special miracles by the hands of Paul:
> So that from his body were brought unto the sick handkerchiefs or aprons, and the diseases departed from them, and the evil spirits went out of them.

This again is phenomenon. That doesn't mean that you have little old handkerchief healing services now. This was specific to Paul, special to Paul. You don't go around and take a nice little sheet and pinking shears and cut out nice little squares. Then lay your hands on them and call them anointed handkerchiefs. Did any of you ever get those in the mail? Yeah, good. I got them too. I have been at meetings where they have taken these (what they call anointed handkerchiefs, people wrote in for them) and they'd have a whole stack of them laying here. And all of us preachers would lay our hands on them to bless them good! And then they'd take them and put them in an envelope. Lick'em shut and throw them in the mail. And then they'd send them out to the people that had asked for them. And I followed up on some of this stuff. And the people who got them many times were completely healed!

That bothered me because I knew the rigamarole that

went on behind the scenes. I knew all the baloney. And I got to thinking, well how come those people got healed? They didn't get healed because we laid our hands on them and anointed them. You know why they got healed? Because they *believed* that when they got that handkerchief and put it on (put it on their ear balls) that they'd hear again! And they did hear! One woman got one and laid it on an open cancer and was completely healed of cancer! It wasn't the handkerchief, it was her what? believing! That's it! Now why can't we get our believing beyond the handkerchief stage into the greatness of God's Word? The Word will never let us down! But the principles of believing are all the same. If you believe that eating that piece of chalk would heal you of ulcers, if you got ulcers, come and eat it! You'll get rid of it (the chalk as well as the ulcers). That's right! It's our believing in what we believe God is able to do.

Well, verse 13. This really shook that community.

Acts 19:13a
Then certain of the vagabond Jews, exorcists [who were exercising devil spirits], took upon them to call over them which had evil spirits...

Now that is quite a story. Here are people who got evil spirits going to call over those who've got evil spirits!

Acts 19:13b, 14
...the name of the Lord Jesus, saying, We adjure you by Jesus whom Paul preacheth.
And there were seven sons of *one* Sceva, a Jew, *and* chief of the priests, which did so.

He was the chief priest! Now his sons were sure out of alignment and harmony, weren't they? He was the chief priest! No wonder they had a little trouble in that old synagogue, huh? Sure. But here were the sons of the chief priest and they were the ones who were operating devil spirits, and they were calling over those who had evil spirits: we command you little old evil spirits to come out of them in the name of Jesus that the Paul fellow preacheth!

Verse 15.

> **Acts 19:15**
> And the evil spirit answered and said, Jesus I know, and Paul I know; but who are ye?

Who in the world are you? I bet that shook their old cookies, huh? Look, the old devil spirits here, they are in those people. And you know they used their lips and their mouth.

> **Acts 19:16**
> And the man in whom the evil spirit was leaped on them, and overcame them, and prevailed against them, so that they fled out of that house [without their pants] naked and wounded.

Wouldn't that have made a good TV story? I can just see that guy running outside without his pants on! Hot footing it! Sure. And then while he's running out, the guy's throwing an ink bottle or something at him and hitting him in the back. Maybe he's throwing a knife at him, just hitting him there that the blood squirts out so he's wounded, you know? That one fellow licked all seven of those guys. That's right. That's something!

> **Acts 19:17**
> And this was known to all the Jews and Greeks also dwelling at Ephesus; and fear fell on them all, and the name of the Lord Jesus was [what?] magnified.

Why? Because the Apostle Paul dared to stand on the Word of God! And he broke that synagogue right down the middle, went to the school of Tyrannus. They really started moving, believing God's Word. Things began to happen. Even to the end where these fellows said, we command you to come out in the name of Jesus that the Paul fellow preaches. They got licked good and proper! And when they saw that power of God that was resident, even in the name of Jesus living in men, they got a little holy respect for the men of God and the Word of God! You bet your life, because the next verse says:

> **Acts 19:18**
> And many that believed [that got saved, born again] came, and confessed, and shewed their deeds.

Do you know what they confessed? Not their sins, they simply came and said, here's our *Life*, *Look* and *Times*, *Saturday Evening Post*, here's our *Playboy*, here's our astrology magazines. Here's all of this baloney we have been reading! The newspapers, the *New York Times*, the *Dayton Herald*, and the "*Saint Mary's Evening Liar*," all of these things we have been reading. That's right! "They came, and confessed, and shewed their deeds." That's right!

Because class, let me ask you, what are you reading? If you spend all your time reading that other baloney, what are you going to believe? How much time are you giving to the Word of God? I tell you this gets to be a real bother! And I'm not preaching at you, I'm just telling you God's Word. I think many times we're all in the same boat. I got the big fight in my house all the time. Not all the time, but usually. About three times a year I get real mad. Everybody wants to sell us magazines. Everyday somebody comes or sends us a notice trying to get us to buy another magazine. Then the high school kids come around to sell me one so they can go on a trip. And they embarrass me. You know why they embarrass me? I didn't want to take their magazine. I said I would give them five dollars, and they wouldn't take my five bucks unless I'd take the magazine. I'd give them five dollars (get them to go on their trip) but, I didn't want the magazines! Why? Got too doggone many now! And it bothers me.

When you get your old house all loaded with magazines, how much time do you get to read God's Word? And it isn't the magazines that are going to set the power of God in our lives! Every time you read a magazine, you get more negative! Usually. It's like watching TV. I watched one show before supper and didn't even enjoy supper. Then I'd sit there at the supper table and say to myself, "Wierwille, how stupid can you be?" And it's surprising how stupid I can be! That's right. The show was so bad even I felt bad. That's right! It was miserable! And I felt miserable. Dotsie made a tremendous supper and I couldn't even enjoy it because I felt miserable. That was number two; number one was we ate too much. And that wasn't her fault; it was simply because the crazy TV show was on. The kids wanted to see it, and I wanted to see it because I got involved with the plot and wanted to figure it out.

Verse 19.

> **Acts 19:19a**
> Many of them also which used curious arts…

Curious arts—do you know what that is? Black arts, Ouija boards, a few other minor little details.

> **Acts 19:19b**
> …[they] brought their books together [they brought even the books that tell how to do this black art stuff], and burned them before all *men*: and they counted the price of them, and found *it* [to be] fifty thousand *pieces* of silver.

They had spent a lot on their magazines, hadn't they? I think many times this is what bothers me the most about the magazines. How they tell us we can buy them 50% off, you know. And still it's four or five bucks. And then you buy ten or twenty of them, and you've got a hundred dollars involved. And low and behold, what couldn't we publish in the Ministry with a hundred dollars? We could publish another book on the accuracy of God's Word on a subject. But, here we are buying their other baloney. We just get so limited!

Well, when they got through with it, fifty thousand pieces of silver. That was a real burning ceremony, people! They really cleaned out their attics and their houses. They got rid of that baloney. And that's when verse 20 says, that's when the Word of God began to grow.

Acts 19:20
So mightily grew [what?] the word of God and prevailed.

Not *Reader's Digest*, *Life*, *Look* or *Times* or *Saturday Evening Post*, or *Atlantic Monthly*. No. No. But the thing that prevailed then, was the Word of God! Why? Because now they were reading the Word of God, they were talking the Word of God, they were thinking the Word of God, they were working the Word of God. Before that they were reading *Life*, *Look* and *Times*, *Saturday Evening Post* and the rest of it. No Word. Well, really something, isn't it?

Acts 19:21-25a
After these things were ended, Paul purposed in the spirit, when he had passed through Macedonia and Achaia, to go to Jerusalem, saying, After I have been there, I must also see Rome.
So he sent into Macedonia two of them that ministered unto him, Timotheus [Timothy] and Erastus; but he himself stayed in Asia minor for a season.
And the same time [that he stayed there in Asia minor] there arose no small stir about that way. [Why?]

FREED FROM THE LAW 201

> For [because] a certain *man* named Demetrius, a silversmith, which made silver shrines for Diana, brought no small gain unto the craftsmen;
> Whom he called together with the workman of like occupation,...

And now you've got a union! A union meeting. And he says to them:

> **Acts 19:25b, 26**
> ...Sirs, ye know that by this craft we have our wealth [our income].
> Moreover ye see and hear, that not [only] at Ephesus, but almost throughout all Asia, this Paul hath persuaded and turned away much people, saying [that those things that we make with our hands] that they be no [not] gods, which are made with hands:

And you know that Paul fellow is absolutely wrong! But he's persuading the people, and he's beginning to hurt our income! That's why he's got them all together in the union meeting.

Verse 27.

> **Acts 19:27a**
> So that not only this our craft is in danger to be set at naught; but also that the temple of the great goddess...

You've got to get religion in here. You see, it isn't quite enough in a union meeting to get the finances up, you've got to hit some emotional, some moral issue, some spiritual issue, so you can really whip them into line! He said, you know we get our wealth from this, but that's not just it.

> **Acts 19:27b**
> ...[don't you know] that the temple of the great god-

dess Diana [in Ephesus] should be [is going to be] despised, and her magnificence should be [is going to be] destroyed, whom all [all] Asia and the world worshippeth.

Quite a speaker, isn't he?

Verse 28.

Acts 19:28
And when they heard *these sayings*, they were full of wrath, and cried out, saying, Great *is* Diana of the Ephesians.

Great is Diana of the Ephesians, Great is Diana of the Ephesians. That whole town just rang with those words!

Acts 19:29-31
And the whole city was filled with confusion [a real mob!]: and having caught Gaius and Aristarchus, men of Macedonia, Paul's companions in travel, they rushed with one accord into the theatre.
And when Paul would have entered in unto the people, the disciples suffered him not.
And certain of the chief of Asia, which were his [Paul's] friends [because Paul had converted them], sent unto him, desiring *him* that he would not adventure himself into the theatre.

In other words, Paul it is the will of the Lord, don't you get involved! Don't you enter into that area!

Verse 32, the union meeting.

Acts 19:32a
Some therefore cried one thing, and some another: for the assembly [the church, the *ekklēsia*] was confused;…

Remember how I teach you this in the Foundational Class that the word "church" means "called out"; *ekklēsia*.

If you're called out for a union meeting, it's called a church. If you're called out to a bowling alley for a bowling party, it's called a church. The word church, (*ekklēsia* in Greek) is an assembly! And it says:

> **Acts 19:32b**
> …and the more part knew not wherefore they were come together.

That's usually the truth, that's right!

> **Acts 19:33, 34**
> And they drew Alexander out of the multitude, the Jews putting him forward. And Alexander beckoned with the hand, and would have made his defense unto the people.
> But when they knew that he was a Jew, all with one voice about the space of two hours cried out, Great *is* Diana of the Ephesians.

Now, this is the fifth and final record in the Book of Acts. In Acts 20:20 it says they were all zealous for the law. You see, I'm not going into verse 21, but you almost have the first great split that came in the church. And it was only avoided because they were operating manifestations of the spirit. And at that time, if you could really prove that they were speaking in tongues like Peter had proven to them, because of the six witnesses, the church praised the Lord! The people changed when they saw! But, there were also some people who never did get around to changing, verse 19.

> **Acts 21:19, 20**
> And when he [Paul] had saluted them, he declared particularly what things God had wrought among the Gentiles by his ministry.
> And when they heard *it*, they glorified the Lord, and said unto him, Thou seest, brother, how many thou-

sands of Jews there are which believe; [but] they are [still] all zealous [for]…the law [is the text]: [12]

Were they born again? Definitely! But, when they were born again they were still zealous for what? the law. And that would mean whose baptism? John's. It would mean whose circumcision? the Jewish circumcision. It would mean eating unleavened bread at the right time. It would mean keeping all the festivals of the Jewish church year. And that's exactly what killed the early church!

By the time the Apostle Paul died, the greatness of some of this revelation that I read to you from Acts 19, and the ministry of that great man where all Asia heard —by the time Paul died all Asia basically had gone back to making brick without stone! They've gone back to the legalism of Judaism. And for the most part to 1967 the church to this day has not gone beyond the legalism of Judaism. This is not God's fault! This is people's fault. It is God's will to have what the Word of God says we ought to have, and to be what the Word of God says we ought to be. It says that circumcision availeth nothing. Water baptism availeth nothing. Eating chicken on Sunday availeth nothing. But it says that Christ in you, the power of the Holy Spirit, speaking in tongues availeth much!

But, somehow or other Satan is always around to belittle the greatness of the things of God. And he wants to take people and get them into the enslavement of the old legalism, in which they were engrossed before they got saved. Because Satan knows that as long as you stay engrossed within that enslavement of legalism, you will never rise up to be a great man or women of God, standing on the grace wherewith Christ Jesus saved us and his

---

12. "…they are all zealous of the law" is the King James Version.

love wherewith he filled us! This is why in Galatians 5 —he said in verse 31, to those legalists of Chapter 4:

Galatians 4:31
So then, brethren, we are not children of the bondwomen, but of the [what?] free.

Galatians 5:1
Stand fast therefore in the liberty wherewith Christ hath made us free, and be not entangled again in the yoke of [what?] bondage.

The yoke of bondage is the law. If the law could save us class, then Christ should never have come. If the legalism that we go through in our water baptisms and our circumcisions and all the rest of these things which so many of us have from time to time be called upon to do, if that saves us then Christ lived and died in vain! But a man can be born again of God's spirit and still stayed tied up in all that legalism! Why? Because he wants to! It has nothing to do with the new birth; it has everything to do with his flesh. Because to be born again of God's spirit, you must confess with your mouth the Lord Jesus, believe God raised him from the dead. Right?

A man can speak in tongues and still be enslaved with all the legalism. Go through all the water baptism, all the circumcision and all the other legalist things of eating fish on Friday, keeping the holy day on Saturday—you know, there's a million things. But people, God didn't raise me up in this ministry to go through that legalism! When he raised me up, he raised me up to set before God's people the greatness of the revelation that was given to the Apostle Paul! Where we are born again of God's spirit! We are enslaved to nobody except we are sons of God and servants of the Lord Jesus Christ on a horizontal plane.

And once again he says to you, as he does to the church throughout all Asia when they've heard the Word, he says in verse 1, "Stand fast therefore in the liberty wherewith Christ Jesus hath set you free, and be not entangled again in the yoke of bondage." These people in Acts were zealous for the law. They were born again but they were still zealous for the law! And this is why they obstructed the ministry of the Apostle Paul. This is why Paul prayed for them, three times that the Lord would get those crazy thorns out of his flesh. The thorns are never the unbelievers, the unconverted. The thorn in a man of God's flesh is never the man down here at the corner saloon, who doesn't know there is a God in heaven, much less care, and he's having himself a few "extra spirits".[13] He's never the thorn in the flesh.

You know who's the thorn in the flesh? The person who's born again of God's spirit and he's a religious person and thinks he knows the answers when he doesn't know them! He is the thorn, or she is the thorn in the flesh! They are! Like they were to the Apostle Paul! And that's why class, I thank my God that once again in this day and hour, before the Lord's Return, God has raised us up and allowed us to live in this day and hour and time when we can work that Word. To the end that we can once again understand it, and believe it, and know that we can stand fast in liberty wherewith Christ Jesus has set us free. And that we need not be entangled again with the yoke of bondage!

---

13. Alcoholic beverages are sometimes referred to as "spirits".

Spiritual Matters

We turn tonight to the only place in the Bible, really, where there are three chapters put together that teach us basically all that there is to know about the operations of the manifestations of the spirit and the gifts of the spirit.

We turn to 1 Corinthians, chapter 1. I just read my book on these chapters in Corinthians that I'm going to be teaching now, and I truly marvel at the accuracy of the record in the book on *Receiving the Holy Spirit Today*, this fifth edition. It is just tremendous. I almost hate to teach it without the book before me, because we have worked it down so minutely and so wonderfully. There are so many things that are written in the book which I have not completely engrafted within my mind that I do not want to forget whenever I teach. So much of my teaching tonight as I go through, I'm going to be checking back into the book to see that I give you the greatest benefit of the Word of God that is possible for me to share with you.

The first thing you have to recognize when you come to working this Book of Corinthians is that verse 2 of chapter 1 says, it's addressed:

1 Corinthians 1:2a
Unto the church of God…

If it is addressed *to* the church of God, it's specifically to us, the born again believers. It's not just *for* our learning, it's *to* us; it has our name on it. Now I know that it says "Unto the church of God which is at Corinth." But this same church of God at Corinth, is the same church that lives here today! Because the church is made up of born again believers, right? And therefore, even though it would be addressed to the church at New Knoxville, or the church in St. Mary's, or the church in Columbus, it still would be addressed to the church! The born again believers. But it says,

> **1 Corinthians 1:2a**
> Unto the church of God which is at Corinth, to them that are sanctified...

Sanctified means set apart. They're set apart by the new birth. When you're born again of God's spirit you're sanctified, in God, through Christ Jesus.

> **1 Corinthians 1:2b**
> ...called *to be* saints,...

Saints—saints are not those people that one denomination makes after their bones have rotted and everything else. Saints are people that are born again of God's spirit, who have Christ in them.

> **1 Corinthians 1:2c**
> ...with all that in every place call upon the name of Jesus Christ our Lord, both theirs and ours:

So you can see very plainly that the Book of Corinthians is addressed to the church.

Now in 1 Corinthians, chapter 12. These chapters then are written to the church, the saints. And I told you that the Book of Corinthians was written because of the practical error that had crept into the church, due to the failure of adhering to the greatness of the revelation of the Book of Romans. And therefore, you will see that these chapters are all practical. The practical error that has crept in. These chapters correct those practical errors that have crept in among God's people, the church, the believers. Chapter 12, verse 1.

Spiritual Matters

1 Corinthians 12:1
Now concerning spiritual *gifts*, brethren, I would not have you ignorant.

The first thing I want you to note is the word "gifts" —it is in italics. Scratch it out! They added it, that's why it's in italics.[1] And this is one of the great reasons why people have failed to understand these chapters in Corinthians. Because they have looked upon these chapters or these verses, as gifts. And so they have spoken about the gift of speaking in tongues, you've all heard this. Or the gift of interpretation of tongues. The gift of prophecy. The gift of the word of knowledge. They talk about the nine gifts of the spirit. And this is due to the fact that this one verse, first verse, starts out with the word "gifts." So they believe the whole thing deals with gifts. It doesn't! It deals with spiritual, concerning spiritual things. The word "spiritual" is the word *pneumatikos* from the root word *pneuma* meaning spiritual. This word *pneumatikos* however, means "things of the spirit." Spiritual things. Now class, are gifts from God spiritual things? Yes! But are all spiritual things gifts? No. That's the great key! All spiritual things are not gifts. But all gifts of God are spiritual things.

1 Corinthians 12:1
Now concerning spiritual gifts [things of the spirit or spiritual things], brethren, I would not have you [to be] ignorant.

There are only a few things in the Bible that He mentions specifically He would not have us ignorant of. This is one of them. Concerning spiritual things, spiritual matters, things which relate to the spirit—brethren, born again

---

1. Italic text used in the King James Version of the Bible indicates words that have been added by the translators to the Scriptural text, for which there are no words found in the original language.

believers—I would not have you stupid on, I don't want you ignorant. Well, if He does not want us ignorant, He wants us to know the score, right? He wants us to smarten up! He wants us to know the intricacies, the wonderfulness of it. A literal translation of verse 1 according to usage would be: *"Now concerning matters belonging, determined, or influenced, or proceeding from the spirit, brethren, I would not have you ignorant."* [2] Or if you want a more simple translation of verse 1 it would be: *"Now concerning spiritual matters brethren, I would not have you ignorant."* [3] That's the simplest translation literally I know of that verse.

Verse 2.

1 Corinthians 12:2
Ye know that ye were [what?] Gentiles, carried away unto these dumb idols, even as ye were led.

A dumb idol is one that is made of wood or stone or some metal. It cannot speak, that's why it's called "dumb." The reason the Gentiles were worshipping dumb idols, the Word says, is because this is what they were led to worship—"even as ye were led." No one ever goes further in his spiritual quest than he is led. He cannot receive beyond what he believes and he cannot believe beyond what he is taught. These people were serving dumb idols because somebody had led them to do this.

Verse 3.

1 Corinthians 12:3a
Wherefore I give you to understand, that no man speaking by the Spirit of God calleth Jesus accursed:...

---

2. A literal translation according to usage of 1 Corinthians 12:1.
3. Another literal translation according to usage of 1 Corinthians 12:1.

I believe the word "the" is not in the text so you can scratch it out:

1 Corinthians 12:3b
...no man speaking by the Spirit of God calleth Jesus accursed: and *that* no man can say that Jesus is... Lord, but by the Holy Ghost.

There is a really dynamically important verse of scripture. As I said first of all, the King James adds the article "the." If you leave the article out in both places, it almost explains itself: "*I give you to understand, that no man speaking by [pneuma theou] God's spirit, calleth Jesus accursed: and that no man can say that Jesus is Lord, but by pneuma hagion, the gift.*" [4]

Now people, here we have a scripture that hardly anybody wants to believe, until you really get deep in the Word and understand the greatness of the holy spirit field. Just with a casual reading, you will not see what I'm going to unfold. But with a minute, detailed reading and understanding of God's Word, you will see the infinite greatness of it! First of all, from all the records that we've gone through in the Book of Acts, whenever anybody manifested that Jesus was Lord in their life, what was the one thing that they did? They spoke in tongues. This is why the last phrase of verse 3, "no man can say that Jesus is Lord, but by *pneuma hagion*, by the gift," is to say that no man can say that Jesus is really the Lord in his life, except he speak in tongues. Now that is remarkable!

Picking it up in the first part of the verse.

1 Corinthians 12:3a
...I give you to understand, that no man speaking by the Spirit of God calleth Jesus accursed:...

---

4. A literal translation according to usage of 1 Corinthians 12:3.

Why? Well, these people (Gentiles) had been led away to dumb idols as they were being taught, and they would worship these dumb idols. And when the idols wouldn't give them rain, nor food or clothing, nor what they wanted, then they'd come back and they'd curse them! Raise hell with them. Now here were these unconverted people and here were the converted ones. And these converted ones were speaking in tongues. The speaking in tongues, they didn't understand, so what were these people saying about the converted ones? They were saying, "Awe, they're doing just what they did when we were Gentiles, they're cursing their Lord." They're cursing him. They didn't understand, so they said they were cursing him.

And the Word of God says, "I give you to understand that no man speaking by the spirit of God can call Jesus accursed." That's wonderful. You know, I am not now speaking by the spirit of God. I am now speaking by what? the spirit of man. The spirit of Christ Jesus, God in me plus my soul life, I'm speaking to you. But when you speak by the spirit of God, to speak by the spirit of God must be to speak how? in tongues. Sure. Now I was speaking by the spirit of God[5] and "no man speaking by the Spirit of God calleth Jesus accursed:"[6] Now this is tremendous. I do not believe this verse is as urgently important today as it was ten years ago in our ministry regarding what I am going to say now. Because time and time again, ten years ago when I was circulating on an itinerary of teaching, I'd always run into it. They'd say, "Well, when you speak in tongues you can curse God." Because they many times said, "Well, we went to a meeting someplace, and somebody understood what somebody else spoke in tongues, and they said they were cursing God."

---

5. Dr. Wierwille spoke in tongues prior to this statement which was captured on the audio version of this teaching.
6. 1 Corinthians 12:3.

This is what I heard ten years ago. I don't think I've heard this for maybe two years, come to think of it now. I just haven't sat down and thought about it, how long it's been since I've heard it. But, I used to hear it so many times. I believe perhaps because of the increased emphasis in the holy spirit field, and the understanding of it, that there are a lot of Presbyterians, Baptists, Methodists, Lutherans, a lot of other people from different denominations speaking in tongues. They've sort of gotten over the idea of trying to poke each other with that speaking in tongues is of the Devil business. I think it's pretty well perhaps drowned out. I hope so. But this is what they used to say, that you could speak in tongues and curse God. Well that is an impossibility! Because, what you speak in tongues, He has to feed to you, right? And if God gives it to you, God could not curse Himself!

But, speaking by the spirit of God is to speak in tongues!

Verse 3.

1 Corinthians 12:3
Wherefore I give you to understand, that no man speaking by the Spirit of God calleth Jesus accursed: and…no man can say that Jesus is the Lord,…

—is THE Lord! A man could go down the street and say "Jesus is Lord." Could a man on the street say "peanuts" or "apple butter"? Sure! Any unbeliever could say "Jesus is Lord." Therefore, this verse doesn't mean for someone just to say it with their mouth; it has to be a lot deeper than that, and it is! In essence it really is, *"and no man can say that he has really made Jesus, Lord in his life."*[7] The Amplified Version translates it that way, in essence. No man can say that you've really made him Lord in your life, except by the gift, except by speaking in

---

7. A literal translation according to usage of 1 Corinthians 12:3b.

tongues. That's what that verse says, and that's what that verse uniquely and dynamically means! And it's marvelous. You know, no man can say he's really made him Lord. You know why? To make him Lord, you walk out without any feeling, without anything in the senses category. You've simply confessed with your mouth the Lord Jesus, believed God has what? Raised him from the dead. And now, the Word says, you're saved! Now prove it!

You can't feel anything, you can't smell anything, you can't taste anything, you can't touch anything, well now prove it—that he's Lord! Prove it that he's Lord! That you've really made him Lord! So what do you do? You start speaking in tongues! Well, to speak in tongues you really take a "leap out in space!" Because, you can't feel it, you don't know if it's there or not! Now, how do you know it's there then? By doing it. And that's how you make him Lord! That he means what he says and he says what he means, and that he is the Lord of your life! Because, you absolutely believe that you can speak in tongues! And so you speak, and that is what makes him Lord! That's the proof you made him Lord! Do you understand that? Isn't that wonderful? Alright, what other proof do you have that you made him Lord? There isn't any! There isn't a one in the Bible! Well you say, "I do his will." Then you had better be speaking in tongues!

What they mean to say when they "do his will" is they go to church. They go to Sunday school. They go to prayer meetings. They read the Bible once in a while, and they're good to other people! And you know a lot of these other things that any person does and a lot of people do that aren't even converted! Build hospitals. Give money to the poor. You see, there is only one thing that you can really say makes him Lord, and that is that you speak in tongues! When you speak in a tongue, then you have the proof that you've really stepped out, he's

Lord in your life! Because he's the party of the first part. He said, speak in tongues, you did it, you couldn't feel it, you couldn't smell it, you couldn't taste it, but you went right out and spoke in tongues! That's the proof you made him Lord! That's the greatness of that verse of scripture. Isn't that wonderful? Verse 3, "I give you to understand, that [no one] no man speaking by the spirit of God calleth Jesus accursed: and that no man can say that Jesus is Lord, but by *pneuma hagion*, the gift."

Now comes verse 4.

1 Corinthians 12:4
Now there are diversities of gifts, but the same Spirit.

Now, there you have the first usage of the word "gifts." The word "gifts" is the word *charismata*. This is the plural of it, *charismata* is plural. This is gifts. The Greek word *charis* means "grace"; *charismata* means "gifts of grace." Gifts by, or of grace. And all the gifts of grace are given this way down, from God to man. That's its usage all through the Bible. These are gifts of grace this way down. If man would earn them, they would not be gifts of grace. They would be gifts due to merit or something rewarded to us because of our works. But, these *charismata* are always gifts of God's grace. This way down.

There are diversities of gifts. Diversities, which mean that the effects which produced are divers kinds. Different kinds. Here the word is talking about gifts. Are we still talking about spiritual matters? Definitely! But it now specifically says gifts. So we're now talking about spiritual matters that are gifts.

According to my understanding of the Word, there are three major groupings of these gifts of God's grace to man. To the unbeliever, eternal life. Romans 6:23 and I think we ought to read it. These are gifts of God's grace. Romans 6:23.

Romans 6:23
For the wages of sin *is* death; but the gift of God *is* eternal life…

Right! The gift of God. And the Greek word is *charisma*. The gift of God's grace is eternal life. So, I said there are three groupings of these gifts:

1) To the unbelievers, eternal life.

2) Then, when you are a believer this gift to you is the ability to manifest the holy spirit (*pneuma hagion*).

3) And the other gifts of grace we will look up in Ephesians 4:11. These are to the church as ministries, of apostles, prophets, evangelists, pastors and teachers.

Ephesians 4:11
And he gave some, apostles; and some, prophets; and some, evangelists; and some, pastors and teachers;

Now go back a couple of verses, it says gifts. In verse 8, it states:

Ephesians 4:8
…When he ascended up on high, he led captivity captive, and gave gifts unto men.

Then verses 9 and 10 are a parenthesis. Then verse 11 you read after verse 8, he gave gifts. And those "gifts" again are *charismata*. Gifts of God's grace, vertically. And you've got to get this into your mind people, because later on I'm going to show you "gifts" on a horizontal level. Not vertical. When they're vertical, they're always *charisma*. Gifts of God's grace, God to man. So put that in your mind. Keep it straight, up and down, perpendicular.

Now in verse 4.

1 Corinthians 12:4
…there are diversities of gifts, but the same [what?] Spirit.

Spirit—the same Giver. The same Giver for the gifts. It's the same Spirit, the same Lord, the same God in every case where there is a *charismata*, a gift given. It says "diversities of gifts"; it's in the genitive case, "of" is genitive. Genitive case which is uniquely, unique in this verse. It's wonderful! Because both the gifts of this verse, the gifts and the diversities of gifts, both of those words are the effects of God's gracious workings. They are this way down, vertically. Both the gifts and the diversities, the differences in the gifts, both the gifts and the diversities are the effects of God's working! That's why it's in the genitive case.

Verse 5.

1 Corinthians 12:5
And there are differences of administrations, but the same [what?] Lord.

The word "differences" in the Greek, is the word *diairesis*. Now this does not mean effect, like in the verse before. This means that there is a difference in the act of dividing. The act of dividing. And the act of dividing gifts is again in God's prerogative. It's like phenomenon. Phenomenon falls in the category of God's prerogative, right? The act of dividing gifts is God's prerogative, it's God's business. The word "administrations" in this verse, is the Greek word *diakoniōn*, meaning ministries whose services benefit others. Wow, that's a tremendous thing. There are differences of administrations. The word "administrations" is this word *diakoniōn* which means ministries whose services benefit others! On an horizontal level. That's that word "administrations." This simply tells us that the ministries as gifts of God, vertically down in a perpendicular way, are to be absolutely used in service to benefit God's people on an horizontal level. That's what that verse says. Tremendous!

Now, "...but it's the same Lord." Understand? And we're still talking here in verse 5 about what? Gifts. About gifts.

Now verse 6.

> **1 Corinthians 12:6**
> ...there are diversities of operations, but it is the same God which worketh all in all.

Now, the word "operations" is translated "worketh" in this verse: "the same God which worketh all in all." The same word.

Now in verse 10, "To another the working." There it's translated "working." In verse 11, it is translated "worketh," see it? You've got those now in your mind? First of all, back in verse 6, "operations" is translated "worketh" in the latter part of that verse. Then it is translated "working" in verse 10, and "worketh" in verse 11. Same word. This word means: that which is wrought, that which is accomplished, that which is done. That's what the word "worketh" means.

It is that Greek word, which I told you from which we get our English word "energy." *Energōn* is the Greek word for "worketh." In other words, the effects produced are diversities. They're distributed different "kinds." They are deliberate acts of dividing by God of the gifts, like apostles, prophets, evangelists, teachers and pastors. But it is the same God who energizes, who worketh, who puts the "*oomph*," the push, to all the gifts. Understand?

God does not give nine gifts of the spirit! But he gives one gift of *pneuma hagion* (holy spirit) which energizes our spiritual ability to manifest nine operations, in the church, plus energizing the five ministries in the church of apostles, prophets, evangelists, pastors and teachers.

I think you can understand this very simply and very easily, when you realize that this is just about like the battery in your automobile. There is one battery in your automobile. There is electrical energy in the battery. And it is that energy in the battery, which energizes the honking of the horn, plays the radio, engages the operation for the cigarette lighter, cigar lighter. What else does it do? Ignition. One battery, but it has nine operations let's say in the automobile. The battery represents the gift. One gift of God. But, it has nine operations that can be utilized from the energy in that battery! And it's as simple as this. People will say, Well if that's true, why doesn't everybody that's born again speak in tongues? Well we found out they didn't in Acts 8, didn't we? And in Acts 19, they had to have a little help from Paul!

Why don't they all automatically speak in tongues? For the same reason that when you sit down in the automobile, it doesn't automatically honk the horn, engage the cigarette lighter, play the radio, or these other six manifestations of some good automobile. Why? Because to play the radio, somebody has to what? engage it. To honk the horn, somebody has to engage it. To get the cigar lighter to work, somebody has to plug it in, engage it. So it is with the operation of the manifestations of the spirit! We are born again, filled with his holy spirit, why don't we automatically speak in tongues? Because, somebody must engage it! Somebody has to do it! The moment you do it, it's energized by the power that's in the spiritual battery which God has put within. That's the simplicity of it! That's the beauty of it!

Verse 6.

1 Corinthians 12:6a
…there are diversities of operations, but it is the same [what?] God…

The same God. In verse 4, it's the same Spirit. In verse 5, it's the same Lord. In verse 6, it's the same God. Verses

4, 5, and 6. The Holy Spirit is Lord, the Holy Spirit is God. The same Spirit, the same Lord, the same God.

Now the latter part of that verse.

1 Corinthians 12:6b
...but it is the same God which worketh all in all.

It is the same God who worketh, energizes, understand? All the gifts, the *charismata*, in everybody. And the *charismata* are for the unbeliever: eternal life! And as he has eternal life, God energizes: the nine manifestations of the spirit. Then, there are five ministries in the body of the church: apostles, prophets, evangelists, pastors and teachers. And He energizes those! The same Lord. The same God, who operates (or who energizes) worketh all in all.[8] Do you understand? That's what that verse means, that's what it says.

Now, Verse 7.

1 Corinthians 12:7a
But...

And whenever you read the word "but," if it's properly translated as it is here, it always sets that which goes before, in contrast with that which follows. Now here in verses 4, 5, and 6, what has been the subject matter? Gifts. Now the word "but" already tells you that you're no longer going to be talking about what? Gifts. It's going to set something in contrast with it. If it used the word "and"—and by the way if you put the word "and" in here, your Bible would fall to pieces! It's that uniquely important to rightly divide it here. Translation wise too. Because if you put the word "and" in it, it would set it in correspondence with that which goes before. Putting the word

---

8. 1 Corinthians 12:6b—...the same God who worketh [energizes] all [the gifts: eternal life, nine manifestations, five gift ministries] in all [everybody].

"but" sets it in contrast. Now we've been talking about *charismata*, gifts of God's grace. But—but, now we're going to change.

> **1 Corinthians 12:7**
> But [But what? the manifestation] the manifestation of the Spirit is given to every man to profit withal.

Now, we're not talking about gifts, now we're talking about what? Manifestation! And the word "manifestation" means something manifested, something you can see. Some evidence that appears before you. That's manifestation. You can't see spirit, but you can see the what? Manifestation. And here we're talking about the manifestation of the spirit. That's what it says, that's what it means. Then are we talking about gifts of the spirit? No. We're talking about manifestation. And that is really tremendous!

Now the word "manifestation" is in the singular. The reason it's in the singular, as far as I'm concerned, is because it represents a "whole," a "cluster." Just like a cluster of grapes where you have one cluster, singular, but you have nine grapes on that cluster. So the manifestation of the spirit is singular, having nine evidences in one cluster.

It is like Galatians, chapter 5. Please look it up.

> **Galatians 5:22, 23**
> But the fruit of the Spirit is love, joy, peace, longsuffering, gentleness, goodness, faith,
> Meekness, temperance: against such there is no law.

In Galatians 5:22 and 23, how many fruits do you have mentioned? Nine fruits. But you see they are really fruits, but why does it say "fruit" in the singular, in verse 22? Because they make up one cluster of a whole. They make up the "fruit of the spirit." Like the manifestation of the spirit. Singular, yet there are nine evidences. So there is one "fruit" of the spirit with nine fruits. If it seems complicated, get the picture of the grapes in your mind on one cluster and you'll never flip on it or question it again. It's real simple.

I would like for you to note. It may come up again later, but it won't hurt you if it comes up a dozen times because you're really learning. People have always taught that the greatest mark of a Christian is that he can love. That's a bunch of baloney! And the reason they say that, they say: by their fruits, ye shall know them. And by their fruits they mean "good works." This is not the fruit of good works! This is the fruit of the spirit! That's what it says, that's what it means. And every commentary I've ever read says it is works. And it says it so simply and plainly in the King James and in every other translation, it always says, "fruit of the spirit." It's not fruit of the good works of man. It's the fruit of what? spirit! And you get fruit of the spirit by the operation of the manifestation of the spirit. The manifestation of the spirit, produce fruit of the spirit. That's how you get it.

> **1 Corinthians 12:7**
> But the manifestation of the Spirit is given to every man...

In other words, every spirit-filled believer has the privilege, and the responsibility, of evidencing at least one manifestation in the church, for the benefit of all. Because this is God's "least will" for every believer in the church. The manifestation of the spirit is given to what? Every man—every man and please note that! If the manifestation is given to every man, then does every man who is spirit-filled, born again of God's spirit, does he have the God given ability to speak in tongues? Yes! How about interpretation? How about prophecy? How about word of knowledge? Word of wisdom? Discerning of spirits? Faith, miracles and healings? The manifestation is given to every man. I didn't write the Book but that's what it means, that's what it says. The manifestation is given to everybody! To everybody! To everybody!

So, if a man says he is born again of God's spirit, does he have the ability to speak in tongues? Then the reason he doesn't is one of two. Either he doesn't know how, or he's just plain stubborn and doesn't want to! That's right. Either he does not know how to speak in tongues, he doesn't know his job, or he doesn't want to. That's all. The manifestation is given to every man. The manifestation is given to every man! And the manifestation is the nine evidences. They are given to every man. Therefore, every man born again of God's spirit, who is filled with the spirit, could speak in tongues, could interpret, could prophecy, could operate word of knowledge, word of wisdom, discerning of spirits, faith, miracles and healings —every man. Every one!

But you see the recipient has to do the speaking. We have to make him Lord. We have to do the speaking. We have to do the interpreting. We have to do prophesying, we have to receive the word of knowledge, the word of wisdom, the discerning of spirits. We have to minister faith, miracles and healings.

Now, the manifestation of the spirit:

1 Corinthians 12:7b
…is given to every man [to what?] to profit withal.

That is every person operating the manifestation. Every person operating the manifestation will find that they are beneficial. Every manifestation of the spirit has a profit in it! Thus, when you see an evidence, a manifestation in the senses realm, of what people say is spirit, the first thing you look for is the profit! What is the profit? If you'll look for that, and if you'll understand the next few verses we're going to cover after this, and know what the profit is in each one, you will never need to go down the drain on any spiritual thing that God or Satan gives you. You'll always know whether it's from the true God or from Satan. What is the profit? What is the profit? That's what you've got to look for!

For instance, what's the profit? You have never been here before. I've never seen you. What's the profit in my telling Eddie D., his name is Eddie D.? He knows his blessed name! I hope. Alright, now you see, but look at what excitement this would cause in a meeting where I've stood up in front and called out the fellow's name back there. I'd say, "Eddie D., from Columbus Ohio." Mr. D., have I ever met you before? "No sir, I've never seen you before." Have you ever been in a meeting before? "No sir." Have you ever written to me before? "No sir." Mr. D., I believe you live on Draftsmere, is that right Mr. D.? (Now, how did that fellow know that? God must have told him.) And I think Mr. D., I don't only think, I know you work for the Post Office Department of the United States government. Oh yes, and you left your two children at home. Look how wonderful this appeals to the ears of people, right? But what's the profit?

Eddie knows his name, he knows where he works, and he knows how many kids he's got. He knows he left them at home. But all over the nation, they're getting taken in like this! By the barrel full! And they think it's from the true God. Now that man could be born again, he could be operating manifestations of the spirit and be as you know a child of God, but he gets possessed in the upper story, and that stuff that I've just demonstrated to you is straight from the Devil! Straight from the source of the pit of hell! What's the profit in it? You know your name, right? I do too. Look people, I've been through this thing upside down and backwards, and it's a miracle that I was able to separate out this stuff what I'm trying to teach you and share with you tonight! Had I not been able to separate it out, we'd still all be going down the drain.

I know of no other person, outside of this ministry, who believes what I've just told you. And I've been with the biggest in the nation. Old Bill Branham used to be able to tell them their names. Am I right? Some of you have been in the meetings, am I right? Sure I'm right! That information and that kind of stuff were strictly from the Devil. And, yet, at another time, he was walking for the true God. Now you say how can this be? Well you'd better not ask that question this late in the ball game or somebody ought to screw your ear balls to a chair! Or do something. That's right. Because you certainly understand body, soul, and spirit. That's right. It's the *man* that does the operating of the true manifestations of God, while old Satan just possesses. That's right.

Suppose that I was speaking and I would say, "Now to prove that God is here, and God will heal you, we'll get the drapes to move!" God will move those drapes. What's the profit? None whatsoever! None whatsoever! You see, people, that's why you've got to get your nose in the Book and work these profits out. The reason I know these profits so well, is because I know every record from Genesis to Revelation, where these manifestation are in operation, or were in operation, in people. And having traced them all through from Genesis to Revelation, time and time again, you see the profit, and you understand the profit.

Now, the manifestation is given to every man. But they are given for profit, for profit in two ways, class: to you the believer and to God's people, the Body! It's a profit that blesses you this way by God (vertically), and you in turn bless God's people on a horizontal plane. This is the profit! This becomes very, very important people because right there is where you either "flip" on understanding spiritual things, and rightly dividing whether it's from the Devil or from the true God, or you just never know.

Now, Verse 7. "…is given to every man to profit withal." To profit withal. Naturally, to profit withal, you say to yourself, how do I profit? How do I profit? Or how will it profit me? Or what is basically the profit in each of the nine manifestations? And, those profits are given in verses 8 through 10 of this chapter (1 Corinthians 12).

1 Corinthians 12:8a
For to one is given by the Spirit…

And if you add the words "in the church" you'd get great understanding of these verses.

1 Corinthians 12:8-10
For to one is given by the Spirit [the *pneumatikos*, the *pneuma* in the church] the word of wisdom; to another the word of knowledge by the same Spirit;
To another faith by the same Spirit; to another the gifts of healing by the same Spirit;
To another the working of miracles; to another prophecy; to another [the] discerning of spirits; to another *divers* kinds of tongues; to another the interpretation of tongues:

The first word in verse 8 is "For" which is a conjunction setting this verse in correspondence with verse 7, and informing us that God's Word is now going to give the specific information to us how this profit, "to profit withal"—how this profit comes about in the church.

The word "to one" or "for to one" is the Greek word *hō*. Now, I want to explain this to you. I don't particularly care whether you remember all this stuff, but it is really, really uniquely accurate here: *hō* is the dative case of the relative pronoun *hos*. Being in the dative case, the word *hō* can be translated either "to one" or "for one." Here in King James it's translated what? to one. "One" is a relative pronoun, and means, and is used interchangeably in language with the word "that." And a relative pronoun refers to the nearest noun as its antecedent. "To profit" is an infinitive. The one in verse 7, "to profit" that's an infinitive. And an infinitive (this is getting a little technical) is a verbal noun. "To profit" used as an infinitive in this particular place, grammatically, is a very cogent expression. As an infinitive, it is used as a noun and yet it has the action of a verb. So that a more vital translation would be, "is given by the same spirit to profit." Given by the same spirit "as to profit," instead of "as a profit." It's that minutely accurate!

Now I know this is a little far-fetched for most people. But look, for some of us who stand in awe of the greatness of God's Word, when you see that thing and you see how beautiful it sets, and when you work this thing down in language, it's just unbelievably accurate! This is what just sets me back and just thrills my soul! And it is as to profit. See everything is for profit, as to profit. It means to profit, and therefore used like I said it was, it connotes an active ingredient. It's always an active ingredient to profit. It's always producing something. That's remarkable! Well I sweat hard on that one and didn't get through, did I? Well that's alright, don't worry. It didn't get through to me the first time either. But, you see if you use the noun in place of the pronoun it would read, everyone would read, "for that profit." And verses 8 to 10 would be much plainer and more accurately presented if they were translated as follows:

Verse 8, *"For a word of wisdom is given by the Spirit for profit;"* [9] That's right! That's literally what it means! *"For a word of knowledge is given by the same Spirit for*

---

9. A literal translation according to usage of 1 Corinthians 12:8a.

228 HOLY SPIRIT—*PNEUMA HAGION*

another profit;"[10] Another profit—not the same profit, understand? But the word of knowledge produces another profit. For profit. It's an active ingredient! Do any of you have the fifth edition with you tonight? Turn to page 151, I've translated it there.[11]

Really it's our friend Reverend Wade that made me work out some of the things in these verses here now. Within the last two years, he made me work them out and write them out, so that he could have them in Australia. And of course when we reprinted the book, I put it in here too. But, one of the things that he was so concerned about, was those people in Australia were all upset about the different word "for another." And you'll see on page 151[12] where it says, *"For faith [believing] by the same Spirit for another [heteros] profit."*[13] And there it's the word *heteros*. I put the words "for another" in italics and brackets. It's the word *heteros* in the first part of verse 9. In the second part of verse 9 it was *allos*. *"For gifts of healing are given for the same Spirit to another [allos] profit; For the working of miracles are given by the same Spirit for another [allos] profit;"*[14]

You see right now I'm wondering if it should be "to" or "for" in that line above. It bothers me whether that is something that we missed in proof reading or not. You mark it and call it to my attention when I get back in the office tonight and I'll check it out. Looks to me like a mistake. I think it ought to read, *"For gifts of healing are given by the same spirit, for another [allos] profit."*[15] Not

---

10. A literal translation according to usage of 1 Corinthians 12:8b.
11. See also *Receiving the Holy Spirit Today*, seventh edition, p. 143.
12. See also Seventh edition, p. 143.
13. A literal translation according to usage of 1 Corinthians 12:9a.
14. A literal translation according to usage of 1 Corinthians 12:9b, 10a.
15. A literal translation according to usage of 1 Corinthians 12:9b.

"to" another profit. I think it's "for." But I'll have to check it. *"For the working of miracles are given by the same Spirit for another [allos] profit; prophecy is given by the same Spirit for another [allos] profit; discerning of spirits are given by the same Spirit for another [allos] profit."* [16] These are all different profits, but each one has a profit in it! That's the point! *"Kinds of tongues are given by the same Spirit for another [heteros] profit; interpretation of tongues are given by the same Spirit for another [allos] profit."* [17]

You will notice that "faith" by the same Spirit, and "kinds of tongues" are the only two of the nine manifestations that have the word *heteros* for another. All the rest have the word *allos*. And working this down was uniquely interesting to me, and for us, because of all nine manifestations of the Spirit there are only two that specifically benefit the operator. One is speaking in tongues. Speaking in tongues specifically blesses me because it edifies God's spirit within me. That's why the word *heteros* is used. The other is the manifestation of faith or believing, as we teach it when we get into the accuracy of it, where God demands of those of us who minister that we believe God for the impossible to come to pass at our command. This is specifically my job. This is why these two are the only ones that have the word *heteros* in it. All the rest are *allos*. And I wrote that as much in here on page 151, bottom of the page:

> Two of the nine manifestations are specifically for only the individual believer to profit. The manifestation of speaking in tongues and the manifestation of faith[18] are a profit only to the one receiving from

---

16. A literal translation according to usage of 1 Corinthians 12:10a.
17. A literal translation according to usage of 1 Corinthians 12:10b.
18. Seventh edition says "manifestation of believing" instead of manifestation of faith.

God. Speaking in tongues profits the believer by edifying his spirit. The manifestation of faith,[19] which is shown forth when a son of God believes for the impossible to come to pass at his command according to the revelation (word of knowledge, word of wisdom, discerning of spirits), received profits only the believer operating it. Other people may profit from the results of the operation, but not from the manifestation itself.[20]

Got it? I profit from the manifestation, you may profit from the results. That's the only line I didn't tell you a while ago else I'd told you everything in here.

Now go to page 22 of your syllabus. In the classes this is where I begin after we have taught the renewed mind, sonship rights, when we begin into the introduction of the manifestations of the spirit. The first thing I tell my people is that the manifestations of the gift from the Holy Spirit, which is power from on high, are nine in number. They're no more and no less, these manifestations. They are not set in order but simply listed in 1 Corinthians 12:8-10, which we have read. Here in Corinthians they are not set in order. They're simply listed; they're simply stated, that's all.

A piano artist is not a gift from the spirit, but a natural ability. Look, you've got to get that! You many times hear people say, like when Rhoda plays the piano, someone would say, "God has certainly given her a gift to play the piano." How ridiculous! I think maybe her great grandpa had more to do with it, and grandma, then on down the line and so forth. But, it's a natural gift, it's a natural ability. Don't confuse natural abilities with gifts from God, or gifts that God gives in the spirit. You see, these

---

19. Seventh edition says "manifestation of believing".
20. Dr. Wierwille reads and quotes *Receiving the Holy Spirit Today*, page 151 [Similarly but not identical: Seventh edition, p. 144].

are not a natural gift. Fruits of the spirit are not gifts. We covered that tonight in Galatians 5:22 and 23. Fruit is a manifestation; the result of the operation of the manifestations of the spirit (of a cultivated spirit filled life) produce fruit. Fruit indicates quality of life in operation with the manifestations.

Gifts are for service. Gifts are functional. The manifestations of the power from on high are not new. Seven of the nine manifestations are clearly in evidence and used in the Old Testament. The manifestations by their nature of operation and administration divide into three groups, with three in each group. The only manifestations that are missing out of the Old Testament are speaking in tongues and interpretation of tongues. You see interpretation of tongues is the companion manifestation of speaking in tongues. Speaking in tongues is severely limited without the companion manifestation of interpretation, as we will see later on when we get into 1 Corinthians 14. It is limited to one specific job. But with the accompanying companion manifestation of interpretation, it has a very effective, profitable ministry in the Body as such.

Now, the nine manifestations which fully came when the Day of Pentecost was fully come (people were bornagain and were able for the first time, since they had the gift which is the God given ability). They were now able for the first time to fully manifest all nine manifestations of the spirit! And by their very nature, the manifestations of the spirit divide into three groups. They just fall in line, just fall in pattern. You don't have to squeeze them, you don't have to work hard on them; this is just the way they work. And every place in the Bible where you see the manifestations in operation, you will see them grouped off like that. The characteristics of the manifestation suggest the names.

Group 1:
Utterance Manifestations: speaking in tongues, inter-

pretation of tongues, and prophecy. These are utterance manifestations. The characteristics of the manifestations suggest the name. They're utterance. You utter them. They're speaking. You speak them. They are worship manifestations, which mean that they're used in a worship service in a Body of Believers. They're used in a worship service where we worship Him in spirit and how? in truth. Right. They are inspirational manifestations. You are inspired because Christ is in you! And because he is in you, you can speak in tongues anytime. You can interpret anytime. You can give a word of prophecy anytime. You don't have to reach up in Daddy's cookie jar. It's already in you! These are worked by inspiration. These are in you. That's why they are called inspirational manifestations. And you see they just fall together in a pattern. Tongues has to have with it, what? Interpretation. Which in turn has to have prophecy with it because those three just by their very nature make up the utterance, the speaking, or the worship manifestations.

Group 2:

Revelation Manifestations: word of knowledge, word of wisdom, discerning of spirits. This group is the eyes and the ears of the church. These are the revelation manifestations. Revelation. God has to reveal it to you specifically or you don't know anything. This is not in you all the time. This, God has to give to you by revelation.

Remember 2 Kings, chapter 4 with Elisha and the Shunammite woman. She had her baby to begin with because of the ministry of God's Word in the prophet. She had never had a child. And remember Elisha said to her, "What can I do for you because you've been so good to me, and fed me and gave me the upper chamber, the room for me to say in, when I travel through?" And somehow or other she'd never had a child, and Elisha told her she would have a son within the proper season, which meant nine months from now.[21] So she did. Years later this son died. And she high tails it toward the prophet, and when she comes toward the prophet Elisha, the prophet sends his servant to go ask her what's going on. For the Lord hath not revealed to me what's the matter, but I know there's something wrong. You see, you don't have this information in you all the time! The prophet Elisha didn't have the information on what was wrong with the woman. Had he been born again of God's spirit he could have spoken in tongues, interpreted, and prophesied anytime, right? But, he didn't have the revelation; he didn't have the information what was wrong with the woman.

This is why these manifestations are the eyes and ears of the church. Without these manifestations, people could pull the "wool over" the eyes of a person. With the operation of these manifestations in a man of God, in the church, who ministers the Word of God, nobody pulls the wool over his eyes! All he needs to do is reach up into "Daddy's cookie jar." Then he gets revelation from God to you downward. "Revealing" is what the word "revelation" means. Information, God gives the information. They are instructional manifestations, for our instruction that we can minister to the body effectively. They are knowing manifestations. They teach us the score! By these manifestations you know, that you know, that you know, that you know! Word of knowledge, word of wisdom and discerning of spirits.

Never, never think of them in terms of the "gift of discernment"! Now that's pitiful. I heard that one last weekend. There isn't anything like a gift of discernment. It's the manifestation of the discerning of spirits. It is not even the manifestation of discernment, as I've heard it

---

21. 2 Kings 4:16—And he said, About this season, according to the time of life, thou shalt embrace a son....

used. Discernment means acuteness in judgment. There are many people who are not born again of God's spirit, who are very acute in judgment. This is not to be acute in judgment! This is the manifestation of the discerning of spirits. To discern by revelation whether they're good spirits or bad spirits, and if they're bad spirits to the end that you can cast them out in the name of Jesus Christ.

Those are the eyes and ears of the church, people! This is what kept that early church, that they really knew what was going on. This is how Peter knew that Ananias and Sapphira had cheated the Lord![22] They came and they said, "We brought all of our money that we sold the property for, we've given it all." And Peter said you're lying like a trooper! How did he know? The eyes and ears of the church; God gives the knowledge, God told them. So whenever you hear or you read where "the spirit said to them" or "God said to them," it's always one or the other or a combination of those three manifestations (word of knowledge, word of wisdom, or discerning of spirits) in the Word of God. Remember last session, where we read about the spirit which said to Peter don't hesitate, you go with them. How did the spirit speak to them? by word of knowledge and word of wisdom. It wasn't a matter of discerning of spirits there. See it?

Group 3:

Action Group. I'm still dealing now with 1 Corinthians 12:8-10. All of these are manifestations. Group 3 is the Action group. These are the action manifestations. These are the power manifestations. Or they are the impartation manifestations, where you impart to others what God wants done. You see class, this thing builds so beautifully and so simply when you really understand the Word and oper-

---

22. Acts 5:3—But Peter said, Ananias, why hath Satan filled thine heart to lie to the Holy Ghost, and to keep back *part* of the price of the land?

ate the manifestations. I speak much in tongues in my private life. As I speak much in tongues, I build up the inner man. In a believers' meeting,[23] I speak in tongues and I interpret boldly. Or I bring a message in prophecy boldly, which not only edifies and builds up the whole Body of Believers, but I'm part of the Body and it will build me up too, up here in my mind! Now since I'm built up big and fat on the inside, and I'm built up big and fat in my mind, now I'm ready to walk. So I need information. I reach up in Daddy's cookie jar and he gives me word of knowledge, word of wisdom and discerning of spirits, regarding the situations with which I am confronted. Then, after He gives me the information, now I carry it out to my fellow men. Now I carry it out as a function, a benefit on a horizontal level to God's people, by way of faith, miracles and healings. Isn't it wonderful?

You see, when you are still hesitant about speaking in tongues and interpreting in a believers' meeting, the revelation manifestations will not operate effectively in you. Because, if you're scared to speak in tongues and interpret, among a bunch of believers like this, what in the world would you ever do when you really run up against a devil spirit, and you need the power of God to discern it's a devil spirit, and then need the boldness to get the devil out of there? You'll die in your tracks! You'll just give up. You just won't do it! So you just sit like a cold cucumber.

The thing all starts with speaking in tongues boldly in your private life. Then it graduates into speaking in

---

23. The Bible provides God's guidelines for things that His people are to do when they gather as the Church. Among them are His instructions in 1 Corinthians 14 for how the manifestations of holy spirit are to be operated when the Church meets together to worship Him. Dr. Wierwille referred to those times when the manifestations of speaking in tongues, interpretation of tongues and prophecy are operated within the Church as a "believers' meeting."

tongues and interpreting boldly in a believers' meeting! Or giving a word of prophecy boldly in a believers' meeting. Then you're about ready to start the Advanced Class. I expect my people who take the Advanced Class to have a thorough knowledge of the Bible. I expect them to operate the manifestations in the Foundational Class dynamically! But you see if I waited for our people to get a thorough knowledge of God's Word, I'd be sitting around till I grew a beard like Moses, for the most part! Because, we're still reading our newspapers too much and our periodicals and our society is keeping us too busy, making money to feed the kids, and running here and running there, that we don't take the time to master the stories in the Word of God! I said to some recently, the best thing for you to do to start, is just buy yourself a good Bible story book. Dotsie has one.[24] She reads it to the kids every morning. Get a good Bible story book and read it four or five times. That will give you the fastest picture of the Old Testament and some of the New Testament there is. And then after you've done that, then go pick up the individual stories and read them directly. That's how you get a knowledge of God's Word! You have to study; you have to work it!

Now, the nine manifestations of the gift of the holy spirit in a believer are the power, or the ability of God in you. Remember, the gift is the ability. The manifestation is the result, or the act, the operation of the gift. Now you can be loaded with the gift, and never do a blessed thing, right? Because we are not operating, don't you see it? Because it's when we understand the profit, that you can sniff out the genuine and counterfeit just like that! All the profit, all the manifestations and the profit that they produce always flow in line with the Word of God, never at cross purposes with it. Never does a manifesta-

---

24. Referring to Mrs. Dorothea Wierwille.

tion that is true, contradict what the Word of God says. Never! Never! Understand? It always has to flow in line with the Word. These things and knowing these things have surely cost me a lot of friends in the ministry. And on the other hand I suppose, it doesn't make any difference.

I was teaching one night in Van Wert, and someone whom some of our people loved very dearly, spoke in tongues and then interpreted. They had no more than started the first word and I stopped him. And I said, Look, if you're going to give it from the Devil shut up! Speak in tongues and give me the interpretation of the Lord! The true God. So he spoke in tongues again and he hadn't said the second or third word, and I stopped him again. Now that just blew the lid off of him! I think 10 or 12, or 15 or 20 people walked out and went home, and all the rest of the stuff. And I was just sick on the inside because they were my friends!

But you see, I caught myself doing that thing so quickly, I just cut it off. And the thing went on for about 3, 4 or 5 months. Nothing but trouble, that's all I've ever had in life anyways on this baloney so I enjoy it. But, low and behold some of my people were in a meeting and this same man was giving a prophecy. And the prophecy was, in essence like this, "Yea verily I the Lord thy God am with thee always. And I would say unto thee this night, that the reality of Satan is not a reality." That in essence there is no Devil. That came out in the prophecy of that man! I had stopped this thing months and months before! I'd seen it. But you see, once it really got out into the open, that even the unbeliever that knows a little of the Bible, would know he was off, right? For the Bible says there is a Devil, right? That's why the manifestations and profit are never running at cross purposes with the Word of God! They *always* agree with the Word of God! *Always*—never at cross purposes!

I watch with a sharp ear. And I think maybe this is why half of you are scared to speak in tongues, half the time you're afraid of me. I don't know why you're afraid of me; you ought to be afraid of the Devil, not me. Because there's one thing that I'll do if you're wrong; I'd at least tell you, and that's the best thing you could have a man of God to do! Man, if I didn't love you I'd let you go to hell! But it's because I love people, that I stop them so I can help them! I watched what was said tonight, because there can be a tremendous counterfeit in two words that was used. She used the word "sheep." Am I God's sheep, technically? No! I am God's what? Son. Jesus was the good shepherd, Israel was his sheep! And I listen for these things, I watch them. Because when we're right down the tracking line, it will sometimes say, "Ye are like my sheep."—"You are protected like the sheep." That I understand. But I am technically not a sheep! I am a Son of God! You see why am I sharp on this? Because if I'm going to help you, I've got to know what's going on.

When we get into interpretation, I'm going to show you that one of the greatest mistakes some of our people are making, is that they are going beyond the interpretation. It happens every once in a while, that I see people go beyond the interpretation. And then again, I see people selling it a little short. Last time we were together I was afraid you[25] were going to sell us a little short, but you didn't. I just sat here and waited, because I knew there was another line to fill it out, and you hesitated a little and then you gave it. That's wonderful. But I watch; I'm careful. And it's not bad to go beyond the interpretation, it's just not good. That's right. It isn't bad because when you go beyond the interpretation, you will automatically go into prophecy. And that prophecy will only reiterate what

---

25. Dr. Wierwille is talking specifically to an individual present during the teaching.

you have just given in interpretation. Therefore, it isn't bad it just isn't doing good. I've got to get my people finally to the place that when you give the interpretation you know that's it, that's it! And when you prophesy, you prophesy. Those little lines of demarcation where the one quits and the other starts are sharply marked. But you have to get alive, and as long as you've got an ounce of fear, it will trip you up! That's why the first lesson in the class is always on fear. We've got to master fear in our lives regarding the things of God.

You should not have one iota of fear regarding speaking in tongues and interpretation or prophecy. Not one iota! Don't shake because you're afraid to speak in tongues and interpret or prophesy. Because the moment you fear, who is it from? And you see how you "clamp it up?" Now I don't always say something, I don't always yell at people, just when they get off a little. But, it depends on where I am, too. If I'm teaching a class, I'll watch over it with hawk eyes you know! But if we're having a Sunday night fellowship or any other time, and it goes a little over in prophecy I don't say anything. I may take the person aside, in the next month or two and talk to them a little sometimes. But the point is that when you're really teaching, we ought to become real versatile in this. Because you are the only people I know that have any great knowledge of all of the manifestations and their operations. And you ought to operate them just so beautifully and so naturally that old Satan just can't get in. And that by the operation thereof, your action teaches other people how accurate it is!

These kids learn to interpret. These kids learn to carry out these things from what they see you do. (Maybe we learn it from the children. I'm not sure which, but this is the way it works.) And the interpretation will always have a natural ending. Many times it's in the essence of: "For

I the Lord thy God have spoken."—"I will be with thee always."—"I will never leave thee nor forsake thee."—"I have given thee my Word and it will stand forever." But I'm not into interpretation yet. I'm still in 1 Corinthians 12:8-10. When we get into some of rest of this stuff in Chapter 14, it will explain itself. It will come up and there it will be just as plain.

Now here in 1 Corinthians 12:8 it says, "For to one" in the King James. But you know I have expounded this and I've said to you why it should be, "For for one" and they are all given for profit. You will have to take that holy spirit book[26] of mine, and you're really going to have to work this down (verses 8, 9 and 10) so that you really know what it says and what it means in the minutest detail.

Verse 11 begins with the word "But," and this is really something! The word "but" sets it in contrast. It sets that which went before, in contrast with that which follows. So setting it in contrast technically, verse 11 fits right after verse 7. Don't put it there but that's where it fits. You see verses 8 to 10 are a subordinate clause referring to the profit in the manifestations of verse 7. Isn't that something? It's accurate right down the line. Verses 8 to 10, I'll say it again, are a subordinate clause referring to the profit in the manifestations of verse 7. And technically, verses 8 to 10 should be in a parenthesis. They're there by way of explanation, to explain the profit.

You see, this sets before us why God did not set them in the order like I've put them: speaking in tongues, interpretation and prophecy. God never meant them to be set in the order. These were simply a subordinate clause and they were to be technically in the parenthesis. To explain —to explain why, each one was for a profit. That's why

---

26. See also *Receiving the Holy Spirit Today*, seventh edition, pp. 142-148.

they are set like that. You see, verse 11 really takes up where verse 7 leaves off.

> **1 Corinthians 12:7**
> …the manifestation of the Spirit is given to every man to profit withal.

To profit withal—all of these.

> **1 Corinthians 12:11**
> …all [of] these worketh that one and the selfsame Spirit [the manifestations all work with the one and selfsame Spirit], dividing to every man severally as he will.

In verse 11, we have a *triple reflective*. It's really something, the emphasis. You know what you could do in this field where I've written this holy spirit book? A person could take the figures of speech in the holy spirit field and write another nice little book on it of a hundred pages of just figures of speech. Here you have one. In grammar, in English it's called a *triple reflective*. And it's most uniquely used in the Word of God here, in the following words: but all of these worketh that *one* and the *selfsame* Spirit. Well, if it's one, it's what? self. If it is self, it's what? same. That's the triple reflective "one," "self," "same." Three words used! Look at that emphasis! Wow! I can't yell it loud enough. The emphasis is just ALL of these worketh that ONE! SELF! SAME!—spirit. Isn't that something?

The word "dividing" in verse 11, is the word "distributed" or "distributing" that we've had before. Now, the word "worketh" you know is the word "energize." All of these manifestations, all nine are energized, given the "*oomph*," the power by that one, self, same, spirit (*pneuma*). Would you say that would have to be God's spirit? Sure! (Capital "S".) Right! Now, the rest of the verse:

1 Corinthians 12:11
...dividing to every man severally as he will.

There is the problem. You see people argue, and they still argue today about it. They say verse 8 says, "for to one is given," and "to another" and "to another." So they say, "You see, not everybody has them."

Even upon a casual reading, that couldn't be right. For how could God contradict Himself, for He just said in verse 7, "...the manifestation of the spirit is given [to who?] every man." Then how could "to one be given" and not "to another," if one verse says it, everybody's already got it! When they used to bring this up to me, I'd always say, "Well, then explain to me verse 11? It says, He divides to 'every man [what?] severally'..." Then they couldn't explain it. Because they just said, "Well He gives it to one and not to another." But in verse 11 it says, "He divides to every man severally." One is not several. Right? A couple is only two; several must be more than two. So I'd say, "Well they must have at least three." You see, just to beat them at their argument. One thing you've got to do when you teach is get people to think for once in their life! Because the average person never thinks, he just thinks he thinks! But he never thinks. So you've got to shake them up! You've got to really make them sit down and think! And once they start thinking, then they'll start getting some answers. Verse 7 said, "...the manifestation is given to every man," right? Alright, then he can't turn around and God say, "Well, I'm just going to give to one so and so, and to another." There has to be a deeper reason for it.

Well, I told you that these were addressed to the church, right? And I said to you a little while ago, you read into these verses, in your mind you read their operation in the church. Everybody as an individual has how many manifestations? Nine. Right. But, inside of the church in the Body, where he ministers this way (horizontally, to the Body) every person will operate at least one manifestation, very, very, effectively. He will shine, in one. This will be his "long suit" spiritually, and therefore every person's contribution in the Body will be "real good" at that point. He will have something he can do as well or better than anybody else can do it! That's why it's written this way. "For-for one is given" for profit inside the church.

Let's say Eddie and I are ministering, like we were Sunday night. Eddie has all nine manifestations and I do too, right? But let's say, Eddie shines in word of knowledge and word of wisdom. That's his long suit. He operates all nine, but those two (word of knowledge and word of wisdom), nothing bypasses him when you minister with him. On that word of knowledge and that word of wisdom—*boom*! *Boom*! Let's say I'm very strong on discerning of spirits. I operate word of knowledge and wisdom, and let's say that discerning of spirits was my long suit, my genus. The one I really shine in. Well then Eddie and I just supplement each other perfectly. That's what it's talking about in those verses.

Now the word "severally" isn't the word severally at all! It is the word *idios*. It is used 114 times in the New Testament. This is the only place it's translated "severally." Other places it's translated "his own" or "one's own." For example, "he came unto his own"—"he came into his own country"—"his own servants"—"his own people"—"his own nation"—that's the word *idios*. Also it's used in a very wonderful verse of scripture which we read in the Foundational Class, 2 Peter 1:20.

> **2 Peter 1:20**
> Knowing this first, that no prophecy of the scripture is of any [what?] private interpretation.

The word "private" is the word *idios* (one's own). That's private. If it's yours, it's private, right? If it's your own, it's privately yours.

Back to verse 11, "...dividing to every man [his own, one's own] as he..." and I think the Amplified Bible has "He" as a capital "H." No, no, no, no, no! It shouldn't be. He is a pronoun. A pronoun is always controlled by its closest associated and related noun. The closest noun to the word "he" is the word "man."

1 Corinthians 12:11
...dividing to every man [his own] as he [he who? the man, as the man] will.

We've already known God's will. For God's will was given in verse 7, "...the manifestation is given to [what?] every man..." And inside of the church you operate as a body. And there God divides to every man the manifestation as he (the man) will. If you do not will to speak in tongues, will you? No. You see God divides, distributes to every man as the man wills. Suppose you don't will, God doesn't give you anything. You haven't got anything. Suppose you do not will to receive word of knowledge, you'll never get anything! Because God knows you're not going to, so why should He open His cookie jar? He just keeps the lid on it. Dividing to every man as the man will! Right here is where we limit ourselves. Right here.

Because you know somebody will say, "I just love to speak in tongues and interpret." That's wonderful. As the man will. You really shine then! You know why we really shine in one manifestation and not another? Because we believe it. You know some things come easier to us naturally than others, so we really augment those; we really bolster those up. And so, pretty soon you just become real sharp in tongues and interpretation, let's say. But when it comes to word of knowledge you miss the boat half of the time! I believe God expects us and allows us the privilege of getting our believing up, because He divides to every man, as the man will! So, if we would *will* to receive more revelation, we would do what? Receive more. If we would *will* to carry out the power, the action, the impartation manifestations, we'd get more ministering done. That's what that verse 11 means, that's what it says! "Dividing [in manifestation] to every man as the man will." It's all that is to it.

Now, we have only one more opportunity left in these verses 8-10. And that is where it says gifts in verse 9.

1 Corinthians 12:9
…to another the gifts of healing by the same Spirit;

We have just read in verse 7 that these nine are what? Manifestations. And yet there is one manifestation which is called a "gift." Now this has really confused them! But this is the only manifestation that is a gift. And it is the manifestation of what? Healing. All healing is a gift. Every healing is a gift. No matter when you get healed, or how or why, every time you get healed it's a gift to you! It's a gift from God, and if a man is ministering to you, it's a gift from God through the ministry of that man. That's the only manifestation that's a gift. It's a manifestation that I operate in ministering healing, and I give healing to you and you receive it. Remember Peter at the Temple gate called Beautiful with John? He said to the crippled man:

Acts 3:6b
…such as I have [what?] give I thee: In the name of Jesus Christ of Nazareth rise up and walk.

Every healing is a gift. Now back in Corinthians it says "gifts of healing." Why is it gifts (in the plural) of healing? Because in God's mercy and in God's grace, you get healed, let's say, of the cause of a headache tonight.

That's a gift to you. Now, you continue to live the same way after tonight as you did before. Eat the same baloney or argue with the same man or woman. Then next week you get that "blessed headache" again, and it's just excruciating. So you come back and you get ministered to, and you get healed again. That is twice of the same sickness; that's why it is gifts (with the "s" on it). When you're healed of the same disease twice, it is gifts (plural). That's why it's in here. Whenever you are healed of two different diseases, it is healings (plural). Understand? You get healed of one disease, then you get healed of another, that's why it's healings in the plural. Then it will be gifts of healings, both plural. That's why it's used as a gift.

Do you have any questions on Chapter 12, verses 1 through 11? Or have I covered it from every angle? There is a literal translation of verse 11 in my book[27] which reads, *"But all these nine manifestations of holy spirit in a believer are produced and energized by the one Spirit, distributing to every man his own, and in the effects produced, as the man wills."* [28]

Aren't those tremendous verses? A lot in there. All of those.

Now, from 1 Corinthians 12:12-27, all you have from verse 12 to 27 is an illustration of what he has just told us, in those first few verses. Where he uses the illustration of the human body, to present the same truths as he has just taught us about the spiritual body, which he set forth in those first eleven verses. I believe you should be able to see so clearly, because here you are one body. Your hand is part of the body. Your fingers are part of the body. Your eyes are part of the body. Your ears are part of the body. You wouldn't like to do without any part of that body, would you? Yet it's one body, and yet all

---

27. See also *Receiving the Holy Spirit Today*, seventh edition, p. 153.
28. A literal translation according to usage 1 Corinthians 12:11.

these have different functions, different parts to play, and yet that makes up one body. So is the church. And we'll begin reading with verse 12.

> **1 Corinthians 12:12-15**
> For as the body is [what?] one, and hath many members, and all the members of that one body, being many, are one body: so also is Christ.
> For by one Spirit are we all baptized into one [what?] body, whether *we be* Jews or Gentiles, whether *we be* bond or free; and have been [or were] all made to drink into one [what?] Spirit.
> For the body is not one member, but [what?] many.
> If the foot shall say, Because I am not the hand, I am not of the body; is it therefore not of the body?

This thing is really terrific spiritually! One Christian says, "Well I don't like the way you speak in tongues." Is he therefore not a part of the Body? Wow, what a lesson. It's in here so deep, it's just really tremendous.

> **1 Corinthians 12:16, 17a**
> And if the ear shall say, Because I am not the eye, I am not of the body; is it therefore not of the body?
> If the whole body *were* an eye, where [would be] the hearing?...

You see it? If everybody spoke in tongues only, where would be the interpretation? And all the manifestations, as well as the gift.

> **1 Corinthians 12:17b-19**
> ...If the whole *were* hearing, where *were* the smelling?
> But now hath God set the members every one of them in the body, as it hath [what?] pleased him.
> And if they were all one member, where *were* the body?

If they were all eyeballs wouldn't that be awful? One eyeball!

> **1 Corinthians 12:20-22**
> But now *are they* many members, yet but one body.
> And the eye cannot say unto the hand, I have no need of thee; nor again the head to the feet, I have no need of you.
> Nay, much more those members of the body, which seem to be more feeble, are [what?] necessary:

Wow, that's really something! Those members of your body which seem to be least important are many times most important. The smallest part of your body sometimes is very vulnerable, and when you hurt that it's just painful. Just take your eyeball. Your eyeball is not as big as your head, but look how sensitive your eye is compared to the head. If I hit my eye as hard as I hit my head, I'd maybe need the whole box of Kleenex to wipe the tears!

Verse 23.

> **1 Corinthians 12:23**
> And those *members* of the body, which we think to be less honourable, upon these we bestow more abundant honour; and our uncomely *parts* have more abundant comeliness.

The members we think less honorable, less important, in the matter of the operations of the manifestations. Sense knowledge wise what does everybody say is the least important? Speaking in tongues. And the Word of God says it's most important! You see, the less honorable are what? Just like the human body. He's taking the human body and just teaching you all those spiritual things right down the line.

> **1 Corinthians 12:24, 25a**
> For our comely *parts* have no need: but God hath tempered [put together] the body..., having given

more abundant honour [respect] to that *part* which [would be lacking sense knowledge wise].
That there should be no schism...

The schism is a break, a cut in the body.

1 Corinthians 12:25b, 26a
...but *that* the members should have [the same love, the same respect, the same wholesomeness] the same care one for another.
And whether one member suffer, all the members [what?] suffer...

Isn't that something? When you hurt your finger, the whole body is what? suffering. When one of you, my beloved people is hurt, the whole body is what? suffering. Look, we've never understood it, less believed. Because everybody thinks they can just go on their own merry way and everybody just does what they fool please! But we're fools and we can't please when we go that way. Why? Because we're members, one of another. And when one member hurts, everybody's hurt. When one of our people to whom I've taught the greatness of God's Word (like you people here), if you got sick, I'd feel bad. I sometimes think maybe it's because of my renewed mind and how I've trained myself. But, maybe this is also why God wants me to know many times. I wake up in the middle of the night and I know something's wrong.

I could wake up at four o'clock in the morning and maybe God shows me Thelma. Or maybe God shows me someone else. I know somebody's being hurt in the Body. When they're hurt, I'm hurt! When they're hurt, you're hurt! The same as if you'd take your finger and cut it off; the whole physical body would be hurt. It will finally heal over, but it will always leave a scar. And the Body of Christ, the church, is all scarred up. And I'd tell you they'll never get it unscarred the way they are going because they want the ecumenicity of all the denominations and that doesn't produce it. The Word of God says it's the unity of the spirit that does it. Not the unity of denominations. Somebody said that these people were "ecu-maniacs about ecumenicity"! But the whole body is hurt! Now this is something. Really something. Well, I'd like to tell you something but Father says, Shut up! So I'll do it. Well, bless the Lord!

Verse 27.

> **1 Corinthians 12:27**
> Now ye are the body of Christ, and [yet you are a member] members in particular [particular in that body].

Then are you important? Oh bless you're wonderful heart, you're important! We are members of the Body of Christ. We are the Body of Christ, the Church, but every person in that body is a particular member! Particular means unique. (Not particular that you clean the house properly. Not particular about what you wear. That's not the word "particular.") But you have one place that's your wonderful, big corner. That's your place where you serve God like God wants you to serve! Every member is a particular member, and without that member in there the Body is always hurting. This is why the Body is in such poor shape, it's hurting—all over.

Now, Verse 28 we shift. In Verse 28 we shift back to where we started in the early part of the chapter when we were talking about gifts and manifestations. Verses 12 to 27, he has given us an illustration. In Verse 28, we read:

> **1 Corinthians 12:28**
> And God hath set some in the church, first apostles, secondarily prophets, thirdly teachers, after that miracles, then gifts [*charismata*] of healings, helps, governments, diversities of tongues.

SPIRITUAL MATTERS 251

And so the old critics say, "You see God put diversities of tongues last, because it was least important." When they say that to you, you just hope and pray they're members of a family of a dozen and they're the youngest one in the family! Because the last is the least important! And you have that argument over with! No, no, no…God isn't that stupid! As a matter of fact even in plain English you use it many times, just the opposite. You write a letter and say, well now this is the last point I want to make, but let me remind you it's not the least important! So that's normal. Something has to be last! If you only have two kids, one came first, the other came last. I mean, something's got to be last! So, diversities of tongues happens to be last here.

Now, I've done a literal translation of Verse 28 in my book that is just the simplest thing and it's the only accurate thing that I know. This is recorded on page 163 of the Fifth Edition, at the bottom of the page:[29] *"So God has placed some in the Church having the ministry of apostles, prophets, and teachers. There are some who minister more effectively as miracle workers, some who are very effective in ministering the blessings of healings, some who are very adept in ministering as helps and governments, and some whose ministry is diversity of tongues."*[30] And that is the answer.

You see, there we're talking about some ministries. We're talking about some manifestations. We're talking about the operation of the manifestations in a believer in the whole operation of the church, where every member is a particular member. If, for instance you're going to help in the typing field in the church, you are to type with the operation of the nine manifestations, to do the job the best way. If you're going to sweep the rug, you sweep it

---

29. See also *Receiving the Holy Spirit Today*, seventh edition, p. 158.
30. A literal translation according to usage of 1 Corinthians 12:28.

operating nine manifestations of the spirit. If you're going to be in the government of the church, you operate in that government with the nine manifestations of the spirit.

So this is how the Body is knit together, and every member has a particular job and ministers effectively— whether he is an apostle or prophet. Or whether he's very adept at ministering in miracles and healing. Or, if he's adept in ministering helps and government. Or, if his ministry to the Body (horizontally) is diversities of tongues. The word "diversities" is the Greek word *genos*. That's where he shines! If it's just speaking in tongues like some of us speak, we don't have a *genos* of tongues, we just have a "species." A *genos* is the top echelon. Look, when that person speaks in tongues and interprets in a believers' meeting, you've had it! They just shine! That's the word *genos*.

Now, Verse 29. First of all you will note that the word "*Are*" is in italics. You'll note the question marks were not in the original texts, right? Therefore, you could read it as follows: "All apostles, all prophets, all teachers, all workers of miracles, all have gifts of healing, all do speak with tongues, all do interpret." That would be real simple. But the problem is that in the critical Greek texts we have some negatives. And I don't know if they belong in the critical Greek texts or not, but they're sure in there. So, I have to put the question mark in sense knowledge wise from a grammatical point of view at least. But, it's still very simple to me. Very simple even when you leave it set in the King James.

1 Corinthians 12:29a
Are all apostles [in the church]? [No.]…

But that does not mean that there are not apostles in all the churches. Take the next one.

1 Corinthians 12:29b, 30a

...*are* all prophets [in the church]? [No.] *are* all teachers [in the church]? [No.] *are* all workers of miracles [in the church]? [No.]

Have all the gifts [*charismata*] of healing [in the church]? do all speak with tongues [in the church]?...

It doesn't say they couldn't all speak in tongues, does it? But the question is, *do* they all? The answer is what? No. They don't all speak in tongues *in the church*. Because, if this is the church tonight and you all spoke in tongues here and interpreted, we'd be here another hour yet! We would get nothing else done! That's why in the Word as you'll see later, when we get into Chapter 14, that he has limited speaking in tongues and interpretation to three speak in tongues and three interpret, in a believers' meeting.

1 Corinthians 12:30b

...do all interpret [in the church]? [No.]

But it doesn't mean they couldn't all speak in tongues and couldn't all interpret! That's all. That's all those verses mean.

Verse 31.

1 Corinthians 12:31

But covet earnestly the best gifts; and yet shew I unto you a more excellent way.

"Covet" means to earnestly desire. We are to earnestly desire the best gifts. Well, what are the best gifts? There are only five after you're born again. The gift of apostles, prophets, evangelists, teachers and pastors. Those are the only gifts, right? Now certainly the gift of a prophet is just as good as an apostle or a teacher or a pastor. Right? Therefore, the best gifts could not refer to the gift given, but to the usage of that gift, as a benefit in operation in the senses realm. For instance, if a community has mostly unbelievers, what gift would be the best gift for that particular community? An evangelist, right? But suppose, in this fellowship here now, certainly an evangelist would not be the best gift to you! Why? Because you're all born again! You don't have to get saved! You would need the ministry of a prophet, or an apostle, or a teacher, or a pastor. That could be beneficial to you, but certainly not the evangelist.

Then which is the best gift? It all depends on the need of the particular body at the place where that Body of Believers is located, or that body is to be located. So the best gift will be that which is best for them. So he said, "covet earnestly the best gifts: and yet I shew you a more excellent way." A more excellent way than coveting. Earnestly desiring. And that more excellent way is the one that is set forth in 1 Corinthians and we'll get to that. And when you operate that in 1 Corinthians, you don't have to covet anything. It all comes to you in its proper way and its proper time, just when you need it. That's the answer!

WHAT'S THE PROFIT

I just want to go over something that I neglected to finish the other evening. In verse 28, of 1 Corinthians 12, it says in the King James:

1 Corinthians 12:28
And God hath set some in the church, first apostles, secondarily prophets, thirdly teachers, after that miracles, then gifts of healings, helps, governments, diversities of tongues.

I believe I told you that the word "diversities" is the word *genos* in the Greek, right? *Genos*, which is the Greek word for our English word "genus." When we speak in biology of a genus, we're speaking of a category of life. Where like the bovine family is a genus. Inside of those cattle you have big cattle, little cattle, red cattle, black and white cattle, orange cattle, and this kind of thing. They are called "species." You have species, but the great characteristic is called the genus.

Now there are people who shine in speaking in tongues, let's say, and in interpretation in a believers' meeting. They have a real genus for this. Sometimes I speak of it and say, "They have a long suit." You've heard me use those words. That's what I mean.

Now this verse 28 is real difficult for people because of the way it is written in the King James. In my book on the Holy Spirit, *Receiving the Holy Spirit Today*, in the fifth edition, on page 163 at the bottom, I have given a literal translation according to usage, and this is much plainer, much clearer. I do not know what page this is on in the fourth edition.[1] If anybody knows, if you'll tell me, I'll tell everybody else here. It's a literal translation of verse 28, according to usage, would be: *"So God has placed some in the Church having the ministry of apostles, prophets, and teachers..."*[2] Now those three are gift ministries, this way down (vertical), *charismata* from God to man. But they are still ministries in the church. Do you understand? They may be gifts, this way down from God to man, but as man operates them they minister to God's people. They're ministries in the church, understand? So then, are these other manifestations of the spirit? The manifestations of the spirit are ministries in the church.

Verse 28, continued: *"...There are some who minister more effectively as miracle workers, some who are very effective in ministering the blessings of healing, and some who are very adept in ministering as helps, governments, and some whose ministry is diversity of tongues."*[3] You see, now that's a literal translation according to usage of that verse 28. Now this 1 Corinthians 12:28 is God's order for ministering in the Church Age, which is the age in which we are living. There is no passage of scripture in the Bible which nullifies this order for the Church, of which you and I are a part. As a matter of fact, there are two sections of the Word of God which augment and strengthen even this verse in 1 Corinthians, and those are the scriptures I'd like to cover with you tonight.

Ephesians, chapter 4, beginning with verse 8. Everybody have it?

Ephesians 4:8
Wherefore he saith, When he ascended up on high, he led captivity captive, and gave [what?] gifts unto men.

---

1. See also *Receiving the Holy Spirit Today*, seventh edition, p. 158.
2. A literal translation according to usage 1 Corinthians 12:28a.
3. A literal translation according to usage 1 Corinthians 12:28b.

He gave gifts unto men. This is a tremendous thing. You know, the word "gifts" here "gave gifts unto men," I want to put together for you and with you. When it's a gift of God to man, it's always perpendicular (God down to man) and it's always called a *charisma*. A *charisma* is a gift of God to man. This gift is always by grace. Now when God gives a gift to man and man takes God's gift and works it out on an horizontal level to mankind, this gift becomes a *dorea*. The Greek word *dorea* is the gift of God; the *charismata*, the gift of God which is by grace, manifested on an horizontal level to mankind as a *dorea*. The Latin edition of the Bible translates the word *dorea* as *beneficium*. And that is a wonderful translation of the word *dorea*. *Beneficium* is translated over into our English word as the word "benefit" from the Latin. Isn't that wonderful?

This just thrills my heart when I see how these things fit so beautifully. God gives these as gifts of grace, then man works it and they become benefits to what? Mankind. Now a man could have a gift this way (from God down to man) but if man never works it this way (on an horizontal level), it never gets to be a benefit to mankind. It's a tremendous thing! You see the word "gifts" in verse 8, of Ephesians here, is the Greek word *dorea* and as such they are benefits on an horizontal level to the church. The Greek word *charismata* is a gift of God by grace, in a perpendicular way, and not as a *dorea* or a *beneficium*. It's never a benefit on an horizontal plane, unless put into use, put into practice, operated by the believer.

Now people that is a tremendous thing! You know if it's in the devil spirit field, if it's from Satan, if something is given from Satan this way down, it's always possession. He possesses man. And then man has no freedom of will to carry it out; he automatically has to carry it out because Satan forces him to carry it out. Isn't that tremendous? But when it's from the true God, it's always a gift of grace, not of merit, it's always a *charisma* to man. It stops right here. Now man has freedom of will, and so man by his freedom of the will believes God's Word, and he carries out the gift, which God has given him by his free will, as a benefit to mankind.

You see this is why the *charismata* or the spiritual abilities as ministries of apostles, prophets, evangelists, teachers, and pastors are here referred to as *dorea*. Because these men have carried out or are carrying out their ministry in the church, then they become *dorea*. That's why it's used *dorea, beneficium*. We're going to read it, and the reason I know this is because it says it's for the benefit of the Body of Believers, to build them up. Well, we'd better read from verse 8 on and then it will all fit for you. In Ephesians 4, verses 9 and 10 are in a parenthesis. You see it?

> **Ephesians 4:9-11**
> (Now that he ascended, what is it but that he also descended first into the lower parts of the earth?
> He that descended is the same also that ascended up far above all heavens, that he might fill all things.)
> And he gave some, apostles; and some, prophets; and some, evangelists; and some, pastors and teachers;

Used this way in the critical Greek texts, the only answer I know, and I think it's logical and fits the text and the accuracy with which the word is used, not everybody is an apostle. But when God gives the gift ministry of an apostle, then some in the body of the church worldwide will have the ministry of an apostle. Some will be prophets. Some evangelists. And some pastors and teachers. Every pastor has to be able to teach. But not every teacher needs to be a pastor. That's why it's written as it is here in this verse.

Now in the next verse, it gives you the purpose for these gift *charismata* ministries in operation as *beneficium* or *dorea*.

> **Ephesians 4:12a**
> For the [what?] perfecting of the saints,...

For the perfecting of them. Now, this perfecting, can that be in the spirit? No! Because when you're born again of God's spirit, how perfect are you? Perfect spiritually. Therefore this perfecting can only be where? in the mind, the renewed mind of the Body of Believers. That's where it is. For their perfecting. Understand?

> **Ephesians 4:12b**
> ...for the work of the ministry, for the edifying [the building up]...

The word "edifying" means building up, of the what?

> **Ephesians 4:12c**
> ...the body of Christ.

To build them up that the church people are strong in Christ, that they know the Word and are able to walk on it.

How long will these gift ministries be here? Next verse tells you. "Until" or "till" is the King James, old English. Until we what?

> **Ephesians 4:13**
> Till we all come in the unity of the faith, and of the knowledge of the Son of God, unto a perfect man, unto the measure of the stature of the fulness of Christ:

And we never get unto the perfect man, unto the measure of the stature of the fullness of Christ, until what? His return. Christ's return. When we shall be fashioned like unto his glorious body, remember all those scriptures now? Then we will see him face to face. We're going to hit that one later on tonight. But, until that time, God has put into the church: apostles, prophets, evangelists, pastors and teachers for the perfecting of the body. Then these five ministries are the ruling ministries in the church. These are the five ministries that rule God's body, God's people, God's church! And these five ministries will be in the body until Christ's return! That the body may be edified, built up, strengthened. The reason is given also in the next verse.

Ephesians 4:14a
That we *henceforth* be no more [what?] children,...

You know when you're first born again of God's spirit you're a what? You're a child. You're a son of God but you're a child in the experience. Now, suppose you never have any accurate teaching on God's Word. You will never grow up. You'll always be a baby! And this is why we've got mostly babies. Because we have no teaching accurately on God's Word. You see to get born again, do you need to know God's Word? No. No, no, no. You don't even have to know Genesis is in the Bible. You don't even have to believe in the virgin birth. You don't even have to believe in lots of things. The Bible says there are two things you have to do. What? Confess with your mouth the Lord Jesus and believe in your heart that God raised him from the dead. As long as you do that, do you have to know any Bible? No! That's why. People get born again, and most of them don't know anything about the Word. And naturally, if they don't know anything about it, and if they're not in a fellowship, or a teaching ministry where the Word is taught, they'll forever just stay born, that's all. They won't know anything else. They'll just be little babies, and they'll get tossed to and fro, as that verse says, with every wind of doctrine, and finally somebody gets strong enough and says, "Well you're a

Methodist till you die," so you're a Methodist till you die. And somebody else says, "Well you're a Lutheran till you die," so they're Lutheran till they die. They don't know anything about God's Word, but they are Methodist till they die.

You see, this is remarkable!

But, these ministries were given that the church, the Body of Believers, should not be children; they ought to grow up! Full grown men and women, spiritually. And that they're not:

Ephesians 4:14b
…tossed to and fro, and carried about with every wind of doctrine, by the sleight of men, *and* cunning craftiness, whereby they lie in wait to deceive;

You see how this section from Ephesians, really makes that verse 28 in Corinthians live? Romans 12 does the same thing.

Turn to Romans, chapter 12. These verses from Ephesians and that one from Corinthians, are in essence the same as from Romans 12:4, where were going to read in a moment. They're the same *charismata*, spiritual abilities, given by God to man, becoming *dorea* or *beneficium* ministries in the church on an horizontal level, as the believers operate them.

Chapter 12 of Romans, from verse 4 on. I wish you'd remember this because this is really something! Chapter 12 of Romans from verse 4 on, gives the operator and the believer of the ministries special instruction, not only as to the ministries, but as to the conduct his own life should have in the operation of the ministry. So some time just sit down and read from Romans 12:4 on, through the rest of the book, and then do it exactly! It gives the operator, or the one who has these ministries, the "how to" use these ministries and what kind of a life he must live, or she must live, to operate it. Verse 4.

Romans 12:4
For as we have many members in one body, and all members have not the same office:

Sounds just like reading 1 Corinthians 12, doesn't it?

Romans 12:5-8
So we, *being* many, are one body in Christ, and every one members one of another.
Having then gifts differing according to the grace that is given to us, whether prophecy, *let us prophesy* according to the proportion of [what?] faith;
Or ministry, *let us wait* on *our* ministering: or he that teacheth, on teaching;
Or he that exhorteth on exhortation: he that giveth, *let him do it* with simplicity; he that ruleth, with diligence; he that sheweth mercy, with cheerfulness.

Now that's King James. On page 166 of the fifth edition,[4] I have given you a literal translation according to usage, which again makes these verses remarkably enlightening!

The third paragraph from the bottom on page 166 says: In Romans 12:4 the word "office" means "function" on an horizontal level: "*All members in the body have not the same function [on a horizontal level].*"[5]

Romans 12:6 is translated as follows: "*You, then, in the Church, having charismata, spiritual abilities and functions, differing according to the divine favor or friendly willingness of God that is given you, if it be a ministry of prophecy, keep busy ministering by [doing what?] prophesying according to the proportion of your believing faith.*"[6]

---

4. Seventh edition, p. 161.
5. A literal translation according to usage of Romans 12:4.
6. A literal translation according to usage of Romans 12:6.

There it is. You see you never prophesy beyond what you believe. You never speak in tongues beyond your believing. If you believe you can speak in tongues, you can, and you'll interpret, but be it unto you according to your believing. Dividing to every man as he what? will! See, in believing. So if you have a ministry of prophesying, get busy ministering in what field? in your prophecy field. Giving a word of prophecy. If that's your long suit, the Word says get busy and use it! According to your believing faith.

Romans 12:7 on page 167: *"Or if you have another type of ministry, get busy ministering; or if your ministry is teaching, get busy teaching; or if you have an exhortation ministry, get busy exhorting."* [7]

Romans 12:8 should now begin: *"He that giveth forth in any ministry in the Church let him do it with simplicity; he that has a ruling ministry,..."* This is in the church. *"...let him do it with diligence; and he that has a ministry making him very adept in mercy, let him do it with cheerfulness."* [8] And all the instructions following these verses are on behavior, and that is, conduct.[9]

Perhaps, I ought to just show you Romans 13. I taught on this a number of weeks ago one night. Romans, chapter 13.

Romans 13:1
Let every soul be subject unto [what?]...higher powers....

The commentaries all say this is governmental power, secular world power. But it isn't! In the context of Chapter 12, what are we reading about? the ministries, the ruling ministries in the church, of apostles, prophets,

---

7. A literal translation according to usage of Romans 12:7.
8. A literal translation according to usage of Romans 12:8.
9. Seventh edition, pp. 161, 2.

evangelists, pastors and teachers. So let every soul, the people that are members of the body, let them be subject unto the higher powers. What higher powers? The church ruling ministries in the church, they're the higher powers!

> **Romans 13:1b, 2a**
> ...For there is no power [no ruling ministry (apostle, prophet, evangelist, pastor or teacher) but that it came from who?] but of God: the powers that be [in the church, these ruling ministries] are ordained [or called] of God.
> Whosoever therefore [in the church] resisteth the power [of these ruling ministries], resisteth the ordinance of God:...

Why? Because God put these ministries in the church that the church may receive what? edifying. Right! That they may be built up for the perfecting of the saints, for the work of the ministry. Remember?

> **Romans 13:2b**
> ...and they that resist shall receive to themselves damnation [judgment].

Judgment is the text, not damnation. It's judgment. And that's simply that they will not be rewarded properly.

> **Romans 13:3, 4**
> For rulers [these men with ministries in the body of apostles and so forth] are not a terror to good works, but [they are a terror to what?] to...evil [evil works]. Wilt thou then not be afraid [or respectful is the text, have awe and reverence] of the power [for this authority, this power which God has given in the church]? do that which is good [in the body], and thou shalt have praise of the same:
> For he is the minister of [what?] God to thee for good....

Isn't that plain as day? Isn't it wonderful too? You could never say that Hitler, Stalin, and a lot of others were men of God. And that every soul had to be subject unto them because they were "higher powers." It can only be for those inside of the church.

Now people, God in His foreknowledge knows when people are going to believe. He knows what men and what women will operate, or those who won't. He knows all this in His foreknowledge. This is why we have very few ministries in the so-called church today, because the so-called church is just playing church. They're not really the church. And there's very little believing and so we have very few prophets, apostles, evangelists, teachers and pastors to perfect God's people today, because there is no believing. Why should God give us the ministry of an apostle in our midst for instance, when He knows before time that that man will never carry out his ministry? God would be stupid, wouldn't He? And God isn't stupid. God doesn't give them then, He just doesn't give them. God can only give when men are willing to receive and the man makes himself willing by his own believing, which God knows before the foundation of the world. And therefore, he either has these ministries or he does not have them.

Remember in the Old Testament, there was a period of 400 years where there was not a prophet of God in the world! Malachi was the last one until Jesus Christ. That was a dark age, wasn't it? It's almost as dark today. So these ministries are few and far between. Because, these ministries are what the Word of God says they are, and they produce what the Word of God says they produce, and when these ministries are in manifestation among God's people, they will be in manifestation because there is believing there, and there are men and women who absolutely will not budge on God's Word.

Absolutely not! Well, I wanted to teach you that from Ephesians and Romans.

Now we go to 1 Corinthians, chapter 13. In verse 31 of Chapter 12, it says:

1 Corinthians 12:31a
...covet earnestly the best gifts:...

And I taught this to you. How all of God's gifts are perfect. Therefore the best gifts can only refer to the place where certain ministries are desperately needed, like the ministry of an apostle or a prophet or evangelist or pastor or teacher.

1 Corinthians 12:31b
...and yet shew I unto you a more excellent way [than earnestly desiring them or coveting them].

And the more excellent way is the way of 1 Corinthians 13, which is the love of God. There are two words that are translated "love" and one of those words is the word *phileō*. *Phileō* is simply brotherly love, like the city of Philadelphia. It means "city of brotherly love." Philadelphia is from *phileō*. This is the old philosophy that you scratch my back, I'll scratch yours. You vote for me, I'll vote for you. You vote for my program when it comes up in the government, and I'll vote with your program now. See this is the old *phileō*. The other one is the word *agapeō*. *Agapeō* is the love of God given this way down (God to man). It's the love of God this way down.

A man can have *phileō* love before he is born again. But he cannot have *agapeō* love. That's like hate. No man can have hate except he is born again of Satan's seed. You see, when a person is born again of Satan, that person has hate. While if a person is born again of the true God, that person has *agapeō* love. This is why hate is of the spirit and *agapeō* love is of the spirit. No man can have hate —I'm telling you accurately, biblically, even if you don't understand it, it's still true. No man can have hate, except he is born of the seed of the serpent. We say in our society, "Well, Maggie Muggins hated what so and so did." But if Maggie Muggins hated literally, she'd have to be born of the seed of the serpent, which some people are. But this man over here, the natural man has neither hate nor what? the love of God. But this man has *phileō* love. And it's real wonderful.

Sometimes I tell you, I've seen more good in *phileō* love, than I've seen in Christians who have been born again of God's spirit. Even though they have the love of God in here, they operate very little. Because there's a tremendous thing here. You can be loaded spiritually, right? Remember this illustration? You can be loaded spiritually, but it takes the free will of man to believe it and put it this way. So let's say this man's born again of God's spirit, he has love in here, in the inner man. Will it come forth? No. Not unless this man does one thing, what? Operates it! Now, how's he going to operate it unless he puts it where? in his mind. That's 1 Corinthians 13. It's as simple as that! Anything that you can put on, that you can operate, has to be in the works of man, right? Salvation is not of works, it is of what? grace. And when we're born again of God's spirit we have the love of God, we have the peace of God, we have His justification, we have His righteousness, we have His sanctification, all of that; but we have it where? in the inner man, in the spirit!

Now after I'm born again, I have to renew my what? mind. Which means that I'm transformed up here (the mind) according to the image which God created in here (the body). I gave you all this in the Foundational Class. So, it's the love of God, the amount of the love of God, in the renewed mind that we put on up here that comes into manifestation. And that's why every time in the Bible, when you read the word "charity" in the King

James, or you read the word "love" in another translation, if it's the word *agapeō*, if it's what God does this way down (God to man), it's a *charismata*. A gift of God's grace. If it is what man does, works, it's always a benefit to mankind because it's in the renewed mind category. That's why charity is always "the love of God, in the renewed mind, in evidence, in manifestation." 1 Corinthians 13:1.

1 Corinthians 13:1a
Though I [what?] speak…

Who does the speaking? I do. Are you possessed? No. If it was possession, he would do the speaking. But it's like I teach you in the class, God gives you the ability, you do what? carry it out. I speak with tongues of men and of what? angels. And have not charity, have not the love of God in the renewed mind, in manifestation. Understand? If I'm born again of God's spirit, I've got the love of God in the inner man, haven't I? But, it's not talking about the inner man here; it's talking about my walk. It's about my speaking, not God's speaking. I speak with the tongues of men and of angels. And every time you speak in tongues, you're either speaking the tongues of men or the tongues of angels. If it's the tongues of men, then what you are speaking, could it be understood someplace here upon earth? Definitely! If it's the tongues of angels, no deal upon this earth.

1 Corinthians 13:1
Though I speak with the tongues of men and of angels, and have not charity [the love of God, in the renewed mind, in manifestation], I am become *as* sounding brass, or a tinkling cymbal.

I am doing it. Is there anything wrong with speaking in tongues and interpretation? No. But it's me! You see, this is why many people may speak in tongues, but they haven't got the love of God in the renewed mind. And not having the love of God in the renewed mind, their speaking in tongues is genuine, but they are nothing but sounding brass, or tinkling cymbal. They are nothing. Nothing wrong with their speaking in tongues, the speaking in tongues is still genuine. It's still kosher. It's still right!

But, what's the matter with them? They're out of alignment and harmony because they have not renewed their minds according to the Word of God, and put on the love of God in the renewed mind. And this is why it does not profit them! And any time any of the manifestations, or the ministries, do not profit the person ministering, it's always wrong. Because the person ministering must be profited! Remember that every manifestation is to what? profit withal. And the way it profits the person ministering (and this is the only way it profits the person ministering) is that the person ministering ministers with the love of God in the renewed mind.

And people, please remember that if you're mad some night and you're "out in left field," and you "hate" your wife or your husband ("hate" in quotes to use my terminology accurately here), or if you're off the beaten track, and somebody says, "Well you want to minister?" Then you say "No way, I don't!" Why? Because of what you're giving out anyways, at that moment. It won't profit you any because you're out of alignment and harmony. Do you understand?

That's why when you speak in tongues and interpret in a believers' meeting, you should be hotter than a firecracker, when you do it! In other words, get up and give it with the love of God in the renewed mind because you know how it will bless God's people, including you! And it will always be a profit to you, as well as the hearer. If

I speak with the tongues of men and of angels, but if I do not have the love of God in the renewed mind in manifestation, the speaking in tongues profits me nothing. I become as a sounding brass or as a tinkling cymbal. That's what it says, that's what it means!

1 Corinthians 13:2a
And though I have *the gift of* prophecy,...

"...*the gift of*" is in italics, right? Scratch it out. It makes the whole Word of God fall to pieces. Isn't that something how they could put those things in there and rack and ruin the Word! "And though I have prophecy." We're talking in verse 1 about speaking in what? tongues. And in verse 2 about what? prophecy. Not the *gift* of prophecy, were talking about the *manifestation*. Right? Right.

1 Corinthians 13:2b
...and understand all mysteries,...

If I understood the mystery, I'd have to get it from one or the other of two sources, either by my working of the Word of God or by revelation.

1 Corinthians 13:2c
...and all knowledge [word of knowledge]; and though I have all faith [all faith is the manifestation of what? faith], so that I could remove mountains,...

This is the reason I know that story in Mark, you know, that I always teach in the Foundational Class(go say to that mountain, go jump in the lake, cast into the sea) has to be the manifestation because this is exactly what this corroborates here in 1 Corinthians 13:2.

1 Corinthians 13:2d
...and have not charity [the love of God in the renewed mind in manifestation],...

Prophecy is no good. Word of knowledge is no good. Faith is no good….No, no, no, no! There's nothing wrong with them, it's what? Something wrong with me! Right? You've got to get that! Look, if I were charming a cobra tonight (dangling it around my neck, kissing it) and if I were speaking in tongues, would the speaking in tongues be genuine? Yes! But it would profit what? me nothing. In essence, I would have not renewed my mind according to the love of God. Look, you've got to get it! That's the greatness of 1 Corinthians 13. Nothing wrong with the manifestations, but it profits me nothing for I am nothing! *I* am nothing—me! Look, suppose I sat up here tonight with two pints of whiskey in my hip pocket, one on each side, and I was drunk as a new boot! And if I spoke in tongues and interpreted, would it be genuine? Yes, but I would be out of alignment and harmony because I have not renewed my mind nor have the love of God in the renewed mind, and it would profit what? me nothing! That's it! That's the whole key. When I learned this lesson in my quest, things got real easy.

Because then I could separate out the guys throwing hymnals at each other; they got involved in the spirit, you know. They got all excited about spiritual things. So a fellow one night took himself a hymnal in the third row and threw it in the back, and I ducked! That's right. I was glad I had been an athlete, because I learned how to duck some of those things. The spirit was helping him to throw these things! He was real excited! Well, then I learned it wasn't the holy spirit at all. But when that fellow spoke in tongues, his speaking in tongues was genuine. But his little old song book throwing is not in the category of the renewed mind with the love of God. For if he'd had the love of God in his mind, all things would have been done decently and in order. That's right.

We aren't finished with the love of God in the renewed mind. You're going to get it from now until we go home after this session because it's written all through Chapter 13, and all through Chapter 14. Because people, every manifestation has to profit you, if you're really going to operate. Because, otherwise you're short changed. And God never allows His people to be short changed! Because if you would give your tithe to the ministry and God did not give it back to you, either in plain cash plus interest, or in some other way that it would pay it off, you would have been better off keeping your tithes to begin with; you would have been further ahead! Well that can't be true because then it makes God a liar! Therefore, the key lies in the love of God in the renewed mind in manifestation.

Verse 3.

> **1 Corinthians 13:3a**
> And though I bestow all my goods to feed *the poor* [and "the poor" is right, the people who have need], and though I give my body to be burned,...

This is a figure of speech saying, you just give everything you have, you lay it on the altar, you don't rust out, you'd rather burn out by doing something.

> **1 Corinthians 13:3b**
> ...[but if I] have not charity [the love of God in the renewed mind], it profiteth [what?] me nothing.

But, would it profit the other fellow if he was starving to death and you gave him a thousand dollars? No. It wouldn't profit you any. You see you'd be the loser. And you can't afford to be a loser because God just doesn't want you to lose. He wants the love of God in the renewed mind. If you've got the love of God in the renewed mind, you give your goods to the poor, and then it will bless you! Understand? That's what he's talking about.

Verse 4.

1 Corinthians 13:4a
Charity [the love of God in the renewed mind] suffereth long,...

It means you put up with people a long time. That's right. The love of God—now by the way, well I'll have to read it to you.

1 Corinthians 13:4b
...*and* is kind; charity [the love of God in the renewed mind] envieth not [It doesn't envy anyone.]; charity [the love of God in the renewed mind] vaunteth not itself,...

Vaunteth not itself. Do you know what that "vaunteth" means? Give me a synonym for it. It's in the field of bragging, trying to put on airs when you haven't got any. This kind of thing.

Verse 5, you see the love of God in the renewed mind:

1 Corinthians 13:5a
Doth not behave itself [what?] unseemly,...

That is tremendous! Doesn't behave itself unseemly. And this unseemly is exactly what it says. You know, there are scriptures in the Bible they get all upset about, women cutting their hair, and all the rest of the stuff, and we are not to wear any gold (something or other I forget); it's in Timothy or some place. They get all shook up! The essence is right here. If you have the love of God, in the renewed mind, neither man nor woman ever does that which behaves itself, what? unseemly. That's right. Therefore, a Christian believer always behaves himself according to that accepted custom and well-being of the Body of Believers in the area in which he functions. And this varies.

In some sections of the country that I've been, where I have ministered, men would come to the services with their overalls on. Their work shoes, their overalls, their jackets. At other sections, like for instance where I'm ministering at this time, this would be entirely unseemly, in this section of our country. Now, do you understand what I mean? Now if I'm down in a section of a country where they all drink tea, you know what I'd drink? tea. This is the walk of the love of God in the renewed mind —this is the walk of love of God in the renewed mind! Now suppose you don't like tea? "DRINK IT!!"[10] Renew your mind! This is the way you live. Now this is tremendous! Isn't that wonderful? The love of God in the renewed mind.

Verse 5 continued.

1 Corinthians 13:5b
...seeketh not her own, is not easily provoked,...

It doesn't get upset easily. But it doesn't say you *never* get upset! It said a little while ago, "it suffereth" what? "long"—that's right! But, the love of God in the renewed mind finally reaches the place where it looks at people and says, "You old whited sepulcher, you hypocrite!" How far have you gone? You can answer this yourself any time you want to. Just how far have you gone in thinking evil of others? For instance, somebody said to you, "Well, Maggie Muggins was with Herman Baloko last night at the drug store at 11:30. I wonder what they did?" Thinketh no, what?

1 Corinthians 13:5c
...thinketh no evil;

When you have renewed your mind according to the Word of God and have put on here (in your mind), the

---

10. Dr. Wierwille emphatically yells to the audience.

love of God in the renewed mind in manifestation, you get to that place in your life where you no longer think evil of people! You just don't think evil. It's just as easy to think good of people. Do you know it? Maybe Herman Baloko was with Maggie Muggins at 11:30 at the drug store because there was a tremendous need, there was something God wanted. You see, we're brought up in a society where instead of thinking positively, instead of thinking right, we're always taught to think wrongly. Think the worst! Why? Why don't you think the best of people? Why think the worst? This is the love of God in the renewed mind. And when we have the love of God in the renewed mind, we have to covet nothing, earnestly desire nothing. Why? Because the love of God in the renewed mind will bring to us everything that we could possibly need, at the time we need it!

Verse 6, the love of God in the renewed mind:

> **1 Corinthians 13:6**
> Rejoiceth not in iniquity, but rejoiceth in [what?] the truth;

There are some people who just get a kick out of it every time there's something wrong, or something happens to somebody that hurts that somebody; they feel real good about it. They're glad that you got caught in the rain! They're glad that your old building blew over and that it wasn't theirs! But you see, the love of God in the renewed mind rejoices not in any evil, any iniquity that happens to anybody else. But it rejoices in the truth!

Verse 7, the love of God in the renewed mind:

> **1 Corinthians 13:7a**
> Beareth all things [beareth all things according to God's Word], [and] believeth all things [according to God's Word],…

"Believeth all things" doesn't mean you believe every blessed lie people tell. Oh no! You believe according to God's what? Word. Amen.

> **1 Corinthians 13:7b**
> ...hopeth all things, endureth all things [now "all" is according to God's Word].

Verse 8.

> **1 Corinthians 13:8a**
> Charity [the love of God in the renewed mind, what?] never faileth:...

That's right. See, this love of God in the renewed mind, it just does not fail. It just lives on top of the heap. It just lives abundantly. It just lives dynamically.

> **1 Corinthians 13:8b**
> ...but whether...prophecies [word of prophecy], they shall fail [cease]; whether...tongues, they shall cease; whether...knowledge, it shall vanish away.

The word "fail" means cease. Here we're talking about the manifestations. There's a day coming when prophecies will be no more. When tongues with interpretation will be no more. See, because it says tongues, they shall what? cease. Now the critics, they have used this verse and said that tongues ceased with the dying of the apostles, for instance (like many of the commentaries teach), and that these manifestations went out at that time. They absolutely could not be right! Because, if they went out at that time, they would not have had the knowledge to know they went out! Because the same verse of scripture that says, "tongues shall cease" says that knowledge shall what? "vanish away." And if knowledge vanished away, then how did they know tongues ceased? Right? There's a time coming of course when they'll cease, disappear and we'll show you when.

Verse 9.

1 Corinthians 13:9a
For [now]…

Right now, you know being sons of God, born again of God's spirit, with the love of God in the renewed mind, operating manifestations.

1 Corinthians 13:9b
…we know in part, and we prophesy in part.

With all the operation of the word of knowledge, the word of wisdom, and the discerning of spirits, we still only know a part! And when we give a word of prophecy, we don't prophesy everything! We only prophesy a what? part—that which is needed at that particular time among God's particular people at that moment.

Verse 10, "But," here it's set in contrast.

1 Corinthians 13:10
But when that which is perfect is come, then [then, not now but then, then!] that which is in part shall be [what?] done away.

Wow, isn't that verse plain? Now he gives an illustration for verse 10 and what he's just taught us.

Verse 11.

1 Corinthians 13:11
When I was a child, I spake as a child, I understood as a child, I thought as a child: but [in contrast] when I became a man, I put away childish things.

The manifestations are just like toys for kids. Toys for children. You know, speaking in tongues is just like a toy for a child! Interpretation, prophecy, word of knowledge, word of wisdom. "When I was a child, I spake as a child, understood as a child, I thought as a child, but when I became a man, I put away [what?] childish things." And it said a little while ago, there is a time coming when the prophecies shall cease, tongues shall cease, and word of knowledge shall vanish away. There's a time coming, but it says this will not come until "…that which is perfect is come, then that which is in part shall be done away." [11]

Now, Verse 12.

> **1 Corinthians 13:12a**
> For now [even though we operate word of knowledge, tongues and the rest of it] we see through a glass, darkly;…

With all these manifestations and the greatness of this wonderful evidence among God's people, it's still just like looking through a glass darkly; "but then," then, then is time, when? He returns (for the perfect is come). We shall what?

> **1 Corinthians 13:12b**
> …but then face to face:…

We shall see him face to face. That's right!

> **1 Corinthians 13:12c**
> …now I know in part; but then [when I see him face to face, when the perfect is come, then] shall I know even as also I am known.

How long are the manifestations going to be here? until Christ's Return. Just as long as the gift ministries of apostles, prophets, evangelists, teachers and pastors are going to be here. Wow, that's tremendous!

Verse 13.

> **1 Corinthians 13:13**
> And now [right now inside of the church among God's wonderful Body of Believers] abideth faith, hope, charity [the love of God in the renewed mind],

---

11. 1 Corinthians 13:10.

these three; but the greatest of these [inside of the church among God's people is what?] *is* charity [the love of God, in the renewed mind, in manifestation].

The word "faith" is the word "believing." Every time this is used in the Bible in its proper setting, it's used regarding something that you can believe for now and receive. Hope is always used in the Bible regarding something which you believe for, not now but in the future. That's why we have "faith" for the new birth now. We have "hope" for the return of Christ. Why? Because you can get born again now, but you cannot have the return of Christ now, because he has not yet come. That's why the Bible says, we hope for his return. Understand? It's always used like that. "Hope" is always used regarding that which you cannot have now, but which you can have in the future. This is the word "hope." So then when people come to be ministered to and I say to them, do you think God will do it? They say "I hope." You might as well send them back to their chair. Because they couldn't get it when? Now. They're looking forward in the future! If you hope for something, you can't get it now. Hope is always future. Faith is always now. And the love of God in the renewed mind activates both our faith and our hope!

That's the great 1 Corinthians 13. And how many, many times don't they take the thirteenth chapter out of its context. They preach and teach on the thirteenth chapter, but never touch the twelfth and the fourteenth. And unless you understand 12 and 14, 13 is absolutely meaningless! Because 13 is sandwiched in between 12 and 14. Had God not wanted the thirteenth chapter there, you know where He would have put it? Where He wanted it! It is exactly where God wanted it! (Now I don't mean just the thirteenth chapter, I'm using it as an illustration. He, God, is not responsible for making a chapter. But that's it right there.) You put it any other place in the Bible, and your Bible would fall to pieces! This is why you must understand all the chapters before, and all the chapters that come after, but especially 12 and 14, because 13 just sits like the meat between the sandwich! And it's the love of God in the renewed mind that pays off, for the profit to God's believers operating manifestations of the spirit.

1 Corinthians 14 is the only chapter in the Bible discussing the use and misuse of the worship manifestations of the spirit, namely speaking in tongues, interpretation of tongues and prophecy. And the reason for this is like I gave you at the opening sessions, or when I talked to you once about Corinthians being addressed to God's people, because of the practical error that had crept into the church, due to the failure of adhering to the great revelation that's given in the Book of Romans.

Verse 1.

> **1 Corinthians 14:1a**
> Follow after charity [the love of God in the renewed mind], and desire spiritual *gifts*,…

The word "gifts" again is wrong. It's *pneumatikos*, things of the spirit.

> **1 Corinthians 14:1b**
> …but rather that ye may [what?] prophesy [in the church].

Now, this is what you have to understand. Corinthians is addressed to the church. I read this to you from Chapter 1, verse 2, the other day. Prophecy, in the church, is given in the language of the body of the people present. If this is an English congregation then a word of prophecy will be in what? English. If this was a German congregation, it would be in what? German. And it's a message from God or for God, to God's people in the language of the body of the people.

If everybody is a believer, which is true here tonight and if this was not a teaching center, like where I am teaching, but if this was just a believers' meeting, then the one thing that would happen here would be, we would have only prophecy. (The reason I use tongues with interpretation so much is because this happens to be a teaching center.) No one would speak in tongues and interpret because speaking in tongues and interpretation is designed for something else. Then where everybody is a complete believer, instructed believer and fully knowing believer, prophecy is for a Body of Believers where everybody is fully instructed and knows the score and is operating. Then you use prophecy. Direct. Why speak in tongues and interpret if prophecy will give it to you? Because, you're speaking in tongues isn't necessary with fully instructed believers. You just give it in prophecy and have it over with! That's the greatness of it.

Verse 2.

1 Corinthian 14:2a
For he that speaketh in an *unknown* tongue…

Now the word "*unknown*" is in italics. If you speak in a tongue it's always unknown to you the speaker.

1 Corinthian 14:2b
…he that speaketh in an…tongue [when he speaks in tongues] speaketh not unto men, but [he speaks to whom?] unto God: for no man understandeth *him*;…

"…*him*" is in italics. Scratch it out. Why? Because on the Day of Pentecost, in Acts 2, did they speak in tongues? Did those who spoke understand what they spoke? Nope! It was what to them? Unknown. But did the hearers understand what they spoke? That's why if you leave the word "him" in there, what happens to your Bible? Falls apart, right. But take that "him" out that they added and it fits like a hand in a glove: For he that speaketh in an tongue, speaks not unto men, but unto God: for no man understandeth. That is no man speaking in tongues does what? Understands what he speaks! If he understood what he spoke, it wouldn't be a tongue; it would be a known language to him.

> **1 Corinthians 14:2c**
> ...howbeit [for in spirit] in...spirit [in the gift operation] he speaketh mysteries.

"...mysteries" is divine secrets, to whom? he and God. And class that's why when you speak in tongues, you and "Daddy" talk things over this way (up and down) divine secrets. God feeds your spirit this way (up and down); Satan can't get his nose in it! Satan can't get his nose in it—the only manifestation he can't. You're speaking divine secrets, you and Daddy! Talking things over this way (up and down). God's feeding your spirit, He is spirit feeding it back to you; Satan can't get in. It's a tremendous thing.

Verse 3, "But"—now here it's set in contrast.

> **1 Corinthians 14:3a**
> But he that prophesieth speaketh unto men...

You don't speak to God when you prophesy. When you speak in tongues you speak to whom? God. But when you prophesy it's in the language of the what? the body of the people present. Everybody can understand and therefore when you prophesy, you're speaking to whom? men. "...*to* edification." The word "*to*" is in italics again.

> **1 Corinthians 14:3b**
> ...speaketh unto men...edification,...

Edification means building up. Building up. To build up. We talk about having a big "edifice," a big house. Called a big edifice. Now, in prophecy people are edified by two things: exhortation and comfort. Look, there's the big house![12] A great house. There's the "edifice." There's the edifice. But to get the edifice you have to have some boards, blocks, or brick or something. Alright, the edifice, let's say is built up of brick. Now, the edifying is by exhortation or what? comfort. That's the accuracy with which that is used. Understand? Prophecy edifies. It builds big buildings, but it builds it by way of exhortation and comfort. Therefore, when you prophesy in a believers' meeting you will edify. Edify whom? the Body of Believers. Will you edify them in the spirit? Nope, in the mind, because I hear it with my ear balls! And I understand it because it's in what language? English. Therefore, you edify the mind. This is renewed mind then! It will help us to renew our mind. And you'll be edified by one of two things: exhortation or comfort. Usually it's a combination of both.

To exhort means to encourage toward a more worthy endeavor. In other words, to exhort simply means "get on the ball." Keep pitching. Keep walking. Keep manifesting. To comfort means to give quiet acquiescence to the Body of Believers. Quiet peace. Serenity. Now, just think for a moment, how God's people, the church, really needs that. The church people are many times nervous, frustrated, they're all beat, from the society and life in which they live. Look what that operation of the manifestation of the spirit will do in a Body of Believers, when they know what God is doing and how the Word fits. It will edify them, build them up by exhorting them and encouraging them toward a more worthy endeavor and giving them quiet acquiescence and peace. "Yea,

---

12. Dr. Wierwille draws a big house on the chalk board.

verily I the Lord thy God am with thee." What, do you know anybody better? "I will never leave thee nor forsake thee. Lo, I have called you. I have brought you unto this hour. Nothing shall in any way shall harm you." People, these things you hear all the time, but they go in one ear and out of the other! Why? Because we just don't love God with the love of God in the renewed mind. Just that we really believe this is God talking to God's people, *boom, boom, boom*, right now. It is!

Inside of the Body of Believers, tongues with interpretation or prophecy, will always edify, exhort and comfort the Body of Believers. And it's always for those people who are present, at that time. When someone spoke in tongues and interpreted tonight, was that to our neighbor living across the road? Nope! Was it to those people who are not here tonight? No. It was to the body present here tonight! Not for Maggie Muggins out in Timbuktu. Now, you got it? Prophecy is in the language of the body of the people present. It will not feed your spirit, but it will feed your mind. And enable you to be edified as a body, built up into this great, big, God's wonderful body (house), by exhorting you or by giving you comfort. And it's always a message from God or for God to God's people at that time, and God always means what He says and He says what He means. That's why I say to my people, "we wash our ear balls out," when these things come up. Because this is God's immediate speaking to God's people that night! He has spoken in His Word generally, to all God's people. But that is God's specific speaking, to that specific group, at that specific time. Tremendous thing!

Verse 4.

1 Corinthians 14:4a
…he that speaketh in an…tongue edifieth [what?] himself;…

Edifieth means built up, right? He builds himself up. Where class? In the mind? No—in the spirit. Right. Because he is only speaking to God. We're not talking about interpretation yet, we're talking about speaking in tongues. And when you speak in tongues you speak to who? God. Divine mysteries, secrets. And God is spirit and He can only feed what? spirit. That's why this is God and this is me.[13] Now God's spirit feeds His spirit which is in me, and He edifies; He builds up the inner man, the Bible says. The new creature which is in Christ Jesus, his spirit in you is edified, built up. Made sharp, alive, to the end where it really gets vital, really gets the *oomph* in it. So that God can give you revelation and He can talk to you and all the rest of the stuff. It edifies, not my mind but my inner man, my spirit, which is God's spirit in me. It builds it up. And that's the only thing that builds up the spirit! Speaking in tongues.

Physical food will feed the physical body. Spiritual food will feed what? the spirit body. Right! Does this speaking in tongues feed my mind? No. Only my what? inner man, which is Christ in me, the hope of glory. Christ in you. That spiritual man in you is what it speaks. That is why, unless people speak in tongues they're never going to develop spiritually. They may quote you the whole Bible. That doesn't mean they develop spiritually! The quoting of the Bible would be in the category of what? the mind. See it, how sharply these truths are set in God's Word? How tremendous.

1 Corinthians 14:4b
...but he that prophesieth [does what?] edifieth [builds up] the church.

Why? Because prophecy is in what language? the Body of Believers. And therefore it will edify not the spirit,

---

13. Dr. Wierwille draws a diagram on the chalk board.

but the mind. That's it, the mind. Because you'll hear it. It will build you up in your believing, so that your walk will jell.

Verse 5.

> **1 Corinthians 14:5a**
> I would that ye all spake with [what?] tongues,...

Why? Because tongues will do what? Edify. Build you up spiritually, but verse 5:

> **1 Corinthians 14:5b**
> ...but rather that ye prophesied [where? in the church]:...[Why?] that the church may receive edifying.

If I speak in tongues in a believers' meeting and I do not do anything but speak in tongues, I will be what? edified. But what about the rest of the people? That's why it's not the love of God, in the renewed mind in manifestation if I do that. The speaking in tongues is genuine, right? But, I'm out of alignment and harmony. I'm outside of the will of God because I've not renewed my mind. For inside of the church, the Body of Believers, *everybody* has to be blessed. And if I speak in tongues all the time, who's being blessed? me. But what about you? You're not. That is out of order. That's what happened in the church in Corinth.

That's why he said:

> **1 Corinthians 14:5**
> I would that ye all spake in tongues, but rather that ye prophesied [in the church]: for greater *is* he that prophesieth [in the church] than he that speaketh with tongues [in the church], except he interpret, that the church may receive edifying.

There it is, plain as day. "...that the church may receive edifying." So when I speak in tongues in a church, I've got to do what? interpret. Why? that the church may get built up. Not just me, but the church! This is why tongues with interpretation equals prophecy, with the exception of the prophecy given by a prophet. For the prophecy given by a prophet has the possibility of having "fore" telling in it. Which tongues with interpretation or prophecy generally never has. Tongues with interpretation never "fore" tells! Prophecy may "fore" tell, if that prophecy is given by a man who has the ministry of a prophet. Otherwise, prophecy will not do any more than edify, forth tell, and build up the Body of Believers. That's all.

Now, verse 6.

> **1 Corinthians 14:6a**
> Now, brethren, if I come unto you speaking with tongues, what shall [it] profit you,...

Well, answer me. What shall it profit you? Nothing. Why? Because you don't understand it, unless it would be a miracle. But generally, my speaking in tongues, I don't understand and generally the Body of Believers will not understand, therefore he's given the manifestation of what? interpretation of tongues.

> **1 Corinthians 14:6b**
> ...what shall I profit you, except I shall speak to you either by revelation [word of knowledge, word of wisdom], or by knowledge [that which I have gained from God's Word and can rightly divide and teach], or by prophesying [which is in the language of the body of the people present], or by doctrine [right teaching so you know how to believe rightly]?

Then he gives an illustration. Verse 7.

> **1 Corinthians 14:7a**
> ...even things without life giving sound, whether pipe or harp [or a piano, or an organ], except they give a distinction in the sounds, how shall it be known,...

Whether Rhoda's playing "Standing on the Promises" or "sitting on the tea kettle," how shall it be known?

1 Corinthians 14:7b
...what is piped or harped?

Isn't that simple? Verse 8.

1 Corinthians 14:8
For if the trumpet give an uncertain sound, who shall prepare himself to the battle?

See, a battle array was formally called by the trumpet, blowing of the trumpet. Verse 9.

1 Corinthains 14:9-11
So likewise ye, except you utter by the tongue [which "tongue" is a figure of speech; it stands for your speech, what you say] words easy to be understood, how shall it be known what is spoken? for ye shall speak into the air.
There are, it may be, so many kinds of voices [tongues of men and of angels] in the world, and none of them [not of one of them] *is* without signification [significance].
Therefore if I know not the meaning of the voice, I shall be unto him that speaketh a barbarian [a foreigner], and he that speaketh *shall be* [a what?] a barbarian unto me.

Suppose you know English only, and I know German only. So you talk to me in the English. You're a what to me? a foreigner. And I talk German to you. I'm a what to you? a foreigner. Because you don't understand me, I don't understand you, we don't even communicate.

Verse 12.

1 Corinthians 14:12a
Even so ye, forasmuch as ye are zealous of spiritual

gifts [spiritual things or spiritual matters, *pneumatikos*],…

The word "*gifts*" is scratched out.

1 Corinthians 14:12b
…seek that ye may excel to the edifying of the church.

Don't you see it? Inside of the church in a believers' meeting, everybody has to be what? edified. And we have to seek to excel to the edifying of the body of the believers! Verse 13, "Wherefore let him…" Now you see, if we're going to be edified now watch this:

1 Corinthians 14:13a
Wherefore let him that speaketh in an…tongue pray…

To do what? Because if he just spoke in tongues, who would be edified? He would, and not the Body of Believers. And inside of the church, the whole church must be what? edified. Therefore, in a believers' meeting when that man speaks in tongues, let him pray to do what? interpret. And the word "pray" is to believe. You know pray is not to utter words, prayer is believing.

1 Corinthians 14:13b
…let him that speaketh in an…tongue…[believe, to do what?] interpret.

Right. Now look. If I speak in tongues in a believers' meeting, and you give the message in English, is yours the interpretation of what I've spoken? No. Yours is what? prophecy. But that's where the Pentecostals have gone off in the assembly. Somebody speaks in tongues back there, and somebody up here interprets. They say it's interpretation. It's not interpretation! Because the Word said let the fellow who speaks in tongues do what? interpret! But you see I give the "so called" interpretation. It isn't interpretation! But the reason this has fooled the people is because I give the message in English, and we call it interpretation. It isn't interpretation; it's my word of prophecy! It's my word of prophecy. It's prophecy. It isn't interpretation at all. "Let him that speaketh in a tongue, pray" to do what? to interpret. Why? Because the church has to be what? edified. Otherwise, if he spoke in tongues only, he'd get edified, and the church wouldn't. Now listen, God never asked anybody to do anything they couldn't do, so therefore when He said, speak in tongues and interpret, are people able to interpret? Sure. If they aren't, they better read the Word.

Verse 14.

1 Corinthians 14:14a
For if I pray...

Now people watch this change. He's now no longer talking about speaking in tongues; in verse 14 now he's talking about what? praying, "...if I pray in a...tongue." Now speaking in tongues is two-fold. It's either speaking to God this way (on a vertical plane) divine secrets, which is to pray. Or it's speaking in tongues to God this way, where he gives a message for interpretation this way, on a horizontal plane. Now before you ever speak in tongues, in a believers' meeting, does God know whether you're going to interpret or not? Yes. Therefore, if you spoke in a believers' meeting, like that person we just illustrated a little while ago, and God knows he's not going to interpret, the message that he will be giving will not be a message to God's people, it will simply be a prayer in what? the spirit. It's a tremendous truth! And simple. It's real simple. Do you understand it?

1 Corinthians 14:14
For if I pray in an...tongue, my spirit prayeth, but my understanding [my mind] is [what?] unfruitful.

You see, you get bigger spiritually but not mentally. My mind is unfruitful. You're just as wise, or just as stupid after you get through speaking in tongues in your mind, as you were before. Understand? Because it doesn't affect your mind! Speaking in tongues bypasses the mind. That's why anybody has the proof in the senses world, he's made him Lord, because he just by freedom of his will says, "I'm going to speak in tongues" even though you haven't got a word in your mind. Because if you had it in your mind, it wouldn't be tongues, it would be a known language.

1 Corinthians 14:14, 15b
For if I pray in an…tongue, my spirit prayeth, but my understanding is [what?] unfruitful.
What is it then? [Well, what is it then?] I will pray with the [what?] spirit, and I will pray with [my what?] understanding…

Two kinds of prayer, right? Praying with the understanding is like we had some do tonight. They prayed with their what? understanding. Right. Now, just sit there and speak in tongues silently for a minute. What are you doing now? Praying in what? in the spirit. That's it! Now could you do this out loud? But not in a what? in a believers' meeting. In your own home? sure—because in your own home you can be washing the dishes, speaking in tongues out loud. You're praying in the what? spirit. And in your own home you could also pray with your what? understanding. That's right.

1 Corinthians 14:15b
…I will sing with the spirit, and I will sing with [what?] the understanding also.

Alright. Singing with the understanding, you understand, don't you? Well, what's singing in the spirit? Singing in tongues. Well sing! Just sing in the spirit. If you can speak tongues you can do what? sing in tongues. Right.

You know, I was ministering in England. I had an awful time with those Englishmen. Had them right down there, you know, where they ought to be speaking in tongues and nobody speaks. (This had never happen to me.) Nobody! And it really sort of shook me. So finally, something just clicked and Father said, "Well, sing the Doxology in tongues." I'd taught them 1 Corinthians 14, where it said "sing in the spirit." So I said to them, "You all know the Doxology?" They responded, "Oh yeah." I said, "Praise God from whom all blessings flow." They said, "Yep." I said, "Okay. Now we're going to sing the Doxology, but instead of singing it in English, you sing words to it in tongues." And look, I started them, and the whole class sang! Everybody.

Alright, prove it to yourself. Do you know the Doxology? Alright, sing it in tongues. That's singing in the spirit! Now, you can take any old melody and sing in the spirit. On the other hand, you can make up your own. God's not limited, you know, to a few little tunes. So you want to sing in the spirit, sing! Just start opening your mouth, sing the melody, sing the words.

Verse 16. Remember verse 15.

1 Corinthians 14:15b, 16
…I will sing with the understanding also.
Else when thou shalt bless with the spirit, how shall he that occupieth the room of the unlearned say Amen at thy giving of thanks, seeing he understandeth not what thou sayeth?

I want to find this in my book here, page 190:

The word "else" equals "otherwise," tying this verse directly with the preceding one regarding praying and singing in the spirit and praying and singing with the understanding. The word "when," *ean*,[14] equals "if."

---

14. *Ean* is the Greek word for "when."

> To "bless with the spirit" is to pray in the spirit in tongues. How can anyone else in the room with me say "amen" to my "giving of thanks" as I "bless with the spirit" if he does not understand what is said?...[15]

If I'm praying in the spirit, and somebody else is in the room and they can't understand what I am saying, they couldn't say "amen" to what I'm doing.

> ...Therefore, referring here to the people again, Paul is saying that they should pray with the understanding and not with the spirit, if someone else is present.[16]

Present with them in the room—that's it.

So, if you come into my house, I'm not going to stand there and pray in the spirit. If I want to do any praying, when you're there, I'm going to do what? Pray with my understanding. Right. Not just particularly you, I don't use this in the sense of you personally. But, if some visitor walks in your house, someone else walks in, instead of praying in the spirit, you're going to pray with what? understanding.

1 Corinthians 14:16b
...how shall he that occupieth the room of the unlearned say Amen...

The "unlearned" (now this is important) are those who are born again, but have not yet learned to walk by the Word of God because they lack instruction. The "unlearned" are uninstructed. The word "bless" equals "praise God." A literal translation according to usage of verse 16 is: "*Otherwise, if you by your will choose to praise God with the spirit by praying or singing in tongues, how shall he who fills the position of the personally unlearned in understanding, of the significance of tongues say,*

---

15. Seventh edition, p. 190.
16. Seventh edition, p. 190.

Verily, Verily, at thy thankfulness seeing he mentally, absolutely does not understand what thou sayeth."[17] Wow, that's a tremendous translation!

Verse 17.

1 Corinthians 14:17
For thou verily giveth thanks well, but the other is not [what?] edified.

Right. My praying in the spirit would be the giving of thanks well, but if somebody else was present in the room, that other one is not what? edified. Not built up. Verse 18.

1 Corinthians 14:18
I thank my God, I speak with tongues more than ye all:

In the church? No! A thousand times no! He has just said before if you speak in tongues in the church, let him pray to do what? interpret. But in your private life, "I thank my God; I speak in tongues more than ye all." Why? Because speaking in tongues will do what for me? Edify me. Why, that's it! That's why I keep "barking" at you people all the time, in the classes, encouraging you. I say, speak much in your private prayer life! I don't care if you don't interpret for one year in a believers' meeting. I don't care if you don't even know how to interpret! Speak in tongues! Because the speaking in tongues will edify you.

Interpretation will never edify you at all; it will only renew your mind. Not edify your spirit. And I really, thank my God I didn't know anything about interpretation for a year, or a year and a half, after I spoke in tongues. Because had I known anything about it, I would have most likely been like the rest of the people; I'd want

---

17. A literal translation according to usage of 1 Corinthians 14:16.

to interpret so I might find out from the Lord what I was saying. That's right. You ever had that problem?

But see, when we first started questing in this thing, we didn't know anything. We didn't know anything about how to prophesy, or how to interpret. But we had gone far enough; we knew how to speak in tongues. And, we knew what the Word says, it would edify us. We just believed God's Word. So for a year or a year and a half, we did nothing but speak in tongues! And I think there have been days in my life, when I've spoken in tongues at least five, six hours a day, if I total it all up. Because, it's remarkable how you can be driving an automobile, speaking in tongues. Your wife can be yacking at you and you can still be speaking in tongues. Likewise with the husband. Or someone can be talking in the back seat and yelling at you, or holding a wonderful conversation, and I can be speaking in tongues and understand every word they're saying! Why? Because speaking in tongues bypasses my what? mind. But, when you speak to me in English, it doesn't bypass my mind.

So here I am. Cindy, talk to me.[18] I can't hear you! Well you see, now I can hear you when I shut up. But, I want you to speak up loud enough, so I can hear you over my speaking in tongues.[19] Alright. She said, "My mommy and daddy didn't get home until late tonight. Didn't you call me..." or something like this. I still can't hear her, but that's alright. You see, I couldn't do this unless I understand her English, right? But speaking in tongues bypasses my mind. But her English I registered here, but my speaking in tongues I just keep moving my mouth. You know how I learned this? From my old friend, Esther,

---

18. Dr. Wierwille speaks aloud, in tongues, to the class at the same time that Cindy speaks in English.
19. Dr. Wierwille again speaks aloud in tongues, but this time softly to the class, while Cindy is speaking out loud to Dr. Wierwille.

bless her soul! She was the most "unbelievingest" woman in this field.

And we just had an awful problem with her, or an opportunity or something. And we just knew that she could speak in tongues, and she just knew she couldn't! So we had the thought that I would write her a letter, while she talked to me. So Esther started talking to me and I started speaking in tongues, and then I started writing her a letter at the same time, and I would write down what she was telling me. And here I was speaking in tongues all the time, and when I had quit writing I handed it back to her, and I said, "Is this what you said?" She said, "Yeah!" then she caught the idea that it bypassed. Speaking in tongues bypasses your understanding in your mind. Lo and behold, that night she spoke in tongues!

Well, I've been through the mill in this field. Tried everything! If it didn't work one way, we'd try another way! Because, we just knew it was God's will for everybody to speak in tongues. So we had to learn, well how does God operate among God's people? How is their believing? And we found out it wasn't God who wasn't willing to operate, it was people that had the problem! God was always ready! But He was waiting on people to move their lips, throat, and tongue. And I didn't know that! Then I had to learn what the mechanics of speech were and had to teach it to the adults, never to the children. But the adults I had to teach it to, "Move your lips, your throat, and tongue, make the sounds, make the words, you push it out!" And when we learned that key, that people didn't understand the mechanics of speech, that's when we had the great lever of leading people into the manifestation of speaking in tongues!

Because God had already given it to their spirit when they believed, right? Then why weren't they speaking? Because they didn't know their job. They didn't know how to do it. So we taught them to move their lips, their throat, their tongue, make the sounds, make the words, but the sounds you make and the words you make, are as God gives it to your spirit. And you speak the wonderful works of God! Magnifying God. This is why, Paul says in verse 18:

1 Corinthians 14:18
I thank my God, I speak with tongues more than ye all:

In his private life, he must have spoken like a house of fire. He said, more than the whole church in Corinth. Well, that wouldn't surprise me a bit, because I imagine they weren't speaking very much anymore. They were fighting with each other, you know, whether it was Apollos or Cephas or whether it was a Jesus gang they belonged to, all this stuff. That verse 18 is wonderful! Isn't it?

1 Corinthians 14:19
Yet in the church [Now he's back to the church.] I had rather speak five words with my understanding, that…I might teach others also, than ten thousand words in an…tongue.

Why? Because five words with my understanding would edify the church, how much? Five words worth. But, if I speak in tongues ten thousand words, you'd be edified how much? none! This is the verse they have used to discredit speaking in tongues. Isn't that terrible how people misuse these things? It doesn't discredit tongues at all! It just simply gives an illustration and a truth! Five words with my understanding will edify God's people, five words worth! But ten thousand words in a tongue will edify me, but not the church. And inside of the church, the church must be edified! Excel in the edifying of the body.

Verse 20.

1 Corinthians 14:20
Brethren, be not children in understanding: howbeit in malice be ye children, but in understanding be men.

Right. Grow up! Grow up. Don't be babies your whole lifetime regarding spiritual matters. Grow up. But in malice just continue to be childlike. You know why? Because a child has no malice. It takes an adult to have that. But, grow up spiritually. Verse 21, I'm going to read through something.

1 Corinthians 14:21, 22
In the law it is written, With *men of* other tongues and other lips will I speak unto this people; and yet for all that will they not hear me, saith the Lord.
Wherefore tongues are for a sign, not to them that believe, but to them that believe not: but prophesying *serveth* not for them that believe not, but for them which believe.

On page 194 of the Fifth edition, these are tremendous verses and I'd like for you for once to start understanding the depth of these two verses, so that we can just continue to grow in our knowledge of God's Word, more and more and more. First of all, in verse 21, the apostle is quoting from Isaiah 28:11 and 12. "The quotation differs from both the Hebrew and Aramaic texts, as well as the Septuagint."[20]

You know what the Septuagint is? The Septuagint is the Greek translation of the Old Testament about 240 or 250 B.C. Before Christ was born. They translated the Old Testament into Greek, and this was done by seventy men. And that's why it was given the name Septuagint.

---

20. See also *Receiving the Holy Spirit Today*, seventh edition, p. 194.

It means seventy. That's the Greek translation of the Old Testament before the birth of Christ.

> It is accommodated to the new circumstances by omission of the center section, which was now irrelevant. God has said that men will speak with other tongues, and that the speaking in tongues is the rest which "may cause the weary to rest; and this is the refreshing" for the weary. How wonderful, and yet even this mighty blessing, in the presence and in the midst of the people will not cause them to hearken to the Lord. It should, but it does not. In this verse we have the figure of speech, *synonymia*—synonymous words having the same meaning but differing in sound, "tongues" and "lips." [21]

With men of other tongues and other, what? lips. This is the figure, in English, synonymous. Where synonymous words, different words are used, different in sound but have the same meaning.

Verse 22.

1 Corinthians 14:22a
[Now] tongues are for a sign [in the Church], not to them that believe, but to them that believe not:...

Now people this verse is addressed to the Church and the Church is composed of what? born-again believers. There was my key. Yet, in the Church there are some born-again Christians who are "unlearned" (verse 16 said so) "...occupieth the room of the unlearned." They are still "children in understanding" but they are children, don't forget it. But they are "children in understanding," they are babes in knowledge. They have become members of the Church and have been instructed, but not sufficiently to fully believe. They are "babes in Christ," and

---

21. Seventh edition, p. 194.

they're referred to here in this verse as "them that believe not." They are not unconverted unbelievers, but they are believing unbelievers. They are believers who still are what? Unbelievers, because they have not been fully instructed. Fully taught. They're unlearned. The unbeliever, the Greek word *apistos*; having been instructed but not sufficiently to fully believe. "Unlearned" is the Greek word *idiotēs* from which we get the word, what? idiot. Really he's uninstructed, a believer he's a "babe."

The word "sign" is a sign to the people in the church, the unbeliever. This is the Greek word *sēmeion* and indicates the significance of the work wrought.

"For" is the Greek preposition *eis*. It governs only the accusative case and indicates motion to, or unto an object, with the purpose of reaching or touching it. Tongues are *for* a sign to them that believe not.

"Not" is the Greek word *ou*, meaning "absolutely not," the same as in verse 2.

Tongues are for a sign in the Church to the unbelievers, those who have been instructed but not sufficiently to believe and walk in the light. To these, tongues are for a sign of the object, design, or teaching of the significant work of the Holy Spirit within the Church. This sign of speaking in tongues, is to inspire these unlearned Christians to greater effort to understand and experience this spiritual manifestation.[22]

That's exactly what we have learned in our Research Center here. When people come into this Center, let's say for the first time, they're really God's people and they're born again of God's spirit, but they've never been in-

---

22. Dr. Wierwille utilizes the text from *Receiving the Holy Spirit Today* with some variation in this paragraph and the previous. This section is not directly quoted but very similar within the audio teaching.

structed. When they hear our people speak in tongues, they just melt! They're just flabbergasted! Because, it's a sign to them that there's something more than they have.

It's just the opposite of what some of the so-called denominations teach. I believe in the holy spirit field, that if I speak in tongues out here on the corner of the street, it is a sign to all the unbelievers. You know the unsaved. You know what the unsaved would say? Well, why don't you go inside and shut up! They'd laugh at you. But, inside of a Body of Believers, where they're really born again of God's spirit, and when they see how decent this is and how in order, and how wonderful it is, they'll hear you speaking in tongues, immediately God's spirit says to them, "See? There's more." What was your experience the first time you heard it? Weren't you blessed? Didn't it somehow or other just sort of shake you inside and say, "My goodness, what are they doing that I can't do?" The ability to speak in a tongue is divinely given for the purpose of direct and intimate communication with God at all times.

> Therefore, this divine manifestation is a sign to those in the Church who do not as yet fully manifest the mighty working power of God.[23]

Verse 22 continued.

1 Corinthians 14:22b
...but prophesying *serveth* not for them that believe not, but for them which believe.

Prophesying is the bringing forth of a message, divinely given by God, from or for God to the people, in the language of the people, which will build up their believing by way of exhorting and comforting

---

23. Dr. Wierwille continues to reference *Receiving the Holy Spirit Today*. See also seventh edition, p. 196.

the Body of Believers. Prophecy is a sign to the instructed and practicing believers.[24]

Got that? It's a sign to the instructed and practicing believers, the faithful, because of the significance of the work wrought by the manifestation of prophecy. A literal translation according to usage of verse 22 is: *"Speaking in tongues indicates the significance of the work wrought, not to the faithful, those instructed and walking in the light, but to the unfaithful; while prophecy indicates the significance of the work wrought, not to those who are unfaithful, but to those who are faithful—those instructed and walking by the Word of God."* [25] It's a tremendous thing!

And people, it's real simple. It's like I said to you, some believer, born again believer who has had a little instruction in the Word of God, walks into a wonderful believers' meeting. And you speak in tongues and you interpret, the speaking in tongues is a sign to him of the work wrought. What God has wrought in you. But, if everybody is fully instructed, you don't need that sign, right? But you still need to hear from God regarding the specific situation, so in that group you would what? Prophecy. See how it all fits?

Now back to verse 23.

1 Corinthians 14:23a
If therefore the whole church be come together...

The whole church. Now the whole church, the church is made up of born again what? believers. But inside of that born-again believer bunch, some are more fully instructed than what? others. Now, understand that a man could be 60 years old, just born again yesterday, with no

---

24. Dr. Wierwille continues to reference *Receiving the Holy Spirit Today*. Also see seventh edition, p. 196.
25. A literal translation according to usage of 1 Corinthians 14:22

real knowledge of God's Word. But others may be only 25 or 30 years old, and they've been instructed for 5 or 6 years in the accuracy of God's Word. Now you've got to remember, the whole church. Now you've got the picture?

> **1 Corinthians 14:23b**
> …come together into one place, and all [the people] speak with tongues, and there come in [to this church]…unlearned, or unbelievers, will they not say that ye are mad?

Will they not say you're off your rocker? Will they not say you are mad? Will they not say you're out in left field? Why? Because everybody is talking in tongues at the same time! The "unlearned" are those who (though born again) have not yet been sufficiently instructed to be transformed by the renewing of their minds. The "unbelievers" are those who have been instructed, but not sufficiently to believe to the end of manifesting.

When they, the unlearned and the unbelievers, hear everybody speaking in tongues at the same time they will indeed say that you are mad! They'll say you're out of your mind! Because, inside of the church we're not all to speak in tongues at the what? same time. Inside of the church, we are to speak and let one speak and that same one do what? interpret. Now, I know what you're going to ask. So why does everyone speak in tongues here at Headquarters then? Because, I run the outfit for God. I have ministries in the Body. And these ministries make me responsible for rulership of God's Body. And God's man determines what kind of meeting it is. God makes me responsible to Him, as to what the show is I'm supposed to run. That's right! So if I determine it's a believers' meeting, then what is it? A believers' meeting. If I determine it's a receivers' meeting, it's what? If I determine it's a practice session, it's what?

That's it.[26] This is how God gives ruling ministries and this is how the ministries are responsible for the growth of God's people, that the people be edified.

I know the Word on this stuff, because, you see, when I have everybody speaking in tongues, how many unbelievers have I got left? Better not have any around because I've taught you the Word for two weeks or three. By that time you ought to get to believing at least one paragraph of the Word. You've been instructed. You're not unlearned. If you're unlearned it's because you don't want to learn, and other stuff, because I've bled my heart out for two weeks minimum, in teaching God's people the greatness of God's Word! So you can't say you're unlearned! Because I've taught you the Word! The only thing you could say is that you've rejected God's Word! That's a horse of a different color; we're not talking about that. Here we're talking about those that are unlearned or unbelievers. We never have a receivers' meeting when those "birds" are present, as far as I'm concerned. I don't know, because if they were, what would they say? You're mad; you're off your rocker. That's what the Word says! We've got to stick by what? The Word. The Word is our rule of faith and practice. How we know how to operate.

But, suppose there are unlearned and unbelievers.

1 Corinthians 14:24a
[And]…all prophesy,…

---

26. Dr. Wierwille distinguished between the operation of the manifestations of holy spirit in different contexts. He called a gathering of people who want to receive into manifestation for the first time, such as happened in Acts 2 on the Day of Pentecost, as a "receivers' meeting". When the Church is gathered to worship Him and the worship manifestations of speaking in tongues, interpretation of tongues and prophecy are operated, he termed this a "believers' meeting". God's guidelines for how the manifestations are to be operated in this context can be found in 1 Corinthians 14.

That doesn't mean everybody in the church, but all who speak, do what? prophesy. Yes. So if John spoke, he would prophesy. If Mrs. Muggins spoke, she would prophesy. If Mr. Herman spoke, he'd prophesy. "…and there come in"—see prophecy is the language of the body of the people.

Verse 24.

> **1 Corinthians 14:24b**
> …and there come in [among the church] one that believeth not, or…unlearned, he is convinced of all, he is judged of all:

How? Because the prophecy is in the language of the people. They're already born-again; they hear this prophecy. God's people hear this prophecy; those that are fully instructed hear this prophecy. And the prophecy would encourage, exhort and comfort.

Alright. Then the exhortation. God knows what He's doing and if you watch prophecy carefully it's always right down the line. When you've got unlearned and unbelievers in the prophecy, many times it will just be almost straight exhortation. It would say something like, "Yea, verily I say unto thee, study the Word of God to show yourself approved. Be bold in your walking on the Word." Ever hear this? Why? Because the people who are present have not been fully instructed sufficiently enough to believe completely. That builds up old Joe. That builds up Mr. Bowen. That builds up all of those fully instructed people, and say, there's people in here that really need our enthusiasm. So, when it's all over with, you've prophesied, the unlearned are convinced of all those who have spoken, and they're judged, weighed in the balance, weighed you know. They say, "Well look, I had better get on the ball because I'm not walking boldly enough!" Or I'm not doing this well enough. I've got to get on the ball! That's how it's judged of all. Judged is the word "weighed, evaluated."

Verse 25.

> **1 Corinthians 14:25**
> And thus are the secrets of [their] heart[s] made manifest; and so falling down on *his* face he will worship God, and report that God is in you of a truth.

"So falling down on *his* face" is a figure of speech. You'll just praise God that God is in you, and in the believers! Verse 26.

> **1 Corinthians 14:26a**
> How is it then, brethren? when you come together, every one of you hath a psalm, hath a doctrine, hath a tongue, hath a revelation, hath an interpretation....

That's exactly what had happened in the church at Corinth. Everybody wanted to have a psalm, everybody wanted to yack on doctrine, everybody said they wanted to speak in tongues, everybody said I've got a revelation, and everybody said I want to give an interpretation. They're all out of order. That's why he said:

> **1 Corinthians 14:26b, 27**
> ...Let all things be done unto [what?] edifying.
> If any man speak in an...tongue, *let it be* [the speaking] by two, or at the most *by* three [people], and *that* by course [Do you know what course means? one, two, three]; and let one interpret.

The word "one" is the word "each." He has just told us a little while ago, in verse 13, "Let him that speaketh in an...tongue, pray that he may [do what?] interpret." God couldn't deny Himself now and say, three of you speak and one interpret over there. Because He's just said, "let him that speaketh" do what? pray that he may interpret. And they've sure taken this out of its context and they've done just the opposite. One fellow spoke over there and somebody else interpreted. No. No. No. "...and let one interpret." The Greek uses the word, *heis*, meaning the one and the same. Not someone else. Thus, "let each one who speaks in tongues, that one and the same interpret."

Verse 28.

> **1 Corinthians 14:28a**
> But if there be no interpreter,...

In other words if a fellow speaks in tongues, and he's not going to interpret.

> **1 Corinthians 14:28b**
> ...let him [shut up] keep silence in the [what?] church;...

Right. Because if he speaks out loud in the church, he is to do what? interpret. But if his believing faith, or if his instruction is not sufficient to interpret, then instead of speaking out loud in the church in tongues, "let him speak" what? silently.

> **1 Corinthians 14:28c**
> ...let him speak to himself, and to [what?] God.

Sure. Now, we shift from manifestations for a moment to the ministries, to illustrate both the manifestations and the ministries. Verse 29.

> **1 Corinthians 14:29a**
> Let the prophets [the ministry of a prophet] speak two or three, and let the other judge.

The other prophets judge. Judge what? What these men are saying, whether they're speaking according to the Word. The only way we have of judging one another, the man of God says, is by what? The Word.

Verse 30.

1 Corinthians 14:30, 31a
If *any thing* be revealed to another [prophet, that is] that sitteth by, let the first [prophet] hold his peace. For ye may all…

All who? All the prophets. If you have four prophets, in a believers' meeting, all four prophets would be privileged to do what? prophecy. But, they would still have to:

1 Corinthians 14:31b, 32
…prophesy one by one, that all may learn, and all may be comforted.
And the spirits of the prophets are subject to the prophets.

That's what it says, that's what it means. And this is true in all the manifestations, the ministries. The spirits of the prophets are subject to what? the prophets. If a thing gets out of order it's because the people allow it to what? If I stood up on this chair, would this be God doing it or me? The spirits of the prophets are subject to who? That's a tremendous truth, you got it? I think in the Aramaic the word "spirits" is in the singular, isn't it? That's alright. The spirits of the prophets are subject to the prophets. Why?

Verse 33, "For God is…" the author of confusion—no, no, no! Now you'd think He was, right?

1 Corinthians 14:33
For God is not *the author* of confusion…

The word "author" is fairly accurately given. "God is not confusion." So any time you've got confusion, can it be of the true God? No. Now you see why if you lay down on the floor with your dress up to your neck, and say you've been struck down by the spirit, it's unseemly, out of order, and it causes confusion. Who's doing it? It's that sharp! You see why when I teach you the Foundational Class, I know all this stuff. So I many times say things that sound peculiar to your ears, but if I just have you long enough to teach you, we'd finally get around to all of this. But anytime anything is out of order, it's always of the Devil. A man throwing a song book, because he's sincerely questing after the spirit, what's the matter with him? It's of the Devil. He can be speaking in tongues like a house of fire. The speaking in tongues would be what? genuine. But the other is confusion. And confusion is of the Devil. Wherever there is confusion, there is every evil work!

Verse 33 continued.

> **1 Corinthians 14:33**
> For God is not *the author* of confusion, but of peace, as in all churches of the saints.

I'm going to finish Chapter 14 so don't leave. Now you'll like verse 34. I promised you women we'd get to you sometime, here you go.

> **1 Corinthians 14:34, 35**
> Let your women keep silence in the churches: for it is not permitted unto them to speak; but *they are commanded* to be under obedience, as also saith the law.
> And if they will learn any thing, let them ask their husbands at home: for it is a shame for women to speak in the church.

There you got it! So now we got a new denomination or an old one, which teaches that no woman is ever allowed to preach. No woman is ever allowed to teach. And yet I want to tell you, how many church doors would not be closed if the women hadn't stood faithful and did the teaching! Because the men have been staying home all along, chewing tobacco or doing something. That's right! A handful of faithful women teach Sunday school class after Sunday school class, week after week. But you see, not working the Word they never get to the truth. And so they have preconceived ideas like, "throughly" or "thoroughly"[27] or something. They have these preconceived ideas, and so when they read this scripture they never see its context!

For instance, how can you ask your husbands at home if you aren't even married? Cindy here. How can you ask your husband at home? You don't have one! How could any woman ask her husband, if she didn't have one? So, first of all it has to talk about women who have what? husbands. Yes! Now, how in the world could you ask your husband at home, if your husband hadn't been there? That's right. Suppose he hadn't been at church this morning. How are you going to ask him about stuff? You've been there. The wife's been to church, the husband slept in! How are you going to ask him if he hasn't been there? So you see when you look at this thing it gets to be real funny. If I had more time I would illustrate it for you. But I won't. So, we'll go right to work on the greatness of it. It's talking about the women of the prophets. The subject is prophets. Once again, the subject is prophets.

> **1 Corinthians 14:34, 35a**
> Let your women [the women of what? the prophets] keep silence in the churches: for it is not permitted unto them [the women of the prophets] to speak [That's right!]; but *they are commanded* to be under obedience [to their husbands, who are the prophets], as also saith the law.

---

27. Dr. Wierwille is referring to 2 Timothy 3:17—"That the man of God may be perfect, thoroughly furnished unto all good works." This verse if often confused or mistranslated saying "throughly" instead of "thoroughly."

> And if they [the wives of the prophets] will learn any thing, let them ask their [what?] husbands at home:...

Sure, they live with them. They sleep with them. They drink coffee with them. They can talk to them because the prophet's been there, right? So, if the woman wants to know anything about what he spoke, or what he said, instead of doing it publicly, she asks him at home. And she says, "Hey, honey, what's this thing mean that you said this morning? What's the score here?"

1 Corinthians 14:35
> ...if they...[want to] learn any thing, let them ask their husbands at home: for it is a shame for women [what women? the women of the prophets] to speak in the church.

And the word "speak" is the word *laleō* which means to have the running off of the mouth. That's what it means, literally. That's right.

You know what was happening in the church at Corinth? It's a tremendous TV show! Here were these prophets, giving the greatness of God's Word, and there was the prophet's wife back there, standing up saying, "Honey, will you wait a minute and let me speak a little, honey. You know, I'm your wife. Remember me? I'm your little old honey bunch. I cook your stew for you and burn your toast! Remember me? I want to speak a little bit because after all, I'm your wife. I have a little right to this." That's what happened in the church at Corinth. And God said to the women of the prophets, shut up. If you want to have the running off of the mouth, ask at home. But inside of the church, it is a shame that you, the wife of a prophet act like this. Why? Because when God gives men ministries, that woman may be the sweetest thing in the world, but she's entirely out of order, when she does that which is contrary to God's Word. She belittled the prophet. She made God's prophet look like he wasn't quite as big as he ought to be, because she was the wife that had made him! You know, behind every good man stands a better woman. What about the failures?

Verse 36, puts it right on the line. It says to the wives of the prophets.

1 Corinthians 14:36a
What? came the word of God out from you?...

Well did it? No! It didn't come out of the wife of the prophet; the Word of God came from whom? the prophet! It came from the prophet.

1 Corinthians 14:36b
...or came it unto you only?

Yes, it came unto you only, because the prophet's wife is just like any other woman inside of the Body of Believers. Well, that's all that's to the story, about you women.

Now, we're back to verse 37. And from here on out, it's really sharp! Like it's been all the way through. The apostle Paul by divine revelation, writing to the church says:

1 Corinthians 14:37
If any man think himself to be a prophet, or spiritual, let him acknowledge that the things that I write unto you are the commandments of the Lord.

"I would that ye all spake in tongues" then, is a commandment. That's it! Inside of the church, let him that speaketh, interpret, is a what? a commandment. If they're just a Body of Believers, I would that ye all prophecy is a what? commandment. Let them speak, one, two, three, in course, order, let each interpret, is a commandment of what? The Lord! That's what it says, that's what it means! It's a tremendous thing, isn't it?

And then comes our favorite verse, in 38. "But if any man…" after all this teaching, and all this wonderful Word of God, if they still want be stupid, what are you going to do about it? Let them be stupid and quit stewing about it.

> **1 Corinthians 14:38a**
> But if any man be ignorant,…

If they do not want to recognize it as God's Word, if you taught them the accuracy and set it forth before them, just like I have before you, suppose there is somebody in here who doesn't want to believe, you know what I'm going to do with you? Forget about you! If you want to stay stupid, stay stupid! If any man will to be ignorant, after all of that knowledge of God's Word that you have related to them, they still want to be ignorant, what are you going to do about it?

> **1 Corinthians 14:38b**
> …let him be ignorant.

That's right. Don't cry your eyeballs out. Just let them be ignorant.

Verse 39 and 40.

> **1 Corinthians 14:39**
> Wherefore, brethren, covet [earnestly desire] to prophesy [inside of the church], and forbid not to speak with tongues.

But inside of the church it must be what? interpreted. And now for the third time in one chapter, they must have needed it! Maybe we do too, huh?

> **1 Corinthians 14:40**
> Let all things [in the church] be done [absolutely] decently and in order.

Let all things be done decently and in order in the church. Isn't that tremendous? Three times in one chapter, talking about decency and in order.

Well these are the great chapters.

BENEFITS OF SPEAKING IN TONGUES

You see the syllabus is just loaded with spiritual "goodies." The only thing you have to do is work it. Really put your mind to work and think things through while you're working that syllabus. But basically, everything that I have taught you is all written either in the holy spirit book, or in the syllabus. It's all there. The only difference is I teach it without the syllabus or the holy spirit book at times, and therefore it has my personality in it, more so maybe than the cold hard book, but the truths are in there! And you ought to take that holy spirit book[1] and go through those sections on Acts and Corinthians and so forth—that this becomes a part of you, that you really understand it, that you know it!

Now, I taught you something. Remember I draw that silly drawing on the board about the man all the time, but this is the only way I can explain it. It's the only way I know that you can make it really fit, all the way through. So here's a man of body and soul.[2] Now when Christ comes in, Christ in you the hope of glory, Christ is in every part of this body. This is spirit on the inside. Now, God is spirit, this we know. And there is a law involved that spirit can only speak to what? spirit. Alright. So God by revelation can speak to this spirit in here. This man of body and soul, now also has spirit; so he's body, soul, and spirit. And part of this man, the part that man operates from and controls his life from, is what we refer to as the

---

1. Referring to *Receiving the Holy Spirit Today*.
2. Dr. Wierwille referring to a drawing on the board.

"mind." I'm not sure that that's right all the way through because this is the word, the best word we use, the best word we have today is the word "mind." But, I think we understand each other, some place above your ears, you control the situation in life. You make the decisions. You make the right or wrong ideas to penetrate in your conversation and so forth.

This is why, in speaking in tongues, no man understandeth, remember? The mind is what? What's the word used in Corinthians? It's unfruitful. So, when you speak in tongues, it is this spirit which is edified in you. The spirit in you is edified, built up. But what about your mind? It is not. But now suppose you're in a believers' meeting and you are going to speak in tongues and you are going to interpret. God knows ahead of time that you are going to do what? That's the difference.

Part of you is mind. Therefore the moment you have a message from God or for God, to the people at that moment, the very moment you speak, God puts these words in your mind, and then you speak out that word in English, in this group, and its interpretation. That's why that great principle on page 23, is just what I have illustrated on the board. God's spirit teaches His creation in you, which is now your spirit, understand? And your spirit teaches your mind, because the man of body and soul has a mind. Then it becomes manifested in the senses realm as you what? act. That is the key!

Now suppose, it won't happen this way, but just suppose it could happen this way. Well, it just doesn't happen but let's say that you could speak in tongues and have ten words in your mind. If you don't give those ten words, the Body of Believers would never have the interpretation. The Body of Believers would never be edified, right? Now, I'm confident of this—that in a believers' meeting, whenever somebody speaks in tongues, that that person will always have at least one word in their mind, when they are through speaking, which will be the interpretation. Not one word, the whole interpretation, but that is the interpretation. And so, if that person will give that one word, then God has the responsibility to have what up there? the second word, the third word, the forth word, the fifth word.

This is why I tell my people, when you're new in this, and you're first beginning to walk, give your interpretation like a house of fire! Just give it as fast as you can give it! Because the faster you give it, the less time you give the Devil to get in your thought pattern and say, "Well now, did you make that up or where did you get that from?" This is all involved. So, give it fast! Sometimes you may have three words, that's all you have. And people say, "Well, I haven't got anything." Well, they're not telling the truth. They have what? And then if you haven't got anything somebody's lying! Look, if you've got one word could you say you haven't got anything? You know how you get more? Speak the one.

The simplest illustration I know is a faucet in a house. You can't get the second drop of water until you accept the first. I don't care what kind of faucet you've got. The second drip won't come until the first one comes. So, you take the first word, give it, the second word will be there. The third word will be there. Why do you want God to give you ten words, when you won't even have the believing faith to give the first one? See how simple this all becomes? It is so simple that the church has missed it a lifetime! Because they were waiting for something to push them, you know. Like they say, "Well if it's of God, God will push me. He'll force me." God never forces. God never pushes. He puts it in there, it's there just as plain as day. You give out one word, two words, three words and as you give it out, He gives it to your spirit. Your spirit is His spirit in you. You are part mind. His spirit teaches your mind; as you act, it comes into manifestation.

Now, by the way this is how all the manifestations operate. They operate the same way. Same way. Prophecy, word of knowledge, word of wisdom, discerning of spirits, all those information revelations operate the same way. He tells your spirit, your spirit tells your mind. Even if it's a picture in revelation, if it's a picture it will still relate itself to your mind. And God will always give in light of your understanding and your experience. For instance, if He's got a man, who is a great athlete or an interest in athletics, and he really knows the field of athletics, God may symbolize it to him in a picture that deals with athletics. Let's say, there is a farmer. God symbolizes to him in the terms of his farm or something he knows real well. God always gives you the information, in the capacity of your understanding. Always! Never fails.

Now on page 23. The manifestation of speaking in tongues, what it is *not*. First of all, it is not gibberish or foolishness. Why? Because no language is gibberish or foolishness. Although to the mind of your senses, the language of one people may sound odd in the ears of the people of a different language or culture. You know, if you don't understand German and if I speak German to you, then to your senses ears that German would sound like gibberish or foolishness. But it isn't gibberish or foolishness, is it? So it is in speaking in tongues. When you speak in tongues, when you hear yourself speak, you may say, "That sounds funny!" But no language is ever funny! No language is ever gibberish or foolishness.

Now there are people in here that do understand German. There are other people that don't. Now for you people who don't, for instance, listen as I speak in German.[3] I almost got stuck on my German. Alright, now to your senses ears, you people that do not understand German, that sounded sort of funny, didn't it? Did it sound real fast to you? or slow? This is just like tongues. This is why no language is ever gibberish or foolishness. That's why in 1 Corinthians 13:1, we read last session:

1 Corinthians 13:1
Though I speak with the tongues of men and of angels,...

Therefore, every time someone speaks in a tongue, it will always be the tongues of men or of what? angels. And it's never foolishness, never gibberish. It is a tongue.

Whenever you speak in tongues, that language you speak will always be perfectly enunciated. The pronunciation of your words will always be perfect! The emphasis or accent of the words will always be perfect. Never fails! Never fails! And of course in this field, I not only know what the Word of God says, but we've had the practical experience of people. For instance, someone speaking in French who knew absolutely no French at all! But when they spoke it in a tongue, they spoke in French. And another person in that auditorium understood French and taught it for years. And there was that person speaking in tongues for the first time, and her enunciation was perfect; it was better than you could learn it in most of the schools. It was just like that person being right from France. Same thing we experienced in High German in a class in California. That woman couldn't speak any more High German than that chair can! And yet, when she was filled with the holy spirit, she started speaking in tongues; she spoke in High German. And her High German was just as fluent and the emphasis was just tremendous, but the language comes from whom? And God

---

3. Dr. Wierwille spoke in German in the audio teaching at this time.

isn't what? stupid. Therefore, when He gives us these things, if we just relax, get quiet, move our lips, our throats, our tongues, make the sounds, don't squeeze it. You know when you want to speak English, you can't squeeze it! See if I squeeze it, I don't speak "too good"![4] Likewise in tongues. If you squeeze it, you don't speak that language too well. So, if you just relax yourself, just let go and let the greatness of God's power be in you, and you speak it out. The words you speak will always be pronounced perfectly, the enunciation will be perfect, the emphasis will be perfect, and you'll be speaking the wonderful works of God, tongues of men or of what? angels. That's it.

Now, speaking in tongues is not a sign of weakness, nervousness, disruption or unintelligence. You see, I put all these in here because these are arguments I've heard against speaking in tongues. They say, "Well, only a nervous individual could possibly speak in tongues or someone with not much intelligence could speak in tongues." And every time I used to hear that, I used to wonder about the Apostle Paul. Poor fella! The Word of God says his education and his knowledge was beyond any of his what? age[5]—beyond any of his buddies, so it's a nice company to be in.

Jude. Look at the Book of Jude, verse 20.

Jude 20a
But ye, beloved, building up yourselves…

Building up yourselves. Remember last time we read in the Word that speaking in tongues does what to us? It edifies. To edify is to build up. This is the same thing.

---

4. Dr. Wierwille uses a squeaky voice to illustrate his point.
5. Galatians 1:14 (ASV)—and I advanced in the Jews' religion beyond many of mine own age among my countrymen, being more exceedingly zealous for the traditions of my fathers.

BENEFITS OF SPEAKING IN TONGUES

Jude 20b
> …ye, beloved, building up yourselves on your most holy faith, praying in the Holy Ghost,

"Praying in the Holy Ghost" is to pray in what? tongues. Pray in the spirit. Read it last session, right? When you pray to God in the spirit, you edify yourself. To pray to God in the spirit is to speak to Him, and when you do you edify yourself. You build yourself up, in your mind? No. In you're what? spirit. Right! "…building up yourself on your most holy faith." That's right.

You know, speaking in tongues is not linguistic ability. I had a professor at Princeton who could speak 22 languages! We had an awful time understanding him in English, but he could speak 22. That man had linguistic ability. Many sinners have linguistic ability. To speak in tongues is not to have linguistic ability. And we have letters and other stuff on file of people who have objected to our speaking in tongues on the grounds that they never we're going to be missionaries!

Well, it's not a gift of languages. Now I better explain this. That you could, for instance, speak in a desired tongue at will. It's not a gift of languages where you could say to God, well now I want to talk in Greek here for a while. So you speak in Greek. So now when you want to go with Mrs. Kennedy to Greece for a vacation, you don't have to learn Greek, you just go over to the Greeks and you say, "Well, now Lord, I speak in tongues, and if you don't mind I'd like to speak in Greek." No, no, no, no!

We do the speaking, but we speak as the spirit gives us what? utterance. That's right! It's not a gift of languages, so that you could go to Africa for instance, and speak in the Afrikaans' dialect at will. No, no, no.

Next, it is not an unusual ability to understand languages. Well then, what is it? It is supernatural. 1 Corinthians 12:11. Look it up.

1 Corinthians 12:11
...all these worketh that one and the selfsame [what?] Spirit,...

That makes speaking in tongues a supernatural manifestation. It's not natural. If I learn a language, that is what? natural. But when I speak in tongues, it is what? supernatural!

Also, it is unknown to you. For instance, if English is your only known language, then any other language is unknown to you, and is therefore, to you, a tongue. 1 Corinthians 14:2.

1 Corinthians 14:2
...he that speaketh in an *unknown* tongue speaketh not unto men, but unto God: for no man [what?] understandeth...

You see, you do not understand what you are speaking, it's a tongue to you. This does not mean that no one on the face of the earth could not understand. Why? Because of Acts 2, which you will remember, don't look it up. Acts 2, you will remember that on the Day of Pentecost when they spoke in tongues, what about the people that were out there who heard them? They understood. If it's the tongues of men, it could be understood some place on earth. If it's the tongues of angels, I think you're going to have to go to a different place.

Now, the manifestation of speaking in tongues, what is it? It is your spirit making intercession with God's will for your good. And that's a tremendous thing! Romans 8:26.

Romans 8:26a
Likewise the Spirit also helpeth our infirmities: for we know not what we should pray for as we ought: but the Spirit itself...

Did I drill you one night, that the gifts should always be "itself," never "himself" or "herself"? Third person singular and so forth.

Romans 8:26b
...but the Spirit itself maketh intercession for us with groanings which cannot be [what?] uttered.

Right. Let's do verse 26 again, "Likewise the spirit also helpeth our infirmities: for we know not what we should pray for as we ought: but the spirit itself..." This spirit of God in me, when I speak to the Father, it is this spirit in me which is His spirit in me, understand? It is this which "makes intercession for us, with groanings which cannot be uttered." In King James, both Spirits are in capital "S" aren't they? I think they ought to both be in lower case. I think we're talking about the gift in the context. Romans 8:26-28. And, I'd like for you to note that the word "infirmities" here implies, and refers, and indicates that the "infirmities" is regarding our what? our prayer life.

Romans 8:26b
...infirmities: for we...[don't know] what we should pray for as we ought:...

This is our infirmity. You see people, just think it through, it's simple. With your senses mind there are many things you do not know about another individual, as to how to pray for him or even yourself! Now suppose if a man is blind you can see that. Right? So if you were going to pray for that, you could pray for his blindness, but what is behind it you may not be able to see. Sometimes the things in your own life, you don't really understand why these things are the way they are in your life. You see, sense knowledge wise we're always limited. For ourselves, as well as for others.

If I were going to pray for Cindy, there's just sense knowledge wise a lot of things I don't know about Cindy. And therefore when I would pray for her, I'd have too much hit and miss. But if I pray for her in the spirit, then it's the spirit that maketh intercession for us. And it's always a perfect prayer, because God's spirit in me knows what V.P. Wierwille needs. God's spirit in her knows what she needs. That's why praying in the spirit, or speaking in tongues in prayer, is the greatest lever of prayer we have. And people, in the Bible this is the only one that makes intercession. It's the only one. It makes intercession for us, as individuals and for the saints. That's all. My praying with my understanding can't make intercession for you. But my praying in the spirit can.

Verse 27.

Romans 8:27a
…he that searcheth the hearts knoweth what *is* [in] the mind of the Spirit,…

There you've got a figure of speech, "mind of the Spirit."

"…he that searcheth the hearts." God. God in Christ in you, the anointing, remember the gift? He knows what's in the mind, the desire of that spirit within you. "…the mind of the Spirit" is a figure. What the spirit knows about you that's in you. Where your need is. What your desires are.

Romans 8:27b
…because he [or it] maketh intercession for the saints according to *the will of* God.

"…*the will of*" is real accurate in the sense in which we understand "will of." Isn't that a wonderful verse? Then when we pray, if we want to pray perfectly, the greatest effective lever of prayer we have is to pray in the spirit. Not only for ourselves, but to stay our mind, for instance on Cindy. And while I have my mind stayed on her, I will pray in the spirit for her. And as we pray, it's the spirit that makes intercession for her, before God. This is why verse 28 is also tremendous in the context of which we're dealing.

Romans 8:28a
And we know that all things work together for good...

Why? Because we are praying in the spirit. Without praying in the spirit, that scripture is null and void! It's out of order.

Romans 8:28b
...to them that love God, to them who are the called according to *his* purpose.

Now, on page 24. To speak in tongues, is to be edified.

You can keep your finger in Romans if you want to because we're coming back to it, but we're going to Corinthians right now.

1 Corinthians 14:4
He that speaketh in an *unknown* tongue edifieth himself;...

To edify is to build up even though your understanding is unfruitful. I showed you this on the board and taught it to you three or four times last night and tonight.

1 Corinthians 14:14
For if I pray in an...tongue, my spirit prayeth, but my understanding is [what?] unfruitful.

See. You're not edified in your understanding or in your brain cells; you're edified in the spirit. And page 24 says, it will edify you before you get to the believers' meeting so that you can edify the believers when you get there. So that you're not cold as a cucumber when you get in the believers' meeting!

1 Corinthians 14:18, 19
I thank my God, I speak with tongues more than [what?] ye all:
Yet in the church I had rather speak five words with my understanding, that *by my voice* I might teach others also, than ten thousand words in an *unknown* tongue.

Because he does not interpret. If he interpreted, it would edify the Body of Believers.

Next, tongues with interpretation is equal to prophecy, with the exception of prophecy given by a prophet. I explained it to you last night. That the prophecy of a prophet could have what in it? foretelling. But the prophecy of a disciple or a believer will not have any foretelling in it. It will have exhortation in it and what? comfort. Tongues with interpretation will never have any guidance in it or foretelling in it. None.

Guidance comes not by the worship manifestations, but guidance comes by what? What manifestations? Revelation manifestations: word of knowledge, word of wisdom, and discerning of spirits. That's where guidance comes. You do not get guidance by speaking in tongues and interpretation. You do not get guidance by prophecy. You get edification, exhortation and comfort by speaking in tongues and interpreting and by a word of prophecy. If there is ever any foretelling,[6] it has to be under the ministry of a prophet, who in his prophecy is giving foretelling which is then no longer the prophecy of just a believer. It is the prophecy of a prophet, which is by

---

6. Dr. Wierwille often spelled f-o-r-e when referring to foretelling to distinguish between foretelling and forthtelling. A man of God operating the ministry of a prophet may forthtell or foretell. The forthtelling is his operation of the *manifestation* of prophecy. His foretelling is the operation of the *ministry* of a prophet. A prophet always has the possibility of both.

what? revelation. Don't you see? Sense knowledge wise, would you notice the difference? No. It would sound just the same. But, if there's ever any foretelling, in the prophecy of a man, that has to be done by a prophet and that foretelling will not be the believers' general prophecy. It will be given to the prophet by what? revelation. It's guidance people, it's instruction, it's information. Understand? Got it?

Remember, Paul wanted to go to Jerusalem, and Agabus coming unto them. Agabus prophesied, but he also had some foretelling in it. Well, how did he get the foretelling? He didn't get it with tongues and interpretation or prophecy. Don't you understand prophecy? Look at the Book again. Settle this thing in your mind. Back to 1 Corinthians 14, verse 3.

> **1 Corinthians 14:3**
> ...he that prophesieth speaketh unto men *to* edification, and exhortation, and comfort.

Then verse 5.

> **1 Corinthians 14:5b**
> ...greater *is* he that prophesieth than he that speaketh in tongues, except he interpret,...

Alright! So if I speak in tongues and interpret, the Body of Believers is going to be edified, exhorted and what? comforted. Okay. When I prophesy the Body of Believers is going to be edified, exhorted and what? comforted. But, if I bring a word of prophecy as a prophet, then the Body of Believers couldn't be edified, exhorted and comforted, then all at once there is foretelling in it, the foretelling is by revelation to the prophet. This is so sharp that we've got to settle this thing.

Because in every "Assembly" group, and every Pentecostal group, and every "Holy Spirit" group that I have ever seen, they all believe that if they want guidance they go to a meeting where they get "lathered up" spiritually. And when the proper person speaks in tongues and interprets, they'll get guidance what to do tomorrow. Or by prophecy, they'll get guidance what they're to do. You see why they go off the deep end? Satan knows that they're out of alignment and harmony. So, here they are "prophesying" and instead of *really* prophesying, old Satan slips it in, you know, because that's what they're expecting. They're expecting what? guidance through prophecy. And so they "prophesy," but the counterfeit has slipped in. So they say, "Well yea verily I say unto thee, it is good for thee to go out fishing tomorrow." Or "sell your farm and give it to the poor." Or do such and such. You see, this is what they call prophecy—getting guidance. You don't get guidance!

If you get guidance with tongues and interpretation and prophecy, then why would we need the revelation manifestations? You need revelation manifestations for the guidance, the information. Word of knowledge, word of wisdom and discerning of spirits, you need that for the guidance. Don't let them fool you, they don't overlap! God ain't stupid! Sense knowledge wise, the prophecy of that prophet with foretelling in it, would sound the same to the senses ears, right? He just utters with his mouth and spits it out, in the language of the body of the people present. But if it gets to foretelling, the Word of God says, it's always revelation. Not inspiration, it's revelation. These lines are pretty sharply marked. You just have to cut them real sharp and keep them there. And you'll never go off the beaten track.

Now, no man understands. That means the man speaking does not understand what he's speaking in tongues. Now comes that little diagram, and I want you to be sure to understand this. In the church, speaking in tongues by a believer is a message from God or for God, because it must be interpreted. And as I told you before, God knows whether you're going to interpret or not, before you speak in a believers' meeting, right? Therefore, if you're going to speak in tongues in a believers' meeting, and you're not going to interpret, then that is a prayer in the church by the unbelieving believer—one who does not believe to interpret or does not know how. Then that is a what? prayer, without believing to interpret. God knows this afore time, by His foreknowledge so it is a what? prayer. And that (the speaking in tongues) will edify his what? spirit. That's why the fellow up in front who said he gave the "interpretation" could not possibly give the what? interpretation. That was prophecy.

People are sincere, they mean well. However they're satisfied with their experiences. So someone in the back speaks in tongues, somebody else over here interprets— no, no. Can't be interpretation! Because God knows before that fellow ever speaks, he's not going to what? interpret. So it's not to the church at all! The man who speaks in tongues, he'll get edified. This other fellow over here who thinks he's giving the interpretation isn't giving it at all! He's giving his own prophecy, the word of prophecy.

To the senses ears, interpretation would be in English, and prophecy is in English. And there's basically no difference in the operation of the manifestation in the senses realm, therefore they wouldn't know the difference. You only know the difference from the accuracy of God's Word, the integrity of the Word. That's the only way you know the difference on what I'm teaching now! This is why a man in the church could be praying in the spirit, right? Sure. Because he's speaking in tongues out loud, but God knows he's not going to interpret, therefore it's not a message from God or for God to the people. It is just a prayer in the spirit which will edify him. But there is someone who is going to speak in tongues in this believers' meeting (God knows before that individual starts) that when they are through they are going to do what? interpret. Therefore, the message God gives to them is entirely different. He gives them a message in tongues, which when it is interpreted, is not a prayer, but is unto edification, exhortation, and comfort. This is real sharp! Otherwise, if speaking in tongues is a prayer, then the interpretation would have to be what? a prayer. But speaking in tongues, if you do not interpret is a prayer. But if you're going to interpret, God knowing ahead of time it's no longer a prayer, then it gets to be a message from God or for God.

Well, I've been through this so much (upside down and sideways) and I think we have 50 people in the Ministry I've lost on this particular issue alone! Because they just think that there is no difference in speaking in tongues, interpretation, and prophecy. There is a difference! And especially this speaking in tongues business. They think it's praying to the Father. It said, "you speak to God."

> **1 Corinthians 14:2**
> …he that speaketh in an…tongue speaketh not unto men, but unto [who?] God:…

Therefore, they say, the interpretation has to be in prayer or praise. They just don't understand!

You know, speaking to God is not a one way track! It's the same as if I said to the people, "I spoke to Mr. Smith today." What does that tell you? That I did all the talking? No, he also talked; we talked things over. When the Bible says to "speak to God," it doesn't mean a one

BENEFITS OF SPEAKING IN TONGUES 331

way deal where you do all the talking! "...speaketh not unto men, but unto God:" means a two-way line! Not just one way.

Now, in private—in private, speaking in tongues is always a prayer or what? praise. Alright, if you're at the shop or if you're at home speaking in tongues, and you're there by yourself, would you ever have interpretation? No. It's always a prayer! And we have people upon people who've gone down the drain because they don't believe that! Because, they go in their house, you know, and they start speaking in tongues. And they'd say, "Well, Lord, I'd sure like to know what I've said, so I'll interpret." So they speak in tongues, and then they interpret, by themselves. Then they go down the drain. It's just not right! Because, speaking in tongues is a prayer! There is no interpretation! It's a prayer! That's all.

Now they say, well it could be prophecy. No! Prophecy is inside of the church, the Body of Believers. The Body of Believers! Right? Therefore, if I spoke in my private prayer life in tongues, and then I'd say, "Well now, I'm going to get the interpretation" and then I give "the interpretation"—I say I give the interpretation of what I just spoke in tongues in my private prayer life. It's not interpretation at all! And it's not prophecy! Because prophecy, God only gives in the body of what? believers. Don't you get God in the soup!

Where does he get the interpretation from then? What he calls "interpretation" or this which he calls "prophecy." Where does he get this from? the Devil. Right down the line. This happens to a lot of good, wonderful people! But, I don't get shook about a lot this stuff, because it's just something you've got to teach people. I teach every class that we go far enough in the same thing: You speak in tongues in your private prayer life, you never interpret! Don't worry about interpretation! Because, when you speak in tongues in your private prayer life, it's a communication between you and God! Divine secrets in the form of prayer. "Praise" is another word that is used in the text. Now, do you understand that little section in there? Alright.

Now, speaking in tongues, what is it for?[7]

- To edify you[8]
- To speak to God divine secrets[9]
- To speak the wonderful works of God[10]
- To magnify God[11]

The reason I've put these in here is to sort of crystallize them all for our people. And secondly, because you ask the average unbelieving believer, what good speaking in tongues is, and he'll ask you, well what good is it? He can't even give you one good reason for speaking in tongues, except that it isn't right! That's the only thing he knows—that it can't be done and shouldn't be done. And yet, the Word of God has all these things to say, about what it's for, exactly how wonderful it is! It's to edify you, it's to speak to God, speak the wonderful works of God, magnify God, to speak divine secrets.

In Romans 8, a little while ago, we found out it was to pray what? perfectly. No selfishness in the prayer, praying in tongues.

---

7. See also *Receiving the Holy Spirit Today*, Seventh edition, p. 35.
8. 1 Corinthians 14:4a—He that speaketh in an *unknown* tongue edifieth himself;...
9. 1 Corinthians 14:2—For he that speaketh in an *unknown* tongue speaketh not unto men, but unto God: for no man understandeth...; howbeit in the spirit he speaketh mysteries.
10. Acts 2:11b—...we do hear them speak in our tongues the wonderful works of God.
11. Acts 10:46a—For they heard them speak with tongues, and magnify God....

BENEFITS OF SPEAKING IN TONGUES   333

- To pray perfectly [12]

It's to overcome our weaknesses in our prayer life, and our knowing of ourselves and others. It is to make intercession to God for us.

- It is to give thanks well [13]

You know, we'd better look at 1 Corinthians 14:17 again. We didn't hit that too hard last time, but there it is. You see he's talking about a man praying in the spirit, in the verses before, when somebody else is around, and he shouldn't be doing that praying business that way. Because the man "understandeth not what thou sayeth." But, in verse 17, even when you pray in the spirit (speak in tongues), you give thanks well.

1 Corinthians 14:17
...givest thanks well,...

It's a prayer and thanks to God, this way up and down. You're praising the Lord and thanking the Lord. That's why when people get up in believers' meetings and say "Let's have a little praise service," everybody gets up and says, "Well, praise the Lord! Praise the Lord, Praise the Lord, Hallelujah! Praise the Lord." I don't know if you've ever been at those services, I have! To praise the Lord is to pray in the spirit. You and the Father. That's right. It's to give thanks well.

Now, the next two are tremendous.

- To have the Spirit bearing witness with our spirit [14]

---

12. Romans 8:26, 27—Likewise the Spirit also helpeth our infirmities: for we know not what we should pray for as we ought: but the Spirit itself maketh intercession for us with groanings which cannot be uttered. And he that searcheth the hearts knoweth what *is* the mind of the Spirit, because he maketh intercession for the saints according to *the will of* God.
13. 1 Corinthians 14:17a—For thou verily givest thanks well,...
14. Romans 8:16—The Spirit itself beareth witness with our spirit, that we are the children of God:

- To know that you are a joint-heir with Christ [15]

Look at Romans 8.

Romans 8:16
The Spirit itself beareth witness with our spirit, that we are the children of God:

God's spirit. When I speak in tongues, who do I get the information from? God. The utterance is from the Lord, right? As the Spirit giveth utterance. Now as I speak, I speak in tongues, it is God's spirit bearing witness with His spirit within me, that we are the children, of what? God. And that's the only verse in the scripture that tells you that you've got the proof, you're a child of God.

The other scripture says:

Romans 10:9
If thou [will] confess with thy mouth the Lord Jesus, and shalt believe in thine heart that God hath raised him from the dead, thou shalt be saved.

Who knows whether you're saved or not? Who? Only God. Now how do you know it? by speaking in tongues. People, when you rightly and sharply divide it, that's the answer. God knows it. That's the deal, God knows it. But what about you knowing it? But when you speak in tongues, it is His spirit bearing witness with your spirit, which is His spirit in you that you're a child of who? God. Wow, that's a tremendous comfort to know! And furthermore, Chapter 8, verse 17.

Romans 8:17a
And if children, then heirs; heirs of God, and joint-heirs with Christ [by our speaking in tongues];...

---

15. Romans 8:17—And if children, then heirs; heirs of God, and joint-heirs with Christ; if so be that we suffer with *him*, that we may be also glorified together.

It's our proof. Not only that we're a child, but that we're a "joint-heir" with Christ. And this all fits where Jesus said, before he ascended, "The works that I do, ye shall do also, and greater works."[16] This is where the "joint-heirship" comes in. Tremendous!

Alright. Back to the list on page 24.[17] Speaking in tongues is:

- To strengthen you with might in your inner man [18] (Ephesians 3:16)

This is just like Jude verse 20.

Jude 20
…building up yourselves on your [what?] most holy faith, praying in the Holy Ghost [praying in the spirit],

Now here in Ephesians 3:16.

Ephesians 3:16
That he would grant you, according to the riches of his glory, to be strengthened with might by his Spirit in the inner man;

I believe "in the inner man" is not in the Eastern Aramaic texts. But, even though it may not be in the Aramaic texts, it is in the Greek text. And I'm confident that even if it wasn't in the Greek texts, the essence is still there if you'll read it: *"to be strengthened with might by his spirit."*[19] I think literally the text reads in the Aramaic,

---

16. John 14:12—Verily, verily, I say unto you, He that believeth on me, the works that I do shall he do also; and greater *works* than these shall he do; because I go unto my Father.
17. See also *Receiving the Holy Spirit Today*, Seventh edition, p. 35.
18. Ephesians 3:16—That he would grant you, according to the riches of his glory, to be strengthened with might by his Spirit in the inner man;
19. A literal translation according to usage of Ephesians 3:16b.

"to be strengthened by means of his, or the spirit of him." Well now, where can I be strengthened by his spirit? Not in my mind, but in my what? spirit, which is the inner man. That's why I like those verses, those words in there very, very much. Is it true Jim that the words "in the inner man" are not in your Aramaic text? I don't think it is. I think that Dr. Lamsa and I, or you and I, checked this before, I forget. But isn't that wonderful?

It is to strengthen you with might in your inner man! Now, physical strength we get from our physical food, right? Our spiritual strength then comes from our what? speaking in tongues, spiritual food. And the only way you can get spiritual food, is to speak in tongues. And the more we speak in tongues, the bigger and fatter we get in the inner man. This is why people, if you and I want an abundance of revelation from the Lord, we've got to build ourselves up spiritually, by speaking much in tongues in our private prayer life! And quit stewing about whether you've got the interpretation or not, because interpretation doesn't build your spirit. Interpretation enlightens the mind of the Body of Believers. Edifying them, exhorting them and comforting them.

Now the next three, I've covered very well. Speaking in tongues is:

- To bring a message from God or for God to the people, must then be interpreted for it would be in public [20]
- To be a sign to the unbelievers [21]

And we explained that last time. And it is also:

---

20. 1 Corinthians 14:5, 13, 27, 28
21. 1 Corinthians 14:22—Wherefore tongues are for a sign, not to them that believe, but to them that believe not:...

- Rest to the soul [22]

It is rest to the person. Speaking in tongues will quiet you down on the inside faster than Anacin[23] or anything else. That's right. When you get shook on something, or when for a moment Satan gets after you in some field, if you can just sit down and start speaking in tongues, and stay your mind on yourself and your speaking in tongues, you can cool yourself off! Quiet yourself down. The Bible says its rest to the weary; rest to the soul.

Now, speaking in tongues, when will it cease? when Jesus Christ comes again. We had that last session: "When that which is perfect is come, then that which is in part…" How is it used most beneficially? love—with the love of God, in the renewed mind. The Word of God is the will of God. The manifestation of tongues is for all born again believers. If people, after being informed about the Word of God, desire to be ignorant, let them be what? ignorant.

I've been asked that when you speak in tongues, is it all the same language or is it different languages? Some people can speak in a multiple number of languages. Because they have what in tongues? the *genos*, right. The genus of speaking in tongues. Remember? But *everybody* can speak in a tongue. Now suppose you never speak but in one tongue, is it genuine? Yes. And when you speak in that tongue in your private life, will it edify you? Yes, that's right. It doesn't say you have to speak in a thousand tongues. How many tongues you speak in, is dependent upon two things. Number one, God, and number two,

---

22. Isaiah 28:11, 12—For with stammering lips and another tongue will he speak to this people. To whom he said, This *is* the rest *wherewith* ye may cause the weary to rest; and this *is* the refreshing: yet they would not hear.
23. Anacin is one of the oldest brands of pain relievers in the United States, first beginning sales in the 1930s.

your believing. Your believing! Dividing to every man as what? he, the man wills.

Someone else asked me, what is intercession? Suppose you and someone else are having a big fight, and I step in between you two and push you apart. I have interceded, intercession. Now, speaking in tongues makes intercession to God for us. In our infirmities, in our weak spots, in our prayer life, in our general walk in life, in our forgiveness with God, He makes intercession. He "goes to bat for us." Maybe that's a good word for intercession. There are no "human" words that could ever do as big an interceding job as speaking in tongues would. He does it with groanings, you know, this which cannot be uttered! It's a bigger intercession than you could ever do for yourself. That's why it says groanings.[24]

I'd like to say to you that our God is a God of love, and a God of understanding. If men have ministries in the Body, we have to know what's going on. Like when I minister the holy spirit to our people into manifestation, I always know whether you are speaking in tongues or whether you aren't. And I know exactly what you are saying in tongues. Why? Because God gives it to me by revelation! Revelation for my guidance, my information, my instruction.

But this is how I know. It's how I watch over people. I get it by revelation but this is in the category of men with ministries. Understand? I would like to say of all of our people who have had this difficulty through the years, I have really never seen anybody go off, if they stayed in the fellowship and with our people. But if they didn't, I've seen them go off! Because your staying in the fel-

---

24. Romans 8:26—Likewise the Spirit also helpeth our infirmities: for we know not what we should pray for as we ought: but the Spirit itself maketh intercession for us with groanings which cannot be uttered.

lowship gives God an opportunity through our ministry to keep instructing you and bringing more light and more understanding to you. Then before you know it, you're right on the ball in the whole field! You see, I never worry so much about people getting off the ball as other people do, you know why? Because we've all been off the ball so long, one more day isn't going to hurt! That's right! For years we didn't do what? speak in tongues. When we didn't speak in tongues we were what? off the ball! We weren't doing the will of God!

Now, suppose I've got a believer in a class who's at least learning a little, and starting to walk a little. Well, suppose they make a mistake? So what! They made one for thirty years before it. That one at that time isn't going to kill him! And God loves you and I do, and that makes a majority. That's right, so you just keep working with people.

Next we are going into interpretation. And I'm going to help you a great deal, so that you can spot when your interpretation is finished, and when prophecy begins. This, I think is the sharpest point of cutting between interpretation and prophecy.

TONGUES, INTERPRETATION AND PROPHECY

When I speak in tongues by myself, it's a prayer. What about if two or more of us are together? Two or more— I just don't know, but I've always sort of thought three. This is really in my heart I guess. I'll tell you where we learned this. You often wonder why these kids from Columbus, Ohio are so bold. You know how they got bold? There were five or six that were in the same class, and they all came from the same Methodist church. And they were all buddies. They always went to dances together, and they went to picture shows together, and they had food together. They were always together! So after they had taken the class, and during the class they were always together. So during the course of that class I told them to "exercise their arm."[1] And that Columbus group, those five kids believed what I said. So, when the class was over with they'd go to each other's house. Every night they'd be at a different house. They'd just sit around and say, "Alright, let's all speak in tongues." So, one would speak in tongues, the next one speak in tongues, then the next one would speak in tongues, and then the next one speak in tongues. That's how they set it up. So they'd just speak by the hour.

Then, after they got real versatile in speaking in tongues and hearing each other speak, they got used to each other. Then they took the next step and they said, alright, now when we speak in tongues, we'll believe God to give the

---

1. "Exercise their arm" is a figure of speech Dr. Wierwille used to encourage the students to speak in tongues much.

interpretation in the Body of Believers so we can become strong for the Lord. And so they'd speak in tongues and they'd interpret. That's why they're still strong and have been all through the years. This is the answer. They exercised! Now, there is no better way of learning than to exercise. And we need to learn, because we haven't been with people from the time we've been born who do this thing. So you've got to learn it when you're an adult, except for our kids that are coming in under us, it's different.

What is the church? What makes the Body? How many do you have to have for a church? Would two make a church? Alright. Someone says, "Where two or three are gathered together in my name, there am I in the midst of them." I thought of that too, but that's in the gospels. That's right.

Alright. Here's another question. Will the one helping the other, without a gift ministry, by revelation know as she helps the other, what the interpretation is? Suppose Emma is helping you or someone. Okay, now, operating all nine manifestations of the spirit, you will speak in tongues, and then you'll start on the interpretation, and you maybe do not know enough, or haven't been taught enough to be fully instructed. Like I taught you tonight, when you can give the interpretation you give it like a house of fire, remember? I said, the faster you give it, the less opportunity Satan has to put doubt in your mind! Alright, so you give three words and you stop. Then Emma comes along and she finishes it out for you. How does she do it? By revelation. But this is how the Body is to help.

Now, I can give you the Word of God on this. "We, who are strong, should bear the infirmities of the weak." And this is in our spiritual life. We're helping one another because I have a little more knowledge than you do, so

I help you. Then you have a little more knowledge than Mrs. Cooper, then you help Mrs. Cooper. Mrs. Cooper has a little more knowledge than my brother Harry, then she helps him. This is what the Body ought to do for one another. Help one another.

And people let me say to you again, I'm not afraid of making a mistake. I'm not afraid of doing it wrong or wrongly. I'm not afraid to be in error, because as I said before, we were in error for 30, 40, or 50 years never even doing it. So if I make a mistake once after I do it, and you help me to correct that mistake or help me to overcome it, I don't worry about the mistake. This is why I don't worry about you people. I sometimes hear people give the interpretation, and I know when they ought to stop, but they don't stop! They keep right on going. Well, why don't I ball them out? I don't have to because I just keep on teaching, and I know they're not hurting anything. They're just not doing the best. And some day when I build them up a little further, then they'll do it a little better. So it's a tremendous ministry.

That's why people, when you really understand our lives and our ministry—I think among our people, there is the greatest love of God in the renewed mind that I've ever seen in the world! I have not seen it any other place. I have seen, "I love you, if you love me!" And if you don't chew tobacco and I don't chew tobacco, we get along good. They call that love. That's not love! That's just chewing tobacco and not chewing tobacco. That's right! The love of God is where we love one another, and then we're not critical of our people. We don't tear them down before others; we don't ridicule our people. And when we can, we help them to overcome at the points where they are weak. I think that's love. And I've never seen any greater love among any of God's people in our day and age in which we live, then I've seen among our people. That's right.

Now, on page 25, the manifestation of interpretation of tongues. This is the companion manifestation of speaking in tongues and is one of the three worship, or utterance manifestations. Speaking in tongues is limited without this operation. What's it limited to? Building yourself up. It is limited to your private prayer life, building yourself up spiritually without the companion manifestation. With the companion manifestation it becomes a worship. Speaking in tongues and interpretation become worship manifestations, where they are used in the worship of believers before God.

What it is not. It is not received by revelation. If it's received by revelation it's word of knowledge, word of wisdom or what? discerning of spirits. You speak as you are inspired by God. They spake as the spirit gave them what? utterance. You speak as you are inspired by God. You just give the message.

It is not an understanding of what has been spoken in tongues. You got that? If you understood it, it wouldn't have to be by inspiration as God gives it to you. It would be a known language.

It is not a translation. A translation is word by word. That's a translation. If you take a Greek word and you give the exact meaning of it, that's a translation. This is why in that whole holy spirit book[2] I say this is "a literal translation according to usage." That's a remarkable way to say that, because it covers a multitude of sins and says nothing. But it gives the people the essence of what I'm trying to say. It is not a translation. If I said that was a translation, I'd be in the soup! I never give a translation in my whole works and my writings, because I do not believe that the translation from one language to another justifies itself. I believe if it was originally given in Aramaic that you cannot give it in English by just taking that

---

2. Referring to *Receiving the Holy Spirit Today* book.

TONGUES, INTERPRETATION AND PROPHECY   345

one Aramaic word, and giving an English word for it. I think you have to give the "gist" of it, the essence. And in the literal sense when I say, "a literal translation according to usage," what I mean is "giving the interpretation thereof." That's what I mean when I say in my book, "a literal translation according to usage." I give the gist, the sum and substance, the accuracy with which it was originally given.

It's like this verse George was asking me about, "but if there be no interpreter" (1 Corinthians 14:28). We set that up in the holy spirit book beautifully. In the last three years within the United States I asked three of the greatest leading teachers of Greek to tell me whether that word "interpreter" could be translated "interpretation" or what we could do with that phrase. Not a one of them knew the answer! They said the word is interpreter and it can only be translated "interpreter." And I knew it had to be wrong because it didn't fit the rest of the Word of God. For the first part of Corinthians, he said, "If a man speak in tongues, let him pray" to do what? Interpret. Therefore that's very plain. Then when he got to verse 28, "if there be no interpreter," could not be right because he already told them when they speak in tongues, do what? Interpret! Okay. Therefore, I said years ago, "if there be no interpretation." It had to be this. Now we came along and worked it this last time, and after I'd asked all those people, I got together with Karen. I said, Karen, there must be something in the grammar here, in the English that I don't understand. If you understood it, if I understood it, we understood it, then it would be accurate. And she said, well, it's simple. It's a subjunctive mood, and it's a conditional clause, and therefore it reads, literally, "if the man lacks the will to interpret." That's exactly what it means. We put it in the book. Tremendous!

What else it is not: Interpretation of tongues is not a knowing of what has been said. That would be sense knowledge. It is inspiration. Well, what is it? It is to speak forth the interpretation of that which has just been given in an unknown tongue by you. It is giving forth in your language, which is the language of the body of people present, the interpretation, the sum and substance, the gist of that which has been spoken by you. Now that's exactly what it is. The interpretation is to give the sum and substance, the gist. It's not a translation; it's just giving an interpretation, the sum and substance. Look, "Lo I am with you always." There's one. Now let me give it another way. "I will never leave thee nor forsake thee." The gist, the sum and substance of those two is the same. That's interpretation. You just give the gist, the sum and substance, the essence of what you said. And you give it in your vocabulary, your English. That's right. And it's always a message from God or for God to the people, the Body of Believers. It's always in the essence of "Thus saith the Lord." Or, the Lord speaking to His people. It's from God, to God's people. It's a message from God, or for God, where God speaks what He wants to say to His people. And you give the gist of it, the sum and substance, the essence in your language.

So let's say you're a hillbilly. You're going to give it in the language of the hillbillies. If you're a Minnesotan you're going to give it in the language of the "Minnesotans." If you're a Bostonian you're going to give it in the "Bostonian" language. See, they use their vocabulary. Just like when holy men of God spake as they were moved by the Holy Spirit. They used their vocabulary, so you use yours! But you give the gist, the sum and substance.

Whenever I teach this I always think of my southern girl. She gave a tremendous interpretation, when she said, "And I hollered, and I hollered, and I hollered, but ye did not hearken unto me." This was God. She gave the interpretation of what she had spoken in tongues. And she said, "hollered." Now the only people that holler have to be down from the hills someplace because they'd holler from one holler to another. And it's their vocabulary! It's their vernacular. Now in my interpretation, I would never have given that, coming up from an area where we just don't use the word "holler." I would have said, "And I called you, and called you, and called you, but you didn't hearken unto me."

But, she coming from her territory said "I hollered and I hollered and I hollered." See? That's wonderful isn't it? The essence is the same, right? Whether she "hollered" or whether you're "called." The sum and substance, the gist, is the same.

Now, take it a step further in here. It is supernatural. It is inspired utterance. It's enthusiastic believing. You've spoken in tongues and you are enthusiastic, now believing to give the interpretation. You speak, and it is given to you as you speak by the Holy Spirit (The Giver) by way of the "power from on high," which is in you. God's spirit teaches your spirit. Your spirit teaches your mind. You just spit it out!

It is God's will for all who speak in tongues to interpret. Let him pray that he may interpret.[3] It is giving the gist. Interpreting what has been spoken in an unknown tongue. It is for the edification of the Body of Christ, the church, even as prophecy. Tongues with interpretation equals prophecy. If he is not able to interpret he must keep silent, pray to himself and to God in the church. You understand that? Having the evidence of tongues, you are under obligation to believe for the interpretation in the Body of Believers.

The interpretation of tongues, when will it cease? when

---

3. 1 Corinthians 14:13—Wherefore let him that speaketh in an *unknown* tongue pray that he may interpret.

Christ comes again. They're all the same in the manifestations at the tail end. And interpretation of tongues, how is it used most beneficially? with love in the church. Now, that's all that's to the whole lesson on interpretation!

Now we go back and we pick it up. Alright, here I am in a believers' meeting, I speak in tongues. And immediately—immediately, when I am through speaking in tongues, I will have one English word in my mind. I don't pay any attention to what that word is. I don't decide that's the right word, or the wrong word. You know what I do? I just say it! I don't even think about it. I just say that word, then I give the second word, the third word, the fourth word, and I just keep on giving! I just keep right on giving, until I get to a point. And what point is that? The point when just for a second it's like a door closes. It's just like the screen comes down, the shade comes down, it just "*boom*"—just for a second. And the key is always that it has a natural ending. It always has a natural ending.

Now, I've watched people get fooled on this. Because when I teach this so minutely, they start thinking more about the natural ending than they think about the inspiration, giving their interpretation. So they're looking for the ending all the time. And, low and behold, the inspiration is such that in the opening part of the message, the Lord says, "I will never leave thee nor forsake thee," so they think that's the natural ending at the beginning and they stop. When he's simply saying, "I will never leave thee nor forsake thee, therefore I wouldest that thou shouldest go on boldly, study my Word and understand for a certainty, that I will forever keep thee and guide thee." Instead of carrying on the rest, they have stopped before they got through.

Now, speaking in tongues, let's say it's a certain length long. Alright, I'll give you an illustration. Let's say you spoke in tongues twelve words. How long will the interpretation be? Now wait just a minute. I can guarantee you one thing that the interpretation will not be in two words. And I can guarantee you something else that if it's much over twenty five or thirty words, you're too far the other way. Everything is within reason. Always. Now class, this I know from language. Take any language—French, Greek, German, Spanish, any of them. If you have twelve words in Spanish, I doubt very much if you can give the translation of those, or the interpretation of those twelve words in two words. On the other hand, if you have twelve words in Spanish, I doubt very much if it takes a hundred words to give the gist of those twelve.

Now, how then do you know when your interpretation is finished? Alright. You start practicing the presence of God like I told you, without any fear. Remember, the first lesson in the class? We overcome fear. As long as you've got a little bit of fear, regarding the interpretation, you better be with somebody who can guide you through. Because the moment fear comes, it's from what side? Satan. And it will always "chop" you. But, you have to get free from fear, and you just start giving it out! You just bubble! You just effervesce it forth. And when it reaches that certain point, you'll always know. The witness of the spirit to you will be, "that's it!" It will always tell you, if you just listen to the witness of the spirit. He'll tell you on the inside to your spirit. It will just be, that's it, that closes it.

The lines of demarcation between interpretation and revelation are sometimes so sharp, that even I can't tell them apart! For instance, that little place where I know you have to stop. Sometimes, I've done this so often that I don't have a question about it, but if I had to teach it, I could not teach you where the inspiration stops and revelation comes to tell you that's all!

But you'll get it from two sources if you're listening. You'll either know by inspiration that's the end of it, or by revelation. God will say, "that's it!" But, you've got the spirit in you, so you're operating (and can operate) word of knowledge, right? So I just expect God to know and tell me when it's over with. But they'll always, more or less, have a real natural ending. The message has been given in tongues, and then the interpretation will give the gist, the sum and substance, the essence of it, which will exhort and comfort God's Body. And it will reach a place when it will naturally end. Sometimes it's like, "For I the Lord, have spoken unto thee." Alright, that's it! At other times it's in the essence of "I will be with you always. I will never leave you. For I the Lord thy God have said this unto thee this hour." It's always in this. And it's always a message from God, or for God, to God's people. You're always speaking to God's people for God. That's the interpretation. Alright, stand, speak in tongues and interpret.[4] "Yea, verily I the Lord thy God, do speaketh to thee my children this very night. I have given thee my Word. I have set it in thy midst. Now hearken unto my Word and walk forth boldly."

Alright. You see, had she gone on now beyond this point, where she said, "Hearken unto me and walk forth boldly." Alright. First of all, do you see the natural ending on her interpretation, "walk forth boldly"? I doubt if you do. It's something I was believing for, a real sharp division, I didn't get it. But, maybe my believing wasn't up. But, I could see this! I mean, understanding the operation of the manifestations, to me it's a real natural ending; "walk forth boldly" is the final end. The interpretation is telling you from here on out: go on, walk boldly. Don't

---

4. Dr. Wierwille calls on someone from the audience to speak in tongues and interpret. Only the interpretation is printed.

hesitate, don't doubt, don't question, just walk on what God has taught us!

Now, suppose she had gone on. That's the end of the interpretation. Now what is it, when we speak in the language of the body of the people and have not spoken in tongues? Prophecy. Then she would go on into what? Prophecy. And the prophecy would only reiterate, go over the same message that she has just given in the interpretation. Now, suppose she goes beyond, in her prophecy, what she has just given in her interpretation? Then where will she go? What would she do? Now look class, I said "interpretation." Now she goes beyond the interpretation. At first, when she goes beyond the interpretation, this prophecy will simply reiterate what she has just given in what? But now she keeps going too far, what happens? It's straight prophecy. It will go beyond the reiteration stage and she will be prophesying. I've watched this thing so sharply through the years. It's just remarkable! Do you understand?

Alright, one more time. Here I am. I speak in tongues and I interpret but I do not stop at the point where the clue is, the queue. So I keep on, now I'm speaking in English right? Okay. Now I get into prophecy. I'm prophesying. And this prophecy will reiterate what I have just interpreted. Now, if I don't stop prophesying at this point of reiteration, I'll keep going beyond the reiteration and I'll be giving straight prophecy. Well, there's nothing wrong with tongues with interpretation or prophecy. But, I believe that we should try to learn the Word and get the Word so deeply within us, and be rid of all fear and anxiety and everything else. Then we can just speak boldly in tongues and interpret, and quit at the time when the interpretation is really finished. Rather than to go on in prophecy which would only reiterate what we've just said in tongues. Or, to go into straight prophecy beyond the reiteration.

Now I'll tell you where we many times get into opportunities along this line. Among our old grads who just love the Lord and get so inspired sometimes, they can hardly stand it. That's right! We have them in here sometimes on Sunday night. I could just take that thing apart, line for line, but I let them go because I understand. They get what I call "hot for the Lord." You know, they get so warmed up inside, they just love the Lord. They love the ministry of His Word. They're just thankful that they can be here and this is God's place with God's people. They're so enthused that they speak in tongues, and they begin to interpret and give it beautifully. Then they don't stop. They go on to prophecy and it reiterates what they've just said, and they still don't stop! They go on for another half a minute, and give straight prophecy! But, that's why I set up this last week where I could teach more of how this stuff operates, so our people could get a greater knowledge. And this is why I'm telling you these things.

Now, speak in tongues and interpret:[5] "Walk forth boldly my children knowing that I am with thee, and I'm guiding thee in everything that you undertake to do." Okay. "Everything you undertake to do." Now to me that's a real natural ending.

Alright, speak in tongues and interpret:[6] "I am the Lord thy God that leadeth thee in the path of righteousness for my name's sake. I am thy constant companion. I uphold thee and strengthen thee, and I'll guide and direct thee until life's end."

Okay. See the natural endings? Now, all of these have been within reason, right? You see in the operation of

---

5. Dr. Wierwille calls on someone from the audience to speak in tongues and interpret. Only the interpretation is printed.
6. Dr. Wierwille has Uncle Harry speak in tongues and interpret. Only the interpretation is printed.

the manifestations, they'll always be within reason. I want to drive the point that you see if I speak in tongues fifteen words, my interpretation is not going to be three words. It's also not going to be a hundred! Now, the Lord could disprove me maybe on this thing, but I doubt it very much. Because I just do not know of any language that I have ever worked, or ever talked to people, or seen work at any time, where you need a hundred words for fifteen, in language. Now I'm sure. God's just witnessed to me it can't be done. So, that's out. Alright.

Now speak in tongues and interpret:[7] "Walk forth children. Be strong in the world…Word, teaching unto others so that they may teach it unto the world." Amen. So that they may teach it unto the world. To me that's a real natural ending. And it's a wonderful thing. Now, you noticed she stumbled over one word. What did she say first? Give me the line, the phrase. I'm going to teach you something if you can recapture the phrase for me. "Be strong in the Word." And she said "world"? Well, it started as that. She started to say world. Alright. She was right the first time and she allowed her mind to say "word" when it should have been "world". That's exactly what was meant when the Lord said be strong in the world. That's exactly what God meant. Why do you want to back up for? Honey, if you'll check yourself, you thought it was the wrong word and it wasn't. It wasn't! Having no fear and no doubt, she had the right word to begin with. Then she questioned it when she gave it and that was the wrong one. It's awful, isn't it? I think it's wonderful you make a mistake like that. I think it's great. That's right. That's how we learn.

You see all of our people, especially on Sunday night, there are two things that has bothered you. Number one

---

7. Dr. Wierwille calls on someone else from the audience to speak in tongues and interpret. Only the interpretation is printed.

is fear. Number two—Well, it's still fear too, I guess in the sense. You're just not quite sure whether you're going to be able to do this as good as Johnny Joe does it. Quit stewing about Johnny Joe! God's your God; the same God that's in Johnny Joe, or anybody else! Same God is in you, so quit stewing about what people think! Be concerned about what God thinks. And if you use the word "ain't," it's perfectly alright with God. Because you give it in the vocabulary you have and use. This is why God never looks disparagingly upon people. It's your own mind that looks disparagingly upon yourself and upon the people in the society, or in the church where you're worshipping.

Alright. Now, give me a word of prophecy:[8] "For verily, I'm the Lord thy God, I shall never leave thee nor forsake thee. I love thee with an everlasting love and shall always be by your side."

Alright, now sense knowledge wise that sounds the same as tongues with what? interpretation. But, instead of speaking in tongues, she just got up and by inspiration gave it in English. That's prophecy. It works the same way as tongues with interpretation, only she doesn't speak in tongues first. She just gives the inspiration—a message from God or for God, to the people unto edification, exhortation and comfort.

Now, is there any question you want to ask about interpretation of tongues? I had her to give the prophecy to show you how it's just like tongues with interpretation. Only, she gives it in English the first time, and hasn't spoken in tongues. Now, where everybody is a believer, fully instructed, then you would always do exactly what she did, right? Because, tongues are only for a sign to the believers who are not fully instructed or they're unlearned. Unbelievers or unlearned as we read last night.

---

8. Dr. Wierwille talks directly to someone else in the audience.

Tongues, Interpretation and Prophecy 355

Now, do you have any question you want to ask on this interpretation of tongues?

Someone in the audience asks that in a believers' meeting where everybody is fully instructed and everyone is a learned believer, should it be just prophecy?

Well, if that is exactly what the meeting is set for then yes, but if I were teaching like I am here, I would still set it up according to the revelation God gives me. But, if we were just doing a believers' meeting here, then I'd have nothing but prophecy. That's right. But very seldom do I just have a straight believers' meeting. It's usually in the field, where Headquarters is a teaching center, as God set it up. And to teach, you have to exercise your arm! The way to teach anything is to get your students to do it. Right? You couldn't get it any more wonderful from God. That's just tremendous.

Someone else in the audience asks, "I've noticed in our prayer life, in tongues with interpretation and prophecy, even amongst the children, it's always in Old English. That bothers me. I don't speak in old English but in my prayer life I do."

I think the answer of course is our minds. You see, you only can give what you have in your mind, you know, I mean, in your vocabulary, understand? And my teaching is from the King James. And so, I build in the minds of our people Old English, King James for the most part. And when we read the prayers in the Bible, we read them from the King James which is in Old English, and I think this is why our messages many times are in Old English.

And how about these younger children that aren't accustomed to reading the Old English yet? Well, they don't have to be accustomed, but Velma teaches them Old English when she teaches the Word. And you teach them Old English, when you teach them the Word, and I think this is it. If we used a modern translation in current English, I think our prophecy would be in that, because we can only give the vocabulary we have in our mind and in our self. And it's Old English vocabulary that we have in the Ministry because of our teaching of the Old English in King James.

In closing, it's been a good six, seven days. Enjoyed it. This is the kind of stuff I like to teach. I mean I like to be with people that are moving and advanced a little bit. Well I enjoy the Foundational Class because I like the fight! But, really when I settle down, you know these nights are really terrific for me because I can take my shoes off and make myself at home. It's like our Thursday night meetings, I just sit with my people and enjoy them. I just enjoy your being here last week and this week, because I can take my shoes off, make myself at home! But, it's a great Word! Tremendous! Well, let's stand for a word of prayer.

SCRIPTURE INDEX

LEVITICUS	
23:10	fn70
23:15	fn70
NUMBERS	
23:19	fn77
JOSHUA	
15:25	fn32
24:15	fn33
2 KINGS	
4:16	fn233
ISAIAH	
28:11, 12	fn337
38:17	105
DANIEL	
5:27	fn63
JOEL	
2:28-32	fn93
MATTHEW	
1:18	101
10:9	52
27:3	53
27:4	54
27:5	54
27:6	54
27:7	54,55
27:8	55
LUKE	
1:38	fn59
6:13	17
6:16	fn17
19:46	42
24:49	20
24:50	31
24:51	31
24:52	43
24:53	43
JOHN	
3:6	49
3:34	58
4:24	fn49,fn110
12:6	52
14:12	fn76,fn335
20:17	fn71
20:22	60
ACTS	
1:1	14,15
1:2	15,16,17,fn32
1:3	17
1:4	17,18,24
1:5	19,20,24
1:6	25
1:7	26
1:8	27,29,30
1:9	30
1:10	31,32
1:11	32,33
1:12	34
1:13	34
1:14	36
1:15	36
1:16	38
1:17	38
1:18	38,51,52
1:19	38,53
1:20	38
1:21	38
1:22	38
1:23	39,40
1:24	40
1:25	40

1:26	40,fn57	5:3	fn234
2:1	41,44,57,59,fn70	8:1	111
2:2	41,42,59,fn60,100	8:2	111
2:3	41,62	8:3	111
2:4	41,fn65,fn70,73,77,79 80	8:4	112
2:5	81	8:5	113
2:6	81,83	8:6	114,117
2:7	83	8:7	117,118,119
2:8-11 (not KJV)	84	8:8	119
2:11	fn332	8:9	119,120
2:12	86,87	8:10	121
2:13	87	8:11	121,122
2:14	44,45,87,92	8:12	122,123
2:15	45,92	8:13	115,123,124
2:16	93	8:14	126
2:17	93	8:15	126,127
2:18	93	8:16	127,130
2:19	93	8:17	127,131,132
2:20	93	8:18	132,134,fn149
2:21	94	8:19	134,135
2:22	94	8:20	135,136
2:23	94	8:21	136
2:24	95	8:22	136,137
2:25	95	8:23	137
2:26	95	8:24	138
2:27	95	9:1	138
2:28	95	9:2	139
2:29	96	9:3	139
2:30	96	9:4	139
2:31	96	9:5	139
2:32	96	9:6	140
2:33	96,97	9:7	140
2:34	97	9:8	141
2:35	97	9:9	141
2:36	97	9:10	141,142
2:37	97,102,103	9:11	142,143,144
2:38	103,104,105,106,107	9:12	145
2:39	108	9:13	145
2:40	108	9:14	145
2:41	35,108,109	9:15	146
2:42	109	9:16	147
3:6	245	9:17	147,148
		9:18	148

10:1	155	10:44	170
10:2	155	10:45	170,171
10:3	155	10:46	fn172,173,174,fn332
10:4	156	10:47	174,178
10:5	156	10:48	178
10:6	156,157	10:34	fn68
10:7	157,158	11:1	175
10:8	158	11:2	175
10:9	158	11:3	175
10:10	158	11:4	175
10:11	159	11:5	175
10:12	159	11:6	175
10:13	159	11:7	176
10:14	160	11:8	176
10:15	160	11:9	176
10:16	160	11:10	176
10:17	160	11:11	176
10:18	161	11:12	fn162,176
10:19	161	11:13	176
10:20	161	11:14	176
10:21	162	11:15	177
10:22	162	11:16	177
10:23	162	11:17	177
10:24	163	11:18	177,178
10:25	163,164	13:2	fn131
10:26	164	18:2	fn185
10:27	164,165	18:24	180
10:28	165	18:25	180,181
10:29	166	18:26	181
10:30	166	18:27	186
10:31	166	18:28	186
10:32	166	19:1	186
10:33	166,167	19:2	187
10:34	168	19:3	188
10:35	168	19:4	188
10:36	168	19:5	188
10:37	168	19:6	fn130,188,189
10:38	168,169	19:7	fn190
10:39	169	19:8	190
10:40	169	19:9	191,fn192
10:41	169	19:10	192
10:42	169	19:11	195
10:43	169,170	19:12	195

19:13	196	13:3	264
19:14	196	13:4	264
19:15	197	**1 CORINTHIANS**	
19:16	197	1:2	207,208
19:17	197	2:8	fn72
19:18	198	12:1	209
19:19	199	12:2	210
19:20	200	12:3	210,211,fn212,213
19:21	200	12:4	215,216
19:22	200	12:5	217
19:23	200	12:6	218,219,220
19:24	201	12:7	220,221,222,223
19:25	201		226,241
19:26	201	12:8	226,fn227,fn228
19:27	201,202	12:9	226,fn228,245
19:28	202	12:10	226,fn229
19:29	202	12:11	241,242,244,fn246
19:30	202		322
19:31	202	12:12	247
19:32	202,203	12:13	247
19:33	203	12:14	247
19:34	203	12:15	247
21:19	203	12:16	247
21:20	203,204	12:17	247
ROMANS		12:18	247
6:23	216	12:19	247
8:16	fn333,334	12:20	248
8:17	334	12:21	248
8:26	322,323,fn333	12:22	248
	fn338	12:23	248
8:27	324,fn333	12:24	248,249
8:28	325	12:25	249
8:29	152	12:26	249
8:30	152,153	12:27	250
10:9	103,fn117,334	12:28	250,fn251,255,fn256
10:10	103,fn117	12:29	252,253
12:4	262	12:30	253
12:5	262	12:31	253,266
12:6	262	13:1	268,319
12:7	262 fn263	13:2	270
12:8	262,fn263	13:3	272
13:1	263,264	13:4	273
13:2	264	13:5	273,274

13:6	275	14:35	309,311
13:7	275,276	14:36	312
13:8	276	14:37	312
13:9	277	14:38	313
13:10	277,fn278	14:39	313
13:11	277	14:40	313
13:12	278	15:23	fn71
13:13	278,279	**GALATIANS**	
14:1	280	4:31	205
14:2	281,282,322,330 fn332	5:1	205
14:3	282,327	5:22	221
14:4	284,285,325,fn332	5:23	221
14:5	286,327,fn336	**EPHESIANS**	
14:6	287	2:1	22
14:7	287,288	2:12	22
14:8	288	3:16	fn78,335,fn335
14:9	288	4:8	216,256
14:10	288	4:9	258
14:11	288	4:10	258
14:12	288,289	4:11	216,258
14:13	289,fn336,fn347	4:12	259
14:14	290,291,325	4:13	259
14:15	291,292	4:14	260,261
14:16	292,293,fn294	**PHILIPPIANS**	
14:17	294,333	2:10	fn105
14:18	149,294,297,326	**COLOSSIANS**	
14:19	297,326	1:27	22
14:20	298	**2 TIMOTHY**	
14:21	298	2:15	fn165
14:22	298,299,301,fn336	3:5	fn72
14:23	302,303	3:17	fn310
14:24	304,305	**HEBREWS**	
14:25	306	2:4	116
14:26	306	**2 PETER**	
14:27	306,fn336	1:20	243
14:28	307,fn336,345	**1 JOHN**	
14:29	307	1:5	fn151
14:30	308	**JUDE**	
14:31	308	20	320,321,335
14:32	308		
14:33	308,309		
14:34	309,310		

Made in United States
Orlando, FL
29 November 2021